D0301344

Theatre and Postcolonial Desires

This book explores the themes of colonial encounters and postcolonial contests over identity, power, and culture through the prism of theatre. The struggles it describes unfolded in two cultural settings separated by geography, but bound by history in a common web of colonial relations spun by the imperatives of European modernity. In post-imperial England, as in its former colony Nigeria, the colonial experience not only hybridized the process of national self-definition, but also provided dramatists with the language, imagery, and frame of reference to narrate the dynamics of internal wars over culture and national destiny happening within their own societies.

The author examines the works of prominent twentieth-century Nigerian and English dramatists such as Wole Soyinka, Femi Osofisan, David Edgar, and Caryl Churchill to argue that dramaturgies of resistance in the contexts of both Nigeria as well as its imperial inventor England, shared a common allegiance to what he describes as *postcolonial desires*. That is, the aspiration to overcome the legacies of colonialism by imagining alternative universes anchored in democratic cultural pluralism. The plays and their histories serve as filters through which Amkpa illustrates the operation of what he calls "overlapping modernities" and reconfigures the notions of power and representation, citizenship and subjectivity, colonial and anticolonial nationalisms, and postcoloniality.

The dramatic works studied in this book embodied a version of postcolonial aspirations that the author conceptualizes as transcending temporal locations to encompass varied moments of consciousness for progressive change, whether they happened during the heyday of English imperialism in early twentieth-century Nigeria, or in response to the exclusionary politics of the Conservative Party in Thatcherite England.

Theatre and Postcolonial Desires will be essential reading for students and researchers in the areas of drama, postcolonial, and cultural studies.

Awam Amkpa is currently an Associate Professor of Drama at the Tisch School of the Arts, New York University. He trained in Nigeria under Wole Soyinka and completed a Ph.D. in Drama at the University of Bristol. He is the author of critical essays and plays – *Not in My Season of Songs* and *Ajasco*, a director of film documentaries – *Winds Against Our Souls*, *It's All About Downtown*, *National Images/Transnational Desires*, and the feature film *Wazobia*.

Routledge advances in theatre and performance studies

1   **Theatre and Postcolonial Desires**
    Awam Amkpa

Theatre and Postcolonial Desires

Awam Amkpa

Routledge
Taylor & Francis Group

LONDON AND NEW YORK

First published 2004
by Routledge
11 New Fetter Lane, London EC4P 4EE

Simultaneously published in the USA and Canada
by Routledge
29 West 35th Street, New York, NY 10001

Routledge is an imprint of the Taylor & Francis Group

© 2004 Awam Amkpa

Typeset in Baskerville by
Florence Production Ltd, Stoodleigh, Devon
Printed and bound in Great Britain by
Antony Rowe Ltd, Chippenham, Wiltshire

British Library Cataloguing in Publication Data
A catalogue record for this book is available from the British Library

Library of Congress Cataloging in Publication Data
A catalog record for this book has been requested

ISBN 0–415–31287–6

In loving memory of Alice "Mama Aba Road" Amkpa
And to Festus Amkpa and Rebecca Amkpa

To inspiring teachers – Wole Soyinka,
Yemi Ogunbiyi and Biodun Jeyifo

And to Abraham and Kader

Contents

Illustrations

Foreword

Placing theatre at the center of postcolonial theory and modernist discourse

By Ngũgĩ wa Thiong'o, author of *Decolonizing the Mind*

Colonialism and the forces it generated have always been part of capitalist modernity. But that modernity, seen through a Eurocentric prism, tends to see colonialism as that Other, and Western civilization, as a linear development, untouched, in its formation and character, by colonial encounters. And yet the genesis of capital as the dominant mode in the production and reproduction of wealth, power, and values in modern society is simultaneous with colonial explorations and settlement, in fact colonialism is its external manifestation.

The other side of the same coin is to see African developments as linear until disturbed by ninteenth-century imperialism, often marginalizing the effect of slavery and plantation slavery on the formation of African identities.

In his book, *Theatre and Postcolonial Desires*, Awam Amkpa rejects a modernity seen through a Eurocentric prism and reads theatre and performance through the prism of these colonial encounters and their historical descendants, postcolonial aspirations. For him modernity is pluralistic and multi-layered. So also is Africa. Awam takes as his heritage, for better or worse, the multiple legacies Africa's interaction with a plethora of global systems from antiquity to the present.

In the process Awam Amkpa makes two important interventions in discourses on theories of the modern and postcolonial. His discussion of Africa's transition to modernity demonstrates the powerful influences these global systems have had on the evolution of the continent's cultural, political, and economic landscapes and thus tempers the tendency to reproduce the Hegelian notion of Africa as a region outside human history. His situating dramatic texts at the center of postcolonial cultural production is a welcome development since theatre texts tend to be neglected by theorists of postcoloniality.

The notion of "postcolonial desire," the act of imagining, living, and negotiating a social reality based on democracy, cultural pluralism, and social justice, is the unifying theme of this book. African theatre and performance are in fact best placed to interrogate this pluralistic modernity and postcolonial desire.

African performance has always been central to questions of social being. Performance was part of the anti-colonial resistance and after independence part of the questioning of the new postcolonial realities, with theatre becoming the site of struggle for social democracy. Not surprisingly, Africa's performance was the first to be assaulted by the cultural forces of colonialism to give space for construction of a colonized being. The same colonized being, mutating into a neo-colonial dictator sees theatre as a threat, and he often sends theatre practitioners into prisons, exile, or death in some cases. But theatre refuses to die either as text or as practice. It becomes a crucial part of the entire process of decolonization and understanding of modernity.

The Africa that has produced this theatre is one of overlapping modernities. It is a product and an expression of multivocal pluralistic modernities and throughout his very intriguing analysis, Amkpa insists on the centrality of the plurality of the African experience. It is because he himself is a product of these overlapping modernities that Awam is able to brilliantly use colonial encounters to interrogate both Africa and Europe guided by his belief that socially conscious art is an essential tool for creating and sustaining democracy.

This book, using Africa and England as the basis of its inquiry, places theatre at the center of postcolonial theory and modernist discourse. Students of literature, theatre, performance, the politics and economies of art should find it useful.

Ngũgĩ wa Thiong'o
Director, International Center for Writing and Translation
Distinguished Professor of English and Comparative Literature
University of California, Irvine

Irvine, 2003

Acknowledgments

This book is shaped by my nomadic existence as a theatre artist and scholar on three continents: Africa, Europe, and North America. It began as a doctoral dissertation at the University of Bristol funded by a fellowship from the British Foreign and Commonwealth Office for the study of Alternative Theatre companies in England. John Marshall's warm friendship and encouraging supervision of my work made Bristol University a home away from home. I am also grateful to Ted Braun, Andrew Quick, James Gibbs, Frances Harding, Nick Owen, Dave Pammenter, Lizbeth Goodman, and Claire McDonald for their willingness to put up with my endless curiosity about the politics of alternative theatre in England, and for drawing my attention to interesting dramatists and theatre archives.

The ancestor of this book was developed in two places – Ile-Ife and Zaria. There, I encountered teachers who changed my life. They include Wole Soyinka, Yemi Ogunbiyi, Biodun Jeyifo, Kole Omotosho, and Chuck Mike. I also wish to thank other friends and associates that I met at Ile-Ife – Adeniyi Coker, Tejumola Olaniyan, Kemi Ilori, Deolu Ademoyo, Owei Lakemfa, Dapo Oluyomi, and Dele Layiwola. My former colleagues at Ahmadu Bello University, Zaria – Brian Crow, Jenkeri Okwori, Oga Abah, Egwugwu Illah, Salihu Bappa, Jummai Ewu, John Haynes, Yakubu Nasidi, Mbulelo Mzamane, and Steve Daniels – added up to a heady atmosphere for my growth as a community theatre artist, activist, and scholar.

My special thanks to Victor Merriman, Tim Prentki, Su Braden, Martin Pumphries, and Erica Carter – friends and colleagues at King Alfred's University College and the University of Southampton – for providing and sustaining a pedagogic environment within which the thoughts contained in this book began to take final shape.

Another trip and relocation across the Atlantic Ocean brought me to South Hadley, Massachusetts. I benefited from intellectual exchanges with a very supportive family of friends at Mount Holyoke College – Samba Gadjigo, Joyce Devlin, Kavita Khory, Eugenia and Robert Herbert, Alberto Sandoval, Nina Gerassi, Tom Wartenberg, Vanessa James, Deborah Battaglia, Amy Kaplan, Don O'Shea, Girma Kebbede, John Grayson,

Barbara Bunyan, Leandro Soto, and John Howard. South Hadley would, however, have lost much of its meaning without the special comradeship and friendship of Elizabeth Young, whose support for this and other projects I gratefully acknowledge.

It was during my short tenure as a Rockefeller fellow under the direction of Arjun Appadurai at the University of Chicago that I polished my thesis on "colonial" and "overlapping modernities." I thank Arjun and several colleagues including Miriam Hansen, David Scott, and Tejaswini Niranjana at the Chicago Humanities Institute for providing me with a base from which to rethink my ideas on theatre and film. Dudley Andrews' mentorship aided that process further during a visit to the University of Iowa.

I thank colleagues and friends at New York University for providing me with a new home that is as intellectually stimulating as it is culturally exciting and personally fulfilling. They include Manthia Diawara, Ngũgĩ wa Thiong'o, Una Chaudhuri, Jan Cohen-Cruz, Bob Vorlicky, Carol Martin, Laura Levine, Ted Ziter, Sandy Bowie, Beth Turner, Arthur Bartow, Kevin Khulke, Chris Jaehning, Jeffrey Jenkins, Bevya Rosten, and Robert Stam. I am also grateful for the faith that Talia Rodgers and Joe Whiting of Routledge displayed in this project.

I dedicate this book partially to my sons Abraham and Kader, who have borne the tribulations of relocation not simply with fortitude, but also with the appearance of excitement. I thank Françoise Douka for lovingly taking care of them. I also appreciate the consistent support of my close friend Christopher Vaz and his partner Anjna Kirpalani.

It is, however, to Gunja SenGupta – a soul mate and ardent scholar whose persistent support facilitated the completion of this book, that I owe my greatest gratitude. Her companionship, intellectual sparring, and ability to decode my thoughts rescued me from the tyranny of translating between multiple borders and linguistic landscapes too often to enumerate.

New York, 2003

Introduction

From colonial modernity to postcolonial desires: oppositional theatre in Nigeria and England

The alarm went off at 5 a.m. It was an unusual Monday morning over three decades ago in northern Nigeria's Islamic city of Kano. I woke up to a lingering sense of the merrymaking that had taken hold of our home since the Friday before. My parents had thrown one of their usual lively parties, climaxed by the performance of a nostalgic masquerade native to their hometown of far-away Lokoja. Masquerades and the mysterious pre-Islamic, pre-Christian African legends they represented, had early cast a spell upon my childish mind, which no amount of Sunday School admonitions against "pagan" rites could ever break. Imagine then, my exhilaration that weekend, upon discovering that it was *my* bedroom the performers had chosen in which to bedeck themselves in the magnificent insignia of the make-believe world about to happen. As I watched them put on their masks from a corner of my room, I heard someone express the apprehension that the lead actor's real-life conversion to evangelical Christianity may have drained him of the ancient mystical powers demanded by the role he was about to play.

Yet, if the performer was culturally "inauthentic," so was his audience. For, like him, the rest of us – my family and the guests who were waiting to be entertained – straddled multiple worlds of what I would later describe as "overlapping modernities." Recent converts to Christianity, we had emigrated to the Islamic and Hausa city of Kano from Lokoja and the surrounding Bassa-Nge villages at the confluence of the Niger and Benue rivers in central Nigeria, where the masquerades originated. Lokoja was itself heir to a pre-European modernity – a cultural pluralism shaped by the area's successive encounters with global systems and internal migrations long before the English created Nigeria. Over the ages, waves of newcomers to the region – the Bassa-Nges, Bassa-Komos, Igbiras, Igalas, Nupes, and Gwaris, many of them refugees from the trans-Saharan slave trade in the north and later the Atlantic slave trade in the south – forged a multi-ethnic society, overlaid in the nineteenth century by the culture of European colonialism. Indeed, Lokoja became colonial Nigeria's first political capital. It was, however, a primordial Lokoja, a "pure" indigenous cultural entity, that the masked performers and their audience imagined and celebrated with song and dance in my parent's home that Friday afternoon thirty years ago. The aboriginal protagonist (neo-Christian in real life) gyrated to the "pagan" songs rendered by his neo-Christian on-lookers with a gusto that swept away anxieties over authenticity on all sides. It signified instead, a sense of alienation from Islamic Kano, a rejection of the marginalization faced by non-Muslim and non-Hausa immigrants to that teeming city, and a nostalgic longing for the comfortable familiarity of the participants' Lokoja "home." That weekend's festivities were, for me, an early lesson in theatre's role in opening up and reflecting a *desiring process* through which we imagine and live alternative universes. Years later, as a cross-Atlantic denizen of both my native Nigeria and its imperial inventor England, I would use theatre as the principal vehicle for registering my postcolonial desire for a democratic Africa and a pluralistic Europe.

But let us return for a moment to the Monday morning following the masquerade. For I was about to cross cultural borders – from a world of make-believe, nostalgic Lokoja "authenticity" in Islamic Kano into a cultural space fashioned by the Euro-modernity of Nigeria's recent colonial past. I attended a school run by an American Evangelist group called the Sudan Interior Mission (SIM). That Monday marked the beginning of an annual religious retreat at the school – an occasion that attracted many visiting pastors from the United States. For me, the most attractive feature of the event consisted in the singing. I especially liked one song known as "The Song of Colors." It was a simple song, yet when sung by the entire school in unison with the choir, it never failed to send a tingle down my spine. Its presentation held a special import for me that day, for I, of all the children in the school, was selected to hold the special book from which we sang the hymn. The book contained no words but rather had pages splashed with different colors, each of which provided a cue to the singing of a particular verse of my favorite song. According to the missionaries, the "black" pages stood for the color of sin in which we were all born; "red" represented the blood of Jesus Christ which He sacrificed for us; "white" symbolized the purity of Christ's intentions and the state of sinlessness all of God's children, but heathens in particular, must aspire to attain. We were also told the "gold" colored pages signified the immense wealth awaiting us in the kingdom of God when we achieved "whiteness" in our hearts. It was a beautiful song, rendered in call and response by my starry-eyed schoolmates and our sacred interlocutors. We sang joyfully, secure in the knowledge that the wisdom and guidance of our American evangelical teachers would lead us, black children born in sin, all the way to heaven.

A few years later, I moved to St Thomas, an elite secondary school run by the Catholic Church, with Irish priests as well as Catholic teachers from England and India. It was there that I became conscious of the ambiguities of my state of being and place of belonging, of the trauma of identity in a crazy, complex, paradoxical postcolonial state. Every morning at assembly, students from a variety of cultural backgrounds including my closest friends – Amir Qureshi from Pakistan, Ralph Bailey from Guyana, Raphael Bassey from south-east Nigeria, Nasiru Hamza from north-east Nigeria, Akinloye Ogubanjo from Western Nigeria, and Patrick Akusu from mid-west Nigeria – congregated in the same school uniform of white pants, white shirts, and white shoes. There, as we said our prayers, we were supposed to meld into one community under a Catholic God – united in heart, mind, and spirit. Yet, no less a person than Father James Gillick, the school Principal and teacher of Literature and Religious Studies, disrupted any simple, unitary notions of identity that such an exercise may have implied. One day, in an attempt to capture the rhythmic beauty of a nostalgic English poem, he chose to speak in his native Gaelic rather than in English. His insistence that he was not "English" confused me. The colonial education I inherited from my parents suggested that Europeans spoke only a few languages: English, French, German and Portuguese, and of course the classical Latin, "the language of God and the church." Father Gillick's choice of Gaelic over English somehow made him an "inauthentic" European. I could not understand why he of all people – to all appearances a white man from the English Isles – would want to disavow an English identity.

My bewilderment over the Irish Father's rejection of Englishness stemmed at least in part from the success with which English colonialism in Nigeria had succeeded in acculturating my family to its cultural assumptions. My parents embraced Christianity and Englishness with enthusiasm. While my mother managed a large family at home, my father worked for the English as a telephone engineer in the then Department of Post and Telegrams. I recall the colonial uniform he sometimes wore on special occasions: khaki shorts, long knee-high brown socks, black ties, and jackets with large buttons emblazoned with the English coat of arms and the inscription "HM's Government" (Her Majesty's Government). He also had the same helmets the English brought to their colonies and the cross-body belts colonial administrators wore on official duties. We were assigned a house in the exclusive Government Reservation Area once occupied by Sir Bryan Sharwood Smith,[1] a former communications and intelligence officer who later became the colonial Governor of Northern Nigeria. My father spent his final working days in post-independence Nigeria lamenting the departure of the English, who alone, in his opinion, knew how to manage the "modernity" they had created for us. As a teenager, I discovered his uniforms, training manuals, and other colonial memorabilia neatly packed into boxes in a closet where they had been consigned after Nigeria became independent in 1960. These items included a wind-up gramophone emblazoned with the image of a dog singing into what appeared like the open end of a large trumpet with the words "his master's voice" scribbled on a brass plate at the base of the equipment. I also found very fragile playing records, telephones, tools, and airmail letters from his former bosses in retirement homes in England, as well as assorted books. Most interesting of all was a manual entitled *The Book of Don'ts*, a master-piece of prescriptive literature designed to assimilate natives into colonial norms of hygiene and etiquette.

These treasures represented the legacy of what I would later recognize as "colonial nationalism," – an essential cultural corollary to England's invention of what we know as the state of Nigeria. The colonization of West Africa was part of the larger story of Western imperialism, driven by European power rivalries and the economic imperatives of the Industrial Revolution – an often violently competitive quest for markets, raw mater-ials, and sites for the investment of surplus capital. In 1884, the German Chancellor Otto Von Bismarck convened a landmark conference of Euro-pean nations at Berlin to regulate the terms of Western engagement in Africa. The Berlin meeting effectively formalized the "Scramble for Africa" by demarcating spheres of political influence and economic interest that the various European powers would subsequently consolidate by force and chicanery. The region that became Nigeria fell to England's lot. In order to facilitate colonial administration, the English divided the Nigerian region into two sections. They established direct control over the southern part which provided access to the sea. There, the native authorities were reorganized and subordinated to a coercive colonial government. The North, by contrast, was run indirectly through existing Islamic chieftains, to whom the English offered military support and safe passage for their articles of trade through southern ports onto European markets. It was not until 1914 that Governor General Frederick Lugard, with a mandate from the Crown, amalgamated the two sections into the single state of Nigeria, named after the great river originating in the Fouta Djallon mountains of Guinea and "discovered" by the English missionary and adventurer Mungo Park.

As in Asia, England faced the formidable challenge of reorganizing the diverse peoples and cultures that inhabited this geographical space into a homogeneous entity readily governable from London. To that end, trade, education, and Christian missions, promoted by the Royal Niger Trading Company on the one hand, and the Anglican Church on the other, served as significant vehicles of "civilization." Most importantly, forging a unified nation out of over two hundred heterogeneous entities that were them-selves part of other global formations on the continent, called for a lingua franca. Thus, English became the dominant language of administration, socialization, and communication in colonial Nigeria, as well as the defining feature of the "modernity" into which the colonial masters sought to conscript the "natives." These profoundly important cultural trappings of colonialism – from etiquette and dress to religion and language – were fashioned into a discourse of what I call "colonial nationalism" that sought to "modernize" and "civilize" the colonized by assimilating them into Englishness. Colonial nationalism promoted the incorporation of Africans into a version of European modernity that I call "colonial modernity" – a modernity semantically, culturally, and politically synonymous with European values and institutions, especially Christianity, the English language, and a clear consciousness of the boundaries between the secular and the sacred in cultural life. Colonial modernity was inherently hierarchical in that it assumed the natural superiority of European mores over those of the subdued "natives," and therefore, the legitimacy of the West's mandate to govern the colonized. In this context, the colonial regime tolerated indigenous cultural practices to the extent that such practices did not challenge the colonial nationalist project. When not demonized, African cultures were allowed as markers of barbaric difference that were then depoliticized and turned into romantic spectacles. In other instances, they were sustained to signify the very savagery that needed to be overcome by Europeanizing the Africans.

Yet, no amount of assimilation to Anglo-European norms could place Africans at the center of European modernity. The colonized remained trapped in what I describe as an "inter-modernist" landscape on the margins of that modernity, bounded by English constructions of race. Encircled by the Africans' blackness, this "inter-modernist" location marked moments of European intrusion into local civilizations and occasions of cultural fusion between European and African. Yet, it was this very space, set up by colonial modernity to define the limits of assimilation that also became the theatre for confronting colonial domination with tropes of anticolonial nationalism. Within the inter-modernist landscape, colonial epistemologies and their modes of representation encountered what V.N. Volosinov referred to as "a struggle for the sign."[2] In this struggle, the colonized frequently appropriated the words, images, symbols, and institutions of the colonizer to talk about and resist their own marginalization.

Theatre became a significant site of these "inter-modernist" struggles. Ousmane Diakhate and Hansel Eyoh[3] have written that Africans did not name their theatre; rather they "lived it," as an integral part of their everyday lives at home and in public spaces. The singing and dancing, masquerades and folk-tales, the rituals and festivals that peppered family and communal life in West Africa all contributed to a theatre of engagement. As practiced in auditoria, market places, community halls, schools, streets, and in religious and secular ceremonies, theatre came to mean a symbolic interpretation of social reality that facilitated communication, socialization, and community. It bound performers and spectators together in a surreal journey of empowerment that carried real potential for collective action. Borrowing from studies in semiotics, I have come to define theatre as a process of enacting and scoring signifiers which enable audiences to identify or counter-identify with the ideological discourses informing the performance. The dramatic arts, like language, consist of a symphony of signs which make and share "meaning," flesh out identities, and galvanize agency. These signs make up "representations" and without modes of representation, identities make no sense.

Moreover, the system of signification that theatrical practices embodied, endowed them with the capacity to not simply illustrate culture, but to make it as well. In the Nigeria of my birth, culture reflects a condition of in-betweeness within the framework of which identity, citizenship, and representational approaches are negotiated. Identity is never finished. Animated by a culture's production of signifiers, it remains in a state of dynamic flux. Thus, try as they might, colonial representations of African identities did not always succeed in locking Nigerians into a static, passive, debased sense of "self." As Chris Tiffin and Alan Lawson have suggested, the discourse of colonialism did indeed incorporate colonized subjects in a system of representation.[4] Rider Haggard's *King Solomon's Mines*, Joseph Conrad's *Heart of Darkness*, and Joyce Cary's *Mister Johnson* all relegated Africans to the margins of a modernity constructed as exclusively European. Likewise, William Shakespeare's *Othello* and *The Tempest* dramatized an imagery that connected blackness with lust, emotional volatility, and "inherent" intellectual inferiority. Colonial representation sealed African identities and stigmatized them as a dispossessed people with no serious possibilities of agency. Yet, unflattering colonial representations provoked the proliferation of counter texts contesting those representations. Tiffin and Lawson drew attention to this fact when they asserted "[colonial] control is complete only up to the moment of its announcement; once enunciated it can never again be total, since the circulation of the knowledge loosens it."[5] Anticolonial theatre created identities and settings for the negotiation of subjectivity and issues of morality between performances and their spectators.

This theatre of nationalist resistance was profoundly hybridized not only by the Africans' own cosmopolitan brushes with different global systems – the trans-Saharan, the Mediterranean, and the Atlantic – but also by their experience with colonial nationalism. Thus, the "inter-modernist" site of semiotic struggles between the imperialist and the colonized was a culturally hybrid space that, according to Homi Bhabha, had the effect of threatening the very authority of colonial discourses: "The effect of colonial power is seen to be the production of hybridization rather than the noisy command of colonialist authority or the silent repression of native traditions."[6] The political potential of hybridity enables the colonized to imagine and live what Bhabha calls a "Third Space" where "the transformational value of change lies in the re-articulation, or translation, of elements that are neither the One ... nor the Other ... but something else besides."[7] "Pidgin English" – one medium of Nigeria's dramaturgies of resistance – represents a case in point. It deliberately subverted the grammatical norms of the colonizer's language even as it used that language to articulate aspirations for independent nationhood. It was within such spaces of inter-modernist hybridity, spaces that demarcated the limits of "native" assimilation to European modernity, that ideologies and practices of decolonization were conceptualized and developed.

Anticolonial nationalism was by no means a unified, monolithic movement, nor did it win the allegiance of all segments of the colonized population at the same time. My father's persistent loyalty to the English long after the sun had faded upon the British Empire should make this point clear. Indeed, the social cleavages and cultural hybridity of the colonized produced what I call an "intra-modernist" landscape marked by conflict and tensions among the "natives" themselves. Colonialism perpetuated age-old rivalries and invented new ones in many subordinated societies. In Nigeria, the English sought to assimilate their subjects into "modern" social classes, privileging some ethnic groups over others in ways that continue to produce regional and ethnic conflict to this day. The colonial organization of the region's myriad ethnic groups into four categories – the Yorubas, Hausas, Igbos, and the so-called "minorities," with the Hausas at the top – not only shaped a fractious independence movement in Nigeria, but also complicated the postcolonial work of redefining a single Nigerian nation. In this context, it is important to note that non-elites – the "people" or the "folk" – were subject to the same forces of reorganization, relabeling, assimilation and indeed hybridization to which the colonized elites were subjected. Anthony Appiah was quite right to observe, "we must not fall for the sentimental notion that the 'people' have held on to an indigenous national tradition, that only the educated bourgeoisie are 'children of two worlds.'"[8] The hybridity that characterized the "inter-modernist" and "intra-modernist" landscapes thus defied bi-polar constructions of anticolonial struggles as "European versus African." It also complicated essentialist readings of a unified "African" cultural "authenticity" at war with European imperialism. Wole Soyinka in his *Death and the King's Horseman* depicted a people navigating the slippery terrains of "intra-modernism" and "inter-modernism" as they struggled to determine who they were and where they belonged. Rejecting essentialist interpretations of authenticity, Soyinka suggested that European modernity had drawn Nigerians into a constantly shifting, highly pluralistic terrain that made it impossible to reduce nationalist contests into a bipolar "clash of cultures."

The Second World War turned the cultural landscapes of inter-modernism and intra-modernism into hotbeds of anticolonial activity. A global war fought against fascism and racism in defense of democracy, supplied ample rationale to challenge imperialism across Asia and Africa, while Japanese victories in Southeast Asia during the war shattered the illusion of European invincibility. Nationalist movements, fed by resentment against the colonial powers' increasing demand for resources and labor, emerged all over Africa. Colonialism disrupted traditional agriculture, prompting mass migrations of rural populations to wartime shanty-towns, which saw the development of potent anticolonial constituencies of unemployed workers. In the wave of Afro-Asian decolonization that followed, Nigeria itself was born anew as an independent nation state on October 1, 1960.

Yet, formal independence from English colonialism did not bring freedom to Nigeria's hopeful multitudes. Colonialism left the legacy of a dysfunctional parliamentary democracy paralyzed by ethnic and regional rivalries. In the post-Second World War period, Nigeria's English masters had crafted a series of constitutions in the course of their negotiations with various nationalist and other factions in the colony, granting a dispro-portionate amount of influence to their client chieftains in the north. The colonial tradition of privileging one section of the country over another accentuated conflicts among the ethnic groups reorganized by the English – often arbitrarily. Thus, the departure of the English was followed by a series of political crises culminating in the overthrow of civilian rule by military coups from the late 1960s to the 1990s. The anticolonial hope of self-determination yielded to Nigeria's long nightmare of neo-colonial dictatorships.

Oil lubricated the machinery of the neo-colonial state. Military dictators with firm support from European nations who bought the new nation's oil, derailed democratic processes with impunity. Conscripting their subjects into a unitary nationalism that paid no heed to the country's ethnic com-plexity, the dictators turned Nigerians into a people who produced things they could not consume, while developing a taste for consumer goods they could never produce. The unequal terms of Nigeria's ties to the industrial-ized West perpetuated its subservience to the colonial, hierarchical variant of European modernity, itself in the process of reconfiguration by the super power challenge posed by the United States. Kwame Nkrumah was perfectly right when he described neo-colonialism as the "worst form of imperialism. For those who practice it, it means power without responsibility and for those who suffer from it, it means exploitation without redress."[9]

Neo-colonialism reconfigured the nature and function of the inter-modernist and intra-modernist landscapes within Nigeria. Foreign nation states no longer served as the instrument of domination as in colonial times. Rather, multinational and transnational corporations whose economic power translated into political currency across many nation states, became the new vehicles for drawing formerly colonized peoples into a fresh global modernity centered in Europe, but encompassing the United States as well. This neo-colonial context transformed the inter-modernist landscape from a site where anti-imperialist cultures were developed into a conduit through which the new imperialism accessed the nation. The elite class at the forefront of the inter-modernist landscape became as corrupt as the military dictators who ruled the land with an iron fist. On the other hand, the intra-modernist landscape became more chaotic as class and religious differences superseded ethnicities as the primary lines of division. Such changes meant that ideologies of decolonization had to reform themselves substantially in order to maintain the anticolonial culture developed in the late nineteenth and early twentieth centuries.

The neo-colonial order did not, however, go unchallenged. Among the major bastions of democratic activism against the new authoritarianism was the University of Ife (now known as Obafemi Awolowo University) perched in a verdant valley covered with palm trees in the shadow of the hills of southwestern Nigeria. Ile-Ife, the historic birthplace of Yoruba mythology, had long harbored a tradition of radical activism against English rule. Its university was established as the anticolonial alternative to the Anglocentric University of Ibadan modeled on England's University of London.

I arrived in Ile-Ife to begin a long career in politically conscious theatre in the "Rain Semester" of August 1979. Wole Soyinka, Nigeria's greatest playwright and a future Nobel laureate in literature, chaired the University's Department of Dramatic Arts, which I joined. Soyinka, together with a host of other teachers and mentors like Biodun Jeyifo, Yemi Ogunbiyi, Kole Omotosho, and Segun Osoba shook our world with a pedagogy that demanded a sense of social and political responsibility from their students. They helped foster an activist culture of decolonization marked by incessant student protests against the military dictators and empowerment campaigns to uplift the surrounding community. We saw the mission of our education as a simultaneous rebuttal of colonial epistemology and processes of creating decolonizing modes of knowledge for asserting our identity and agency. We studied hard to understand the residual and active narrative of colonial modernity and made all cultural practices arenas for contesting and imagining a postcolonial democracy within which we would be social actors against all forms of oppression. While my primary and secondary school education aimed to acculturate me to the tenets of colonial modernity under the auspices of a neo-colonial state, my university education nurtured a spirit of dissent against our shackled present as much as our subjugated past that powerfully shaped our quest for subjectivity. Decolonization became for us, a perpetual process of contesting and constructing democracy rather than the mere formal severance of our colonial connection with England. Our study of a range of activists and thinkers from Frantz Fanon, Cheick Hamidou Kane, and Kwame Nkrumah to Renato Constantino, Amilcar Cabral, and Ngũgĩ wa Thiongo inspired our understanding of coloniality both past and present, and suggested strategies for denouncing and resisting it.

Theatre became for us, the principal vehicle of decolonizing reform, just as it had served an earlier generation as a prime strategy of anticolonial resistance. The changed context of our neo-colonial world, however, called for rethinking our notions of citizenship. The responsibilities of suffrage and civic virtue – the essence of citizenship and the instrument of change in liberal democracies, had little relevance in an authoritarian milieu.

The texts we studied and the dramatic shows we staged, helped fashion my conception of citizenship as consisting of three kinds. In most societies, *formal citizenship* endows individuals with the cultural capital to arbitrate the terms of the society in which they live. Cultural capital in a neo-colonial Nigeria flowed primarily from class, followed by gender, ethnicity, and religion. The new elites were drawn from upwardly mobile, university-educated heirs to England's mercantile operations, as well as from the military corps. Moreover, Northerners translated their colonial-era privileges into a position of political dominance in the new nation. A self-interested alliance of these interests inaugurated a military broker state, and excluded the masses of Nigerians from the privileges of self-rule, making them what I define as "informal citizens." *Informal citizenship* gives people the right to live in a particular society, but denies them the cultural and political capital needed to narrate their local space and politics. It is a marker of disenfranchisement. For formal citizens, the specter of descent into informal citizenship ensures their acquiescence in the hegemonic discourses of their day.

The most dynamic sense of identity, however, and one most suited to the discourse of decolonization is vested in the notion of *non-formal citizenship*. Non-formal citizenship connotes a fluid, hybrid, sense of "self" that seeks subjectivity and agency in a variety of local and global contexts. It rejects deterministic definitions of identity (such as "working class," "elite," etc.) in favor of multipositionality. Its very flexibility facilitates coalition building, and empowers it to engage and contest authoritarian power across a spectrum of locations.

I venture to suggest that it is this shifting conception of identity that carries the greatest promise for realizing what I call *"postcolonial desire"* – the act of imagining, living, and negotiating a social reality based on democracy, cultural pluralism and social justice. It represents a counterpoint to Robert Young's interpretation of "Colonial Desire." If "colonial desire" consisted in the drive of epistemologies and representational conventions within European or neo-colonial modernity to seek out and dominate its "Other,"[10] "postcolonial desire" signifies an act of refusal to assume the passive, static, essentialist identity of that "Other." Rather, it draws upon the resources of non-formal citizenship to fuel a perpetual act of becoming.

Postcolonial desires begin at the very moment in which the subordinated understand their subjugation and launch strategies of defiance and change. Thus, such reformist desires can very well inaugurate, rather than follow, anticolonial nationalism. As the Irish cultural critic Declan Kiberd has put it in the context of literature, "postcolonial writing does not begin only when the occupier withdraws; rather it is initiated at that very moment when a native writer formulates a text committed to cultural resistance."[11] Thus, postcolonial consciousness can trigger the humanistic aspirations of anticolonialism as well as extend it into the post-independence period.

It embraces an expansive vision of freedom that includes not simply the formal severance of colonial relations, but also the creation of a republican society based on democratic citizenship, equity, and tolerance of diversity. Postcolonial dramatists use their art to discover the democratic interstices from which to launch progressive movements of reform.

Drama students at Ife University, including myself, identified with this postcolonial impulse whenever we encountered it in the texts we studied, and sought to live it through the practical world of our community theatre projects. We saw scholarship as political activism deliberately disrupting European epistemologies whose unquestioned authority colonial and neo-colonial modernity had sought to perpetuate. The theatre we studied and practiced, ritualized subjectivity as a simultaneous act of denunciating domination and enunciating ideas of effective citizenship.[12] I use "subjectivity" politically to suggest a state of consciousness that leads us to think of ourselves as subjects rather than as dominated objects of history and culture. Subjectivity initiates the agency – the free will to act – to seek effective citizenships through performances of representation.

A corollary to the vision of non-formal citizenship connected with post-colonial desire is the conception of identity as a site of perpetual hybridity and translations of subjectivity. My upbringing in Kano as well as the decolonization culture at Ile-Ife prompted me to see my world as the product of what I describe as "overlapping modernities." West Africa was home to an array of pre-European empires – the Songhai, Ashanti, Oyo, Hausa/Fulani – several of which were connected to larger global systems in the Arab world and the Mediterranean through networks of trade and cultural exchange. The Atlantic slave trade extended Africa's international reach to the New World, while European imperialism networked the continent into a new modernity rooted in the Industrial Revolution. The heterogeneity of my lived experiences underscored the coexistence of these multiple legacies. Latin, Pidgin English, Bassa-Nge, Hausa, Yoruba, Ibo, and Nupe; animism, Islam, and Christianity; Bach, Motown, and Fela Anikulapo-Kuti, all constituted a patchwork quilt of cultural land-scapes produced by Africa's interactions with a plethora of global systems from antiquity to the present. It became clear to me that a single modernity was incapable of describing the complex, multilayered archeology of my world. I came to see "modernity" as a dynamic system informed by culturally hybrid residual and emergent traditions whose cadences were always multiple rather than unitary and colonizing. While acknowledging the Eurocentric prism through which the term "modernity" is negotiated, I rejected the colonial fantasy that assumed the existence of a single – and European – modernity. This pluralistic, multilayered conception of modernity has remained with me, and frames the analysis of postcolonial desire made in this book.

I argue that postcolonial desires prised open a space of "in-betweeness" between the overlapping modernities that map our world. At Ile-Ife, we resourced decolonization from the heterodoxies of these overlapping worlds and embarked on large-scale translations between them through drama and theatre. We saw ourselves not simply as pilgrims whose luggage was packed for border crossings between one "time" into another, one "culture" into the other, or one geographical location to the other. Instead, we understood our bodies, psyches, and languages as sites within which various borders – internal and imperial, colonial and anticolonial, were translated. In this context, the act of inscribing a contradictory cadence to the term "postcoloniality" became a symbol of linguistic and cultural defiance as we refused to split the world into pre- and post-European time. We rejected binaries of "traditional" and "modern," of "barbaric native" and "civilized native." We resisted rigid legislation of either spatial or temporal qualifications to our claims on postcoloniality. Our postcolonial desires defied and deliberately made incoherent the geo-spatial divisions of the world into West and East or North and South, or First, Second, and Third Worlds. Such incoherence facilitated our nomadic wanderings across the world in search of pro-democracy allies in distant realms of the globe. The primary division mapping our world was the boundary between neo-colonial subjection and postcolonial desires for a democratic place of belonging and social becoming. The postcolonial project turned acts of representation and cultural practices into what Gilles Deleuze and Felix Guattari called "desiring machines"[13] to crank up symbolic interpretations with which to contest social reality and cultivate agency.

Four years after Ile-Ife when, as an advanced graduate student, I physically crossed national borders from the "Third World" to the "First," from colonized Nigeria to its imperial architect England, I became aware that the tortured legacy of empire had extended the reach of neo-colonialism to its metropolitan center. The very same colonizing mentality that had coerced Nigeria to enter the margins of Euro-modernity, had also dominated and dispossessed various groups of people in the heart of the imperial nation. As Robert Young has observed, colonialism "was not simply a marginal activity on the edges of English civilization, but fundamental in its own cultural representation."[14] In this context, the paradigm of postcolonial desires became more than ever a trans-temporal, trans-regional, transnational space for enacting counter-hegemonic scholarship and political activism, rather than merely a region-specific moment in history.

The England I encountered in the 1980s shattered the illusion crafted by my colonial education of a unified cultural, imperial entity. Instead, I saw many different Englands. When I first stepped on English soil, London's Heathrow airport seemed weirdly quiet compared with the chaotic, noisy city of my departure, Kano. Heathrow's sense of clinical order and silence, however, began to fade slowly into a noisy visual montage of very familiar types – dark skinned cleaners and porters from Asia, Africa, and the Caribbean scurrying about their business amid their "white" compatriots. As I left the airport terminal to board the train to Victoria Station, the population began to resemble the map of England's empire more and more. Glancing sideways from the magnificent monuments signifying the British Empire's imperial greatness and wealth, I caught a glimpse here and there of the less glorious byproducts of that legacy. Over time, that more troubling legacy would assume human faces, by no means all black. I visited inner city London communities inhabited by underclass and working-class people excluded from effective citizenship – formal citizenship – by the class structure of English society. I saw starving "white" men in what was dubbed the "cardboard" city beneath the stairwells of the National Theatre, some from the industrial "North," others from the wealthy "South," and many from Scotland, Wales, and Ireland. The significance of the title of the late John MacGrath's theatre company 7:84 dawned on me: only 7 percent of the population owned 84 percent of the country's wealth. At the same time I came to understand the contestatory and conflicting overlaps between Celtic and Anglo-Saxon modernities, English and European senses of modernity, and how narrations and representations of nationhood excluded the voices of a subordinated majority living in the islands surrounding England. I understood Father Gillick as I had never done before. The mosaic of peoples from various parts of the non-European world touched by English imperialism and empire complicated the picture. They greeted my curiosity with defiant stares that seemed to say, "we are here because they were there."

When I finally settled in Bristol to get a doctorate in drama at the University there, I heard many tales of trauma – reverberations of imperial history. My local corner shop was run by a South Asian expelled by the fury of anticolonial nationalism in Kenya. There, as in Uganda, a settler English colonialism had brought in indentured labor from what became India and Pakistan, and established a hierarchy of privilege that discriminated against Africans in favor of Asians. The tradition of mutual distrust that grew up between "blacks" and "browns" culminated in East Africa's purge of Asians as part of its nationalist drive. To the exiled, England thus became a new home more geographically distant than ever from the native lands of their ancestors in Asia. East African Asians joined with their postcolonial kith and kin from the Caribbean and the Indian subcontinent to form raucously diverse ethnic enclaves throughout England.

Immigrants from the English Commonwealth, invited to fill the metropolis's needs of manual labor in construction, transportation, and nursing during and after the Second World War, molded a multi-ethnic English working class. Not surprisingly, the heterogeneity of national origin, ethnicity, and religion divided England's post-empire proletariat. Native-born "white" workers resented not only the middle class, but also their class compatriots from other lands, who they believed, had come to take the little they had. A former Oxford don-turned Conservative politician named Enoch Powell exploited these divisions for political gain.

His infamous "Rivers of Blood" speech at a Conservative Party convention offered an exclusionary vision of English nationalism anchored in the purity of "race" – a vision that sought to deny the reality of England's increasingly multinational identity forged in the crucible of empire.

Powell's unitary conception of the English nation also obscured the relations of internal colonialism that marked England's historical interactions with Ireland, Scotland, and Wales. The labels "British" and the "United Kingdom" overlaid centuries of internecine conflict and collaboration within the British Isles. There were perfectly good historical reasons why the Scottish, Irish, and Welsh were British and not English, that the black sprinter Linford Christie was British and not English. In this context, the conception of "hegemony" propounded by Antonio Gramsci, Louis Althusser, Raymond Williams, Terry Eagleton, Chantal Mouffe, and Ernesto Laclau, proved particularly helpful in my understanding of contemporary England's relations of power, and its internal battles over representation and identity.

The works of these theorists persuaded me that England had sought, through acts of representation, to manufacture a consensus among its citizens that they all belonged to an imagined community called Great Britain. This vision of oneness subsumed England's history of internal and imperialist relations of domination and subordination in an identity whose initial frontier of distinctiveness was race followed by gender, class, and sexuality. The Scottish, Welsh, Irish, and other "white" ethnic groups were conscripted into an idea of nationhood that saw the United Kingdom as an "imagined" frame for enunciating subjectivity. English racial nationalism mirrored colonial nationalism in its project to build consensus through assimilation, however forced. Hegemony is colonial in its performance of a dominant culture's power. It names and occupies spaces, influences psyches, determines limits of subjectivity through modes of representation, and where its consensual tangents are rejected or resisted, overtly applies coercive and repressive means of seeking adherence from its citizens. This apparatus of dominance is all too familiar in the colonies, where colonial nationalism entices and coerces subject populations into its logic. I saw England's hegemony vis-à-vis Ireland, Scotland, and Wales as an internal form of colonization, although its performance in the British Isles might seem liberal in comparison to its dictatorial enactment in formerly colonized Afro-Asia.

Margaret Thatcher's racist rhetoric of English nationalism, couched in the language of European modernity, or nineteenth-century liberalism as she put it, bore an indelible imprint of its colonial variant. Her grandiloquent pronouncements dripped with metaphors harking back to the great days of empire, and portrayed her stewardship of the nation as a moment of renewal that would restore Great Britain to a glory befitting its imperial past. She sought to achieve this promise by repressing various groups within England in ways that recalled imperial England's coercive tactics against anticolonial dissent. The European modernist philosophy of nineteenth-century liberalism, which exalted free markets and unfettered enterprise, and sought to limit state power, served as the rationale for her policies. Thatcher's vilification of labor leaders, and the subsequent collapse of the miners' strike under her watch, debilitated labor unions as modes of organizing working-class protest. Her project to dismantle the English welfare state colonized the working class still further. Persuaded that business prosperity would trickle down to lesser folks, she slashed income taxes for the wealthy to encourage new investment and enacted regressive sales taxes that spelled enormous hardships for the poor. Her aversion to education and health programs undermined post-imperial England's quest for social equity.

An overt commitment to white supremacy, justified on the free market grounds of economic productivity, underpinned the Thatcherite imagination of English nationhood. Allegedly unproductive non-white immigrants from England's former colonies were urged to take advantage of "assisted repatriation." Race riots convulsed the nation in 1981. Thatcher then turned to the annals of empire to bolster her plummeting popularity. When Argentina invaded the English Falkland Islands in 1982, the faraway South Atlantic became a new theatre for the Prime Minister's nostalgic performance of Britannic imperialism, cloaked in the stirring language of patriotism. It became increasingly clear to me, a recently arrived post-colonial subject from Africa, that the colonial structuring of society so well developed outside England had become the political template with which England governed itself.

It was against the background of this resurgent xenophobic racialism that I witnessed the inauguration of Bristol city's first black mayor. Like other port cities including Liverpool, Bristol was founded in large part on the wealth flowing from England's role in the trans-Atlantic slave trade, as well as from slave-grown tobacco in the New World. In a city where the exhibition of manacles and other slave-age memorabilia in pubs and streets visibly recalled its part in the history of African bondage, the election of a black mayor was of considerable import. At the same time, the Commonwealth communities of St Andrew's, St Paul's, and Easton joyously and defiantly asserted the new England's multinational identity through festivals like St Paul's Carnival.

These events suggested that the formal exposition of Thatcher's brand of colonial nationalism did not narrate the whole story of contemporary England. That, in fact, marginalized people found many ways to imagine and live an alternative England, even within the constraints imposed by a hegemonic nationalistic discourse. The England I came to know was, like its former colony Nigeria, caught between "overlapping modernities" which created cultural spaces to contest subordination, and articulate postcolonial desires for effective citizenship and agency. Through the medium of my supervisor John Marshall, I immediately found a "home" among English dramaturges and theatre artists, who use their cultural practices to transform their consciousness of domination into acts that "deterritorialize" hegemonic power from its spheres of influence.

Oppositional playwrights like John Arden, David Edgar, and Caryl Churchill all in their own ways used their drama to contest a unitary sense of Englishness. They acknowledged, indeed celebrated, England's emerging postcolonial identity by imagining nationhood through the prism of cultural pluralism. Their works delineated inter-modernist spaces on the margins of Thatcher-style nationalism bounded by the parameters of race, class, ethnicity, and homosexual identity. As in Nigerian drama, these spaces not only marked the limits of access to effective citizenship, but also represented fertile breeding grounds for decolonization movements. Resistant dramatists in England also depicted the intra-modernist conflicts among communities placed at the margins of the dominant culture. By identifying symbolisms of inter-modernity and the crisis that intra modernist hybridity creates, their dramas and theatres opened up a new space for enunciating subjectivity – a non-formal space, where identity and cultural practices fragment, demystify and limit the power of dominance.

Thus, the political and cultural manifestations of a colonizing European modernity or "nineteenth-century liberalism" – the tormented legacy of empire – served as the common standard against which movements of resistance in both Nigeria and England defined themselves and articulated their visions for the future. As far as Nigeria was concerned, imperialism had laid the foundation of a neo-colonial state that failed to sustain the promise of self-determination and social justice opened up by anticolonial nationalism. At the same time, the experience of empire transformed England itself into something of a postcolonial society by fueling a flood of Afro-Asian immigration to England in the wake of decolonization, and prompting contentious controversies over the meaning of "Englishness." I saw dramaturgies of resistance in the contexts of both Nigeria as well as its former master England, as sharing a common allegiance to what I have already described as *postcolonial desires*, that is, the aspiration to overcome the legacies of colonialism by imagining alternative universes anchored in democratic cultural pluralism. Such postcolonial aspirations transcended temporal locations to encompass varied moments of consciousness for progressive change, whether they happened during the heyday of English imperialism in early twentieth-century Nigeria, or in response to the exclusionary politics of the Conservative Party in Thatcherite England.

It is this transnational, trans-cultural reach of the postcolonial impulse that inspired this comparative study of colonial encounters and post-imperial contests over identity, power, and culture through the prism of theatre. The struggles I describe unfolded in two cultural settings separated by geography, but bound by history in a common web of colonial relations spun by the imperatives of European modernity. In post-imperial England, as in its former colony Nigeria, the colonial experience not only hybridized the process of national self-definition, but also provided dramatists with the language, imagery, and frame of reference to narrate the dynamics of internal wars over culture and national destiny happening within their own societies. Thus, while anticolonial nationalism and postcolonial desires helped articulate Nigerian aspirations for democracy in an era of post-independence dictatorships, they offered English radicals a template for describing class oppression in terms of the ethnicization and colonization of workers at home. They unleashed furious debates over the boundaries of an authentic "African" identity in Nigeria, even as they prompted some English writers to re-inscribe "Englishness" with the inclusive spirit of cultural pluralism.

The battle for signs embedded in these cultural contests between the imperialist and the colonized, the elite and the subaltern, and among the subordinate themselves, occurred in what I have explained as inter-modernist and intra-modernist spaces, hybridized in large part by colonial reorganization and assimilation. For instance, the incorporation of the formerly colonized into the English proletariat means that a member of the English working class may also be a Nigerian-English, Pakistani-English, Jamaican-English, or Irish-English. Likewise, in Nigeria, the English colonial ordering of myriad ethnicities into the four categories of Igbo, Yoruba, Hausa, and "other minorities" shaped a highly diverse and often fractious nationalist constituency. Thus, the discourse of decolonization and post-colonial desires is inherently pluralistic.

The book features prominent Nigerian and English playwrights who came of age after the passing of the British Empire. My selection of these dramatists was governed not simply by the extent to which I judged them representative of particular genres, but also by the fact that I, as the narrator, from my location as a postcolonial subject, personally encountered the artists and their works in particular contexts that contributed to the evolution of my thesis. They include such doyens of political theatre as the Nigerian Nobel laureate Wole Soyinka, his celebrated nemesis Femi Osofisan, and the feminist writer Tess Onwueme. My discussion of Nigeria's Theatre for Development draws upon my personal experiences with community theatre to introduce readers to Africa's non-literate theatrical traditions that target post-colonial (after the empire and coloni-alism) poverty. The chapter on Yoruba Traveling Theatres highlights the uses of ethnic identity in anticolonial and post-colonial struggles.

As I shift my gaze to England, I address dramas that most directly engage the interplay between imperial histories and the invention of postcolonial national destinies. They include the works of the social realist John Arden, the socialist aesthete David Edgar, and the feminist author Caryl Churchill, who aimed to craft democratic modes of representation, offer a pluralistic vision of national identity, and demystify the enterprise of imperialism. In an attempt to illustrate the hybridity of democratic identities for which political theatres in England seek spaces, I also examine English theatre groups and plays, which portray feminist, homosexual, and black protagonists. I look at their works as forms of representation in both their corporeal and discursive senses. While the corporeal focuses on a play's artistic conventions, the discursive refers to the deep social and political meanings of its themes. I refer to this dual characterization of representation as its "iconic" and "indexical" nature. I also argue that drama and theatre articulate postcolonial desires through ideological projections in the symbolisms they evoke as well as within the minds of the audiences who watch them.

The productions of the featured Nigerian and English dramatists and theatre movements, and the contexts of their production and reception, serve as the filters through which I aim to illustrate the operation of "overlapping modernities," and reconfigure notions of power and representation, citizenship and subjectivity, colonizing nationalisms, and postcolonial desires as discussed in the course of this Introduction.

I use the tools of postcolonial analysis to understand critiques of European modernity and visions of counter culture not only in the familiar terrain of the formerly colonized, but also in the context of their post-imperial metropolitan masters. Several Western cultural theorists and theatre scholars such as Peter Brooks, Richard Schechner, Eugenio Barba, and Karen Barber, have examined non-European performance traditions by translating them into European frames of reference. By contrast, this comparative work represents an exercise in "reverse ethnography," in that its African-born author trains his critical, and often-personal gaze upon his native culture before applying the analytical paradigms forged in the study of Nigeria to political theatre in England. For, decades after my weekend of symbolic transportation to Lokoja through the graceful gyrations of those masked performers, I, as a teacher, writer, performer, and producer, remain optimistic about the power of performances of representation to spur consciousness and galvanize agency for winning democratic citizenship in a range of local and global spaces.

Part 1
Nigeria

1 Wole Soyinka

Theatre, mythology, and political activism

IYALOJA (the head market woman): (*She turns to the* BRIDE *who has remained motionless throughout.*)
Child.
(*The girl takes up a little earth, walks calmly into the cell and closes* ELESIN'S *eyes. She then pours some earth over each eyelid and comes out again.*)
Now forget the dead, forget even the living. Turn your mind only to the unborn.
(IYALOJA *leaves, accompanied by the* BRIDE. *The dirge rises in volume and the women continue their sway. Lights fade to a blackout.*)
THE END[1]

The head market woman Iyaloja's words of advice to a young bride-turned-widow at the conclusion of Wole Soyinka's complex play *Death and the King's Horseman*, captures a hopeful vision of tragedy unique to Africa's premier playwright. Soyinka's genius in using the tragic myths of Yoruba culture to forge a compelling language of resistance and change has drawn many admirers and a few detractors. His perspective on crisis and chaos as ingredients for social transformation, rather than an Aristotelian lesson on the wisdom of returning to an established order, has been alternately celebrated and vilified.[2] Yet, few can deny his influence in shaping what the historian Nicholas Dirks describes as "the politics of thinking about power and resistance."[3]

Wole Soyinka, born of Christian parents in the Yoruba town of Abeokuta at the height of English colonialism in 1931, is widely acknowledged as Africa's greatest, if sometimes inscrutable, dramatist. Educated at University College, Ibadan, and Leeds University, UK, one-time play-reader for the Royal Court Theatre in London, and a director, actor, teacher, and writer in Nigeria, he is a quintessential denizen of the hybrid interstice that I have called "inter-modernism." His in-between location has arguably shaped his dialectical approach to culture – his resort to "tradition" to argue for change; his use of the English language to subvert Western, rational, epistemologies by breaking down the barriers between past and present, the spiritual and the material; and his recourse to Yoruba particularisms to articulate universalist postcolonial desires. Soyinka's portrayal of the themes of nationalist and transnational crises embodies penetrating philosophical, political, and metaphoric investigations of culture and epistemology in his home continent. No African mixes political activism, art, and philosophical analyses with as much eloquence, energy, and intellectual rigor as does this 1986 Nobel laureate in literature. Taking aim at the overlapping power structures of European and indigenous African hegemonies, Soyinka's works and political activism assume a decolonizing attitude toward emergent and residual tyrannies and forms of domination. They seek to create a space for radical constructions of postcolonial subjectivity – a space that according to the playwright, performs:

> the simultaneous act of eliciting from history, mythology and literature, for the benefit of both genuine aliens and alienated Africans, a continuing process of self-apprehension whose temporary dislocation appears to have persuaded many of its non-existence or irrelevance in contemporary world reality.[4]

Soyinka embarked upon his unorthodox cultural mission of resurrecting postcolonial subjectivities in an age in which intellectual orthodoxies such as Marxism and ethnic nationalism loomed large. From the 1960s through the late 1970s, it became obvious that the nineteenth-century colonial agenda that organized Nigeria had shifted significantly. Anticolonial nationalism had succeeded in developing a republic formally divorced from its imperial relationship with England. Independence offered the new nation a sense of national belonging and global engagement. Academic institutions became locations for developing various schools of critical and creative studies largely framed by the same anticolonial energies that made the new nation possible. Soyinka, like other Nigerian dramatists examined in this book, came from such politically activist academic communities. Before long, however, ethnic rivalries and regional conflict underscored the arbitrary colonial construction of the geo-political entity inherited from the English. Military dictators usurped the first civilian government in 1966, perpetuating the colonial tradition of coercive rule as a tool of unification. A new twentieth-century globalism and commodity fetishism redefined the country solely as an oil-exporting machine, and helped plunge the country into a violent civil war. The eastern Igbos seceded from Nigeria in 1967 and proclaimed the Independent Republic of Biafra, unleashing a three-year civil war that culminated in reunification and savage retribution.

In the aftermath of the civil war, an oil boom gave financial reinforcement to a new wave of state nationalism upheld by a succession of authoritarian regimes. As the country's tiny elite became chauvinistically nationalist, it developed a taste for whatever it did not produce. Buoyed by windfalls from oil revenue, Nigeria imported every consumable commodity, quickly becoming a neo-colonial satellite state clinging to the periphery of the industrialized West. Despite its dependence on economies outside its borders, the nation also developed an arrogant claim to African authenticity. In the 1970s, it hosted the Festival of African Arts and Culture (FESTAC), African Soccer championships, and other events to showcase its coming of age as a nation with the mandate to exuberantly represent Africans inside and outside Africa. Yet, the truth was that it did not speak for all Nigerians, much less the rest of the continent. Excluded from their share in the nation's oil wealth, the masses of Nigerians enjoyed little formal voice in their government.

State nationalism coexisted with cultural practices attempting to understand and critique the state of the nation. Cultural critiques of the official national narrative premised upon Nigerian prosperity and the nation's appropriation of political and cultural leadership in Africa, abounded. Sometimes subtle, at other times brazen, they responded to Nigeria's neo-colonial despair and the sense of social and political alienation experienced by a majority of Nigerians. Artists in a range of arenas crafted alternative visions of nationalism – Fela Anikulapo-Kuti and Sonny Okosun in music; Hubert Ogunde, Ola Rotimi, and Theatre for Development in theatre; "Wonyosi lace" and "agbada" in fashion; oral expressive forms and varieties of the "Nigerian novel" in literature; "Village Headmaster," "Cock Crow at Dawn," and "Icheoku" as well as news in the local languages on television; "Ajani Ogun," "Aropin N'tenia," and "Ikebe" in films.

Within the universities, Marxism and residual forms of anticolonial nationalism offered analytical frameworks for mounting critical challenges to Nigeria's corrupt dominant class and the unitary nationalist ideology it deployed to buttress its regime. Sometimes contesting, at other times complementing each other as they confronted the national government, counter-cultural activists ranged from passionate ethnocentrists to mimics of European political radicalism. Marxist scholarship highlighted issues of class and the neo-colonial economic structure, and presented strategies for defining and empowering working-class identities. Biodun Jeyifo (perhaps the most erudite and politically impassioned of all), Ola Oni, Omofune Onoge, Segun Osoba, Bala Usman, Bade Onimode, G.G. Darah, Chidi Amuta, Ropo Sekoni, and Jibril Ibrahim, all offered interpretations not only of Nigeria's neo-colonial identity in global politics, but also Marxist strategies for democratic change. Trade unionism became a prominent platform for radical activism, as well as a forum for political collaborations between middle-class and working-class Nigerians committed to contradicting and limiting the excesses of the neo-colonial state. The Left not only dominated organized labor but also organized student unionism across the country thus making universities locations for developing counter-hegemonic attitudes. Their writings on history, culture, and ideology depicted a nation in dire need of revolutionary change and international alliances against global capitalism. To the extent that they talked about collectivities, they did so in the context of forming counter-hegemonic blocs, rather than in order to engage issues of the multiplicity and hybridity of individual and group identities.

It was in this milieu that I, as a drama undergraduate at the University of Ife in 1979, first encountered Wole Soyinka. By then, the playwright had already achieved a formidable reputation, not only for creative and philosophical brilliance, but also for his repeated gestures of defiance against Nigeria's neo-colonial masters which landed him in jail in the 1960s. He became an inspiring mentor through my college days and beyond. It was under his tutelage that I learned to develop a healthy skepticism toward essentialisms of all sorts. Within the relative stability of the Marxist tradition of dissent of our day, there emerged a community of social commentators and activists whose ideological "purism" worried Soyinka as much as did the ethnocentrists' uncritical embrace of "tradition" as the path to resistance. His acrimonious exchange with his detractors is well documented in his *Art, Dialogue and Outrage*. Uncomfortable with rigid ideological or cultural orthodoxies of any kind, and of fixed constructs of identities such as "working class" and "middle class" designated by Marxists as agents of change, Soyinka had long offered an alternative approach to thinking about individual and collective identities, about the hydra-headed nature of power, and about resistance and change. He created characters with shifting, multi-positional identities and found, within the paradigm of Yoruba tragedy, conditions and spaces for fostering communal consciousness for transformation without prescribing the precise nature or direction of such change.

Soyinka's revisionist notions of identity, power, and agency unfolded in the course of a versatile body of works spanning well over three decades from the late 1950s through the 1990s which, for the purposes of cataloging, may be placed under three broad but fluid categories. Plays such as *Dance of the Forests, Kongi's Harvest, The Lion and the Jewel, Trials of Brother Jero / Jero's Metamorphosis, Opera Wonyosi, Play of Giants, Requiem for a Futurologist, From Zia with love, The Beatification of Area Boy*, and *King Ubaku* may be classified as "political satire." Others including *The Strong Breed, Madmen and Specialists, The Road, The Bacchae of Euripides*, and *Death and the King's Horseman* may qualify as "metaphysical drama." The third category consists of "political street theatre" skits, which are numerous and include prominent examples like *Before the Blackout / After the Blowout, Priority Projects, Trials and Tribulations*, and *Rice*. Soyinka fashioned the satire of his political sketches into a low-budget film titled *Blues for a Prodigal* and a long-playing record labeled *Unlimited Liability Company*.

Throughout his plays and philosophical pronouncements, Soyinka has consistently sought an adequate language of resistance and the description of an esthetic comprising mythology, politics, and activism. *Kongi's Harvest, The Road*, and *Madmen and Specialists* all suggest elements of this configuration, but it is *Death and the King's Horseman*, in combination with his seminal essay "The Fourth Stage," that offers its most complete and eloquent expression. In the present chapter, I explore Soyinka's creative use of mythic tragedy as an inter-modernist site of contests over "the sign," as well as to devise an empowering discourse of political agency. I read "The Fourth Stage," together with his celebrated play *Death and the King's Horseman* to suggest that Soyinka's dramatic practice represents an inspiring and agitative archeology of postcolonial cultures. Grounded in the conceptualization of mythic tragedy as a site for fueling communal consciousness of marginality and desire for change rather than as a bastion for consolidating tradition for its own sake, his works challenge authoritarianism whether derived from colonial or indigenous sources and enunciate symbolisms of resistance and agency, the birthing, if not the destination of postcolonial desire.

"The Fourth Stage" was first published in an anthology of essays dedicated to the Renaissance scholar G. Wilson Knight in 1969, and later presented as one of a series of lectures at Churchill College, Cambridge. As a philosophical statement offering a decolonizing epistemology, the essay broke controversial new ground in terms of the enunciative space its theory presented for the study of drama in Africa. It evoked a volley of criticism from disparate quarters, most of them located in Africa. Anti-colonial nationalists castigated the essay's dramaturgy as too European. Marxists lamented its alleged lack of class-based antagonism to European colonialism and capitalism.

The frustration of Soyinka's critics lay partly in the difficulty in compartmentalizing "The Fourth Stage" within rigid genres and established esthetic traditions. One was apt to wonder: is the essayist a tragedian or political satirist? Is he a socialist or anticolonial nationalist writer? What are the instrumental values of his mythopoeic writing? Is he sufficiently African? Yet, "The Fourth Stage" suggests that Soyinka's dramaturgy, although inherently political, does not conform to prescriptive models for knowing or describing individual and collective political identities. In the dramatist's own words:

> I have been preoccupied with the process of apprehending my own world in its full complexity, also through its contemporary progression and distortions ... For after (or simultaneously with) an externally directed and conclusive confrontation on the continent must come a reinstatement of the values authentic to that society modified only by the demands of a contemporary world.[5]

In pursuit of his project to apprehend his own world, Soyinka in "The Fourth Stage" takes us into Yoruba cosmology by describing a tripartite structure of the world: the spaces of the unborn, the living, and their ancestors. In such a structure, the acts of being born, of living, and of dying are

seen as natural processes of transition. The birth of a child is an occasion
for celebration as is the death of an old person. The world of the living
is an arena for conscious reparations through sacrifices, rituals, and
mythology codifying the moralities of *being* and *becoming*. In cases of prema-
ture birth or death, oracular wisdom is sought and appropriate sacrifices
are performed to stabilize the world, as the Yoruba know it. Soyinka,
however, complicates and subverts the ontological certainty of this Yoruba
triplicity by suggesting "The Fourth Stage" which in his opinion is fundamentally the most fulfilling of all transitions. Defying temporal linearity,
"The Fourth Stage" is more a desire that catalyzes perpetual action and
focuses on processes of "social acting," than a description of a life stage
or a well-defined historical destination. In other words, it is a process that
summons a consciousness for change without necessarily naming the
manner of such change beyond its immediate anticolonial directions.
Such consciousness can happen in the worlds of the living, and in the
modes of remembering the dead and the ancestors. Its goal is disalienation
as a constant process of deconstructing domination and seeking a language
of equity and justice.

In a conscious act of invoking an epistemology that is indigenous to
Africa and not overdetermined by European colonizing knowledge,
Soyinka delves into a Yoruba legend describing the origin of the world
to support his concept of "The Fourth Stage." According to this legend,
a supreme deity called Orisa-Nla, whose life narrated the cosmic stability
of the universe, symbolized the world. Once, while tending his garden,
his servant Atunda struck the supreme deity with a rock, shattering this
symbol of cosmic unity into a thousand and one pieces. Soyinka had
celebrated this rebellious act in an earlier poem *Idanre*: "All hail saint
Atunda, first revolutionary/Grand iconoclast at genesis and the rest is logic
. . ."[6] He returned to it in "The Fourth Stage," explaining that fragments
of the disintegrated icon of cosmic wholeness symbolize various godheads
in the Yoruba pantheon and are assigned different but complementary
metaphysical functions in the mythologies of Yoruba cultures. Other
smaller pieces and the dusts of cosmic disintegration are thought to form
the world of human beings. Consequently, Atunda's insubordinate act led
to the physical formation of two seismically divided worlds: those of the
gods and of human beings. The helplessness of these disparate worlds was
underscored by the huge gulf separating them. Various frightening
metaphors conjured by Soyinka describe not only the enormity of the
alienating gulf between these two worlds, but the impending violence that
promised to attend any act of transgressing either. The physical gulf and
the social alienation between the gods and human beings that it symbolized became a factor of constant concern for the gods in particular as
they tried in vain to fulfill various functions bestowed on them by Orisa-
Nla's parts. One of the more daring of their number, characterized
simultaneously by creative and destructive impulses, became a prominent

actor in his persistent quest to bridge the chasm between the gods and the humans. That god, Ogun, drew magma from the core of the earth to construct a bridge for that purpose. As Ogun walked the bridge at the head of a brigade of other gods in search of disalienation, however, he was thwarted by the violence of natural elements guarding the structure. Dismembered, but not with the finality of disintegration experienced by Orisa-Nla, Ogun as a regenerative principle, was reconstituted, and came back to enact his walk many times more. This god's indefatigable pursuit of disalienation made him attractive enough for the dramatist to adopt him as his "patron saint."

Soyinka's use and treatment of the legend of Ogun in "The Fourth Stage" illustrate socio-political themes and esthetic features that characterize much of the playwright's dramatic legacy. Several of his works similarly highlight conditions of alienation and go on to problematize the processes of social activism, drawing attention to issues of individual and collective agency. From his *Jero* plays, *Opera Wonyosi*, *Strong Breed*, and *The Road*, to *Before the Blowout* and the *Priority Project* sketches, Soyinka textualizes his passion for social justice with artistic eloquence. It is, however, his conception of "tragedy" and the notion of agency it incorporates that has made "The Fourth Stage" the subject of intense scrutiny as a marker of Soyinka's dramatic style.

For Soyinka, tragedy is a song of lamentation expressing conditions of alienation and stimulating intense motivations for change. Defying teleological structures, the tragic does not signify paralysis or blind adherence to constituted mythology; rather it is a situation setting up ontological certainties, only to destabilize them so as to enable creativity and the pedagogy of self-reproduction. In developing what he calls "African Tragedy," Soyinka proposes an esthetic principle where the objective of tragic art is not to provoke a catharsis that terrorizes and consigns a community to fatalism and to a logocentric description of its world. Rather, it hypersensitizes the community to conditions of inequity and prompts a deliberate inventiveness that seeks to harness cultural resources to achieve disalienation. As Ogun's perseverance suggests, what makes this approach of a constructive, socially activist tragedy unique, is its stress on repetitive, cyclical, and perpetual action as the essence of agency, anticolonial subjectivity, and postcolonial desire. This is quite similar to Fanon's notion of action, which in the context of colonial domination "exposes an utterly naked declivity where an authentic upheaval can be born."[7]

"The Fourth Stage" challenged the rational epistemological assumptions of the West by depicting seamless transitions between past, present, and future, and between the worlds of gods and of humans – transitions rendered in the English language of Nigeria's colonizers. Yet, its epistemological challenge to European modernity did not translate into an automatic endorsement of the supposed purity or supremacy of indigenous mythology. Instead, in a neo-colonial context, Soyinka's approach implies that the quest for decolonizing social and political identities must go beyond essentializing pristine traditions and structures conveniently remembered and kept intact through mythology. Unlike the anticolonial nationalisms of such movements like "Negritudism" and "Afrocentrism," he urges the development of a consciousness of power relations within and between *internal as well as* external discourses of domination. His political attitude and cultural practice highlight the workings of intra-modernist tensions by suggesting that the tyrannical role of power in alienation and social inequity – whether foreign or domestic in origin, must be represented, framed, and possibly subverted by individuals and societies through transformative processes. Mythology, as an ideological and epistemological resource, is a site, not for canonizing tradition and arresting social development, but for energizing the human spirit's desire for self and communal reproduction. As Soyinka himself states, the purpose of the tragic paradigm as he articulates it, is to signify human beings as socially active and "acting" beings. The value of Yoruba mythic tragedy lies in its symbolic representations of the essence of human subjectivity and social agency, the impulse:

> To act, the Promethean instinct of rebellion, channels anguish into a creative purpose which releases man from a totally destructive despair, releasing from within him the most energetic, deeply combative inventions which, without usurping the territory of the infernal gulf, bridges it with visionary hopes.[8]

Soyinka's use of the tragic paradigm of Yoruba mythology to define notions of subjectivity and issue calls for positive social change emerges most distinctly in his classic play, *Death and the King's Horseman*. It is also this work that most clearly illustrates his use of "tradition" as a site for inter-modernist and intra-modernist struggles for the sign. The following pages present an analysis of this work as a key to Soyinka's vision of post-colonial dramaturgy.

Death and the King's Horseman

The city-state of Oyo offers the setting for Soyinka's most elaborate illustration of his concept of tragedy. The play narrates the parable of Elesin Oba, the chief custodian of the king's stables and one of the most highly regarded chiefs after the king. Oyo tradition has marked Elesin, by virtue of his lineage and social status, to serve as a sacrament in a high ritual after the death of the reigning king. The conventions of the land require that the chief, like other specifically designated individuals collectively named Abobaku,[9] commit a ritual suicide at a specific time and place in honor of the dead king and community's sense of self. When the moment for this supreme sacrifice arrives, however, Elesin is unable to perform his prescribed role owing to an act of self-indulgence on his part as well as the colonial administrator's proscription of the ceremony. The colonial officer, Simon Pilkings, imprisons him as the community laments the impending demise of a familiar world they had sustained for eons, a world whose ontological certainties appear to be slipping away. Meanwhile, Elesin's son, Olunde, sent to England to train as a medical doctor, returns to attend to his father's funeral, only to confront his father alive. In an attempt to restore his family's honor and dignity, he, as his father's heir, commits the ritual suicide designated for his parent, thus fulfilling the dictum of his community's existential narrative. As though to contradict the logic of colonial assimilation, Olunde takes his own life in order to re-orient the community's desire for alternative subjectivity. Upon learning of his son's redemptive act, Elesin, languishing in a colonial jail, also commits suicide. The place and manner of his self-execution, thus, occurs outside the prescriptions of the community's codes of ritual. By the play's end, the tragic protagonist cursed with an identity drained of all communal significance, rids the world of his presence by strangling himself with his chains in his prison cell – a cavernous metaphor for colonial subjugation.

Death and the King's Horseman presents dramatic conflict as multilayered and complex rather than a Manichean contest between well-defined heroes and villains. Tensions between Elesin and his community serve as the fulcrum around which the play revolves. Embedded within this larger plot, however, are other smaller but related conflicts over the colonial strategy of assimilation, and the tyranny of patriarchy among the imperial and colonized alike. The play tells a story based upon a well-known folklore that inspired other plays by two popular Nigerian dramatists – Duro Ladipo and Baba Sala. What makes Soyinka's version distinctive is its political setting in Nigeria's twentieth-century colonial world. The historicity of the moment captured by the play complicates its tragic paradigm in interesting ways. By 1944, when the event it describes occurred,[10] Oyo, where Elesin's sense of being and belonging was invented and mythologized, had undergone significant hegemonic changes. No longer the imperial nation it once was, Oyo had been annexed to the English Nigerian empire. Framed by the overlapping modernities of their world, its people found in their residual mythologies, the resources to re-invent and re-establish a community whose signifiers of being had significantly changed. This made "tradition" all the more urgent as a site for reproducing an indigenous cultural world, and the import of Elesin's role all the more poignant. The community's determined efforts to excavate and reinstate the political importance of Elesin's identity and place in its traditions must be understood in this light.

The play opens amid the seductive strains of Oyo music intended to cement our identification with the proud and passionately committed Elesin. The dramatist, employing a meta-theatrical device, portrays a drama in search of an audience. Closely followed by his drummers and

Praise Singer, the protagonist struts toward the market place – a venue where he can maximize audience identification with his performance of the ultimate sacrifice. The Praise Singer's enchanting invocation sets up the promise of a ritual of death:

> PRAISE SINGER: Elesin o! Elesin Oba! Howu! What tryst is this the cockerel goes to keep with such haste that he must leave his tail behind?
>
> ELESIN: (*slows down a bit, laughing*) A tryst where the cockerel needs no adornment.
>
> PRAISE SINGER: O-oh, you hear that my companions? That's the way the world goes. Because the man approaches a brand new bride he forgets the mother of his children.
>
> ELESIN: When the horse sniffs the stable, does he not strain at the bridle? The market is the long suffering home of my spirit and the women are packing up to go . . . You are like a jealous wife. Stay close to me, but only on this side. My fame, my honor are legacies to the living; stay behind and let the world sip its honey from your lips.
>
> PRAISE SINGER: Your name will be like the sweet berry a child places under his tongue to sweeten the passage of food. The world will never spit it out.[11]

As Elesin plunges into his self-motivating rhetoric, which equally attracts our identification, we notice how well prepared he is for his death. As a master rhetorician, he weaves proverb with metaphor to dispel any fear or doubts that his prescribed mission might generate. In an Oyo world destabilized by foreign influences, he asserts his determination to stay the course prescribed him by tradition:

> ELESIN: The world was mine. Our joint hands
> Raised housepots of trusts that withstood
> The siege of envy and the termites of time.
> But the twilight hour brings bats and rodents –
> Shall I yield them cause to foul the rafters?[12]

As if to reassure himself and his spectators, he casts his role in terms of the imperatives of honor:

> ELESIN: Life has an end. A life that will outlive
> Fame and friendship begs another name.
> What elder takes his tongue to the plate,
> Licks it clean of every crumb? He will encounter
> Silence when he calls on children to fulfill

> The smallest errand! Life is honor.
> It ends when honor ends.[13]

Elesin's choice of the market place as a site to publicly reclaim the power and honor vested in his traditional identity as a member of the Abobaku is significant. In a colonial world where traditional sources of authority have yielded to imperial masters, he needs the market women's affirmation of his exalted place in the residual patriarchy and political dispensation of Oyo, a place about to be memorialized by his performance of ritual suicide. The Praise Singer's invocational opening notes that Oyo was once whole and pure with a stable culture complete with its own corpus of myth and rituals. In a rambunctious opening glee to a troubling opera, he even suggests with great pride that Oyo is a place where Elesin's impending suicide is an illustration of its cosmic coherence. Elesin's sacrifice signifies a commitment to cultural persistence unsullied by the monumental changes that have swept over Oyo from within and without – changes wrought by war, European slave traders, and English colonialists:

> PRAISE SINGER: ... the great wars came and went; the white slavers came and went, they took away the heart of our race, they bore away the mind and muscle of our race. The city fell and was rebuilt; the city fell and our people trudged through mountain and forest to found a new home but- Elesin Oba do you hear me?
>
> ...
>
> There is only one home to the life of a river mussel; there is only one home to the life of a tortoise; there is only one shell to the soul of man: there is only one world to the spirit of our race. If that world leaves its course and smashes on boulders of the great void, whose world will give us shelter?[14]

Tejumola Olaniyan in his sophisticated and analytically rigorous study of Soyinka's *Death and the King's Horseman*, has rightly described the Praise Singer's persuasive antics as "navel gazing, the esthetics of the pristine and the naïve."[15] The compensatory nature of the singer's cajoling indicates both despair and desire. The despair of a depoliticized residual colonial power as it gropes to recapture its moment of grandeur and significance, and the desire for a more meaningful identity than the museum hall curiosity it now represents. Yet, the ritual suicide, vested with the whole community's aspirations for cultural autonomy, is not to be. For Elesin notices a pretty woman in the market place and asserts the lingering power of his place bestowed by tradition, by demanding her hand in marriage, despite the fact that she is betrothed to someone else. We are immediately exposed to a contradiction as Elesin, that advocate for the retrieval and sustenance of indigenous tradition, insists on conflating a dying ritual with a marriage ceremony:

> ELESIN: All you who stand before the spirit that dares
>   The opening of the last door of passage,
>   Dare to rid my going of regrets! My wish
>   Transcends the blotting out of thought
>   In one mere moment's tremor of the senses.
>   Do me credit. And do me honor.
>   I am girded for the route beyond
>   Burdens of waste and longing.
>   Then let me travel light. Let
>   Seed that will not serve the stomach
>   On the way remain behind. Let it take root
>   In the earth of my choice.[16]

Intimidated by his power, the women grant his wish. It is at that moment that our identification with Elesin is deliberately complicated. The arrogance he displays in cajoling and imposing iconicity on his identity in the absence of a communal consensus on the appropriateness of his marriage sets us up for the tyrannical contradiction in Elesin's personality. For at that moment, the collective subjectivity Elesin invokes and promises is jettisoned for a solipsistic subjectivity. His patriarchal significance is underscored, not by consensual wedlock but by the terror generated by his authority. He takes a bride, a woman already objectified as someone else's, in a world where gender, class, and ethnicity are signifiers of subjection. The mute bride is the body underlining his phallocratic essence.

The wedding is held and consummated, thereby postponing the death ritual. When at last Elesin gets ready to resume his prescribed mission of suicide as promised at the beginning of the play, the Praise Singer sets the stage for the transition from marriage to death in highly symbolic and embroidered language. As Elesin dances a trance faster than the music, avowing his resolve to die, the Praise Singer assumes the persona of the dead king as he sings:

> How shall I tell what my eyes have seen? The
> Horseman gallops on before the courier, how shall I tell what
> my eyes have seen? He says a dog may be confused by new
> scents of beings he never dreamt of, so he must precede the
> dog to heaven. He says a horse may stumble on strange boulders
> and be lamed, so he races on before the horse to heaven.
> It is best, he says, to trust no messenger who may falter at the
> outer gate; oh how shall I tell what my ears have heard?[17]

Just as the audience is lulled into a sense of conviction that Elesin will die, the colonial state intervenes. Simon Pilkings, as imperial England's representative in Oyo, descends on the scene to stop the ritual's proceedings, and arrest and imprison Elesin. Elesin's Oyo is under the dominion of a Colonial District officer who is playing host to the visiting Prince of Wales. The imperial visit demands that the colonial officer, Pilkings, be able to demonstrate unquestioned acceptance of his rule by the Crown's African subjects.

Imperial England practiced a strategy of indirect rule in most of what became colonial Nigeria. Unlike their French counterparts, the English developed institutions and moralities that reorganized and re-oriented indigenous cultural practices, permitting the persistence of "traditional customs" drained of political meaning. As Nicholas Dirks has observed, "much of what has been taken to be timeless tradition is, in fact, the para-doxical effect of colonial rule, where culture was carefully depoliticized and reified into a specifically colonial version of civil society."[18] Pilkings' previous encounters with Elesin had left him in no doubt as to the horseman's political pretensions and potential for subverting the colonial order. What spurred the English administrator's proscription of Elesin's ultimate act of social commitment was thus the political connotation of Elesin's impending action, particularly its timing. The play reveals the markings of dominance not only on subordinated bodies and spaces, but also in the conception and practice of *time*. In Pilkings' own words: "Damn! If only the Prince hadn't picked this time for his visit"[19] or as Elesin himself confirms: "You were waiting for dawn white man. I hear you saying to yourself: only so many hours until dawn and then the danger is over. All I must do is keep him alive tonight."[20]

But for the Crown Prince's visit, it would have been a relief for Pilkings to see Elesin die in a depoliticized cultural practice, but the timing of the horseman's sacrifice infused it with political meaning, and hence rendered it a challenge to colonial authority. Soyinka's introduction of this historic dynamic of time and the politics of cultural symbolism testifies to his dramaturgic inventiveness. English colonial regimes in India, Nigeria, and Ghana made significant use of symbolic manifestations of power. Through its "durbars" and parades, the British Empire presented a spectacle of domination at once inclusive and exclusive of the dominated natives. As Helen Callaway has noted:

> Imperial culture exercised its power not so much through physical coercion, which was relatively minimal though always a threat, but through its cognitive dimension: its comprehensive symbolic order which constituted permissible thinking and action and prevented alter-native worlds from emerging.[21]

Soyinka's depiction of Pilkings offers trenchant insights into the psyche of colonial administrators. Trained in English public schools followed by Oxford or Cambridge, several of these officials saw local colonial power structures, in Bradley's words, as "the prefectorial system writ large, and *mutatis mutandis*, the District Officers as masters, the Chiefs as prefects, and the tribesmen as the boys."[22] From Pilkings' perspective, not only was the prevention of ritual sacrifice in keeping with imperialism's civilizing mission, but, coinciding as it did with the Prince of Wales' visit, might with some luck, even earn him a title to validate English approval of his action. His character brings to mind Margaret Perham's depiction of Governor General (Lord Lugard), architect of the colonial state of Nigeria: "Lugard and his envoys seem to dash about the country like knight errants, punishing wicked people and liberating the oppressed, overthrowing cruel kings and elevating good ones."[23]

Yet, in *Death and the King's Horseman*, Pilkings' pretensions to fulfill the obligations bestowed by "the white man's burden" à la Lugard, appears, ironically enough, to be abetted to some degree by Elesin himself. For it is Elesin's moment of self-indulgence – his insistence on postponing death for marriage – that by coinciding with the English Prince's visit, creates the occasion for Pilkings' intervention. Even as Elesin desperately desires to signify, arrest, and stabilize the moving social world woven into a new globalism, the one he and his community inhabit, he becomes solipsistic. He prises an individualistic self from a communally derived iconicity. At such moments we notice that while Elesin likes the honor vested by the community in his identity, he is reluctant to fully accept the communal obligations prescribed by tradition that flow from that honor. Iyaloja reminds him after his arrest:

> IYALOJA: You have betrayed us. We fed you sweetmeats such as we hope awaited you on the other side. But you said No, I must eat the world's leftovers . . . We said you were the hunter returning home in triumph, a slain buffalo pressing down on his neck, you said wait, I first must turn up this cricket hole with my toes . . . We said, the dew on earth's surface was for you to wash your feet along the slopes of honor. You said No, I shall step in the vomit of cats and the droppings of mice; I shall fight them for the left-overs of the world.[24]

It is Pilkings of all people, who exposes the real excuse for Elesin's hesitation: "the elder grimly approaches heaven and you ask him to bear your greetings yonder; do you really think he makes the journey willingly?"[25] Indeed, Elesin confirms his unwillingness during his confession to his new bride:

For I confess to you, daughter, my weakness came not merely from the abomination of the white man who came violently into my fading presence, there was also a weight of longing on my earth-held limbs. I would have shaken it off, already my foot had begun to lift but then . . .[26]

It is Elesin's son Olunde who fulfills his father's mandate. Olunde, in many ways the central character in the saga, is the very embodiment of an inter-modernist struggle for the sign. Oyo's colonial masters have chosen this character to assume an altogether different mandate from the one he ultimately discharges – that reserved for select members of the colonized who are socially mobile and acculturated to English norms and practices. Soyinka's invention of the character of Olunde is laden with multiple layers of meaning flowing from this dynamic. Pilkings sends Olunde to England to train as a medical doctor, thus symbolically usurping the authority of Elesin's paternal role, and that of the local elites the African represented. Yet, Olunde proves far less malleable a subject of cultural assimilation than Pilkings could have anticipated.

We first meet Olunde in Act Four of the five-act play, when he returns to Oyo, expecting to bury his martyred father. Entering an ostensibly binary world of imperial master and colonized subject, Olunde's foreign education gives him a hybrid identity carrying cultural capital that he can ill afford to squander in a project of Oyo cultural resurrection. Soyinka's Olunde, loosened from the communal moorings anchoring his father, appears at first glance to be a "sign in the making," seeking the most appropriate context for attaining full signification. In the end, it is his native culture that provides that context. Far from severing his cultural affinity to Oyo traditions, Olunde's experience with colonial assimilation and alienation creates in him an ever more fervent desire to redefine himself in local terms. Fanon's description of the colonized subject's alienation in *Black Skin, White Masks* offers an insight into Olunde's trauma of being, or non-being:

> I had to meet the white man's eyes. An unfamiliar weight burdened me. In the white world the man of color encounters difficulties in the development of his bodily schema . . . I was battered down by tom-toms, cannibalism, intellectual deficiency, fetishism, racial defects . . . I took myself far off from my own presence . . . What else could it be for me but an amputation, an excision, a hemorrhage that spattered my whole body with black blood?[27]

Like a rebellious son seeking attention from his domineering father, Olunde arrives at Pilkings' official residence, the seat of his hospitality to the Prince of Wales, to proclaim his defiance of the identity the acculturated native received from his surrogate father and colonial master.

Olunde is possessed with the simple desire to defy colonial identification. Within such desire resides a sense of agency and identification with the native environment from which he is alienated. Frantz Fanon again comes in handy in describing such desire:

> As soon as I desire I ask to be considered. I am not merely here and now, sealed into thingness. I am for somewhere else and for something else. I demand that notice be taken of my negating activity in so far as I pursue something other than life . . .[28]

Olunde's act of suicide – that "negating activity" in the pursuit of "something other than life" underscores his desire for something other than colonial "life." The betrayal of Oyo tradition by his other father (Elesin) provides the occasion to fulfill Olunde's quest for recognition, not just from Pilkings and colonial discourses, but also from the Oyo community from which he is excised. In an unequivocal recognition of Elesin's personal failure to uphold the honor of his family and community, Olunde declares, "I have no father, eater of left-overs."

As one whose body is a signifier emptied of its indigenous contents, but whose act of self-sacrifice confers upon him a new identity within his native context, the question that Olunde raises is, what kind of agency does he exercise? Sympathizers of Oyo nationalism might applaud Olunde's action. Yet, it is useful to remember that the discourses of European and Oyo colonial regimes left Olunde and his father with little room for individuality. Soyinka complicates our identification with either character by challenging Negritudist investments in an allegedly binary division between European and African traditions. Indeed, Olunde embodies overlapping cultures defining not only Oyo, but also Nigeria, the new colonial entity into which it is conscripted. His character belongs in a world that is simultaneously local and global. His role introduces incoherence into colonial domination, but not because Soyinka is interested in essentializing and authenticating Oyo myth and ritual. Rather, my reading of the dramatist suggests that he seeks to politicize his audiences into rejecting the ascendancy of colonial logic, which describes the world in Manichean terms of good and bad, civilized and barbaric, European and native. Tejumola Olaniyan is correct in arguing, "Olunde's suicide in affirmation of the indigenous culture is . . . a deflation of the colonialists' pretensions to ethical superiority."[29] The deflation of colonial ethical superiority entails an inherent challenge to imperial epistemologies that embraced neat polarities of the civilized European and the savage Other. More significantly, Olunde's act of sacrifice, however inconclusive and ambiguous its nature, signifies empowerment – a will to act, especially in light of his colonized identity.

Thus, Olunde's action must not be read as a celebration of essentialist indigenous identities and cultural spaces. Indeed, Soyinka has assumed a distinctly anti-essentialist stance elsewhere, most famously in his response to Negritudism: "A tiger does not boast its tigritude." In *Death and the King's Horseman*, if he appears to deploy an essentialist paradigm, it is to advance an anti-essentialist thesis on subjectivity. As the drama unfolds, the mesmerizing language and structure of the ritual of death begins to look dubious and, like the Praise Singer, we notice a "double speak" on the part of the dramatist. Within the seductive foundationalist "grand recit" of traditionalism, subtle critiques and doubts about the true meaning and worth of Oyo rituals, strategically inserted into the drama, gradually evolve into an anti-foundationalist attitude.

Soyinka's treatment of intra-modernist power relations, too, undermines the binary construction of Europe and its African Other. The fields of signification portrayed in the play do not simply represent the old Oyo versus the new English, rather traditional Oyo is itself a product of internal colonial structures and external colonial accommodation. The dynamic between English colonial characters on the one hand, and a ripening anticolonial nationalist moment in the aftermath of the Second World War on the other, suggests the presence of an archeology of overlapping colonial powers – one residual and the other emergent. After all, the patriarchal authority bestowed upon Elesin by Oyo tradition and tolerated by colonial authorities – as long as it did not translate into anticolonial political behavior – enables him to tyrannize the market women into endorsing his ill-conceived wedding.

Indeed, it is Soyinka's depiction of the workings of patriarchy in a variety of social and cultural contexts, both indigenous and colonial, that does most to muddy the boundaries between the worlds of imperial master and colonized subject, and to introduce a crisis of intra-modernism into the story. Pilkings infantilizes his wife Jane as much as he does his servant Joseph, his constable Amusa and all other non-Europeans. Indeed, the character of Jane Pilkings evokes Anne Stoler's description of the role of colonial wives as markers of race, class, and gender.[30] Portrayed as a simpleton whose body is the signifier of limits, Jane's identity like Olunde's is assumed to be "spoken for" by the European colonizing project. As the natives offer Pilkings a community to be domesticated, so also it is important that his wife serve as an exemplar of blissful domesticity. Helen Callaway's brilliant anthropological study of "colonial wives" stresses the marginalization of European women in the imperial project: "The conquering soldiers and visionary empire-builders of these vast, roadless, not yet fully mapped territories had to be men, not boys and certainly not women . . ."[31] The only form of agency allowed Jane Pilkings is a total submission to her husband's colonial mission. Jane seems to be adhering to Emily Bradley's advice to colonial wives in *Dearest Priscilla: Letters to the Wife of a Colonial Civil Servant*:

You must be happy to be alone, yet glad to put everything aside and be at anyone's disposal. You must be interested in the work, and yet a refuge from it, knowing nothing and yet everything about it. You may shed the light of your charming personality on the company, but more often sink into a shadowy corner, still, anonymous and non-existent, concerned that these creatures are fed and refreshed, with everything arranged so that your triumphs are unnoticed and you are utterly taken for granted.[32]

While Jane has a speaking presence but no seriously proactive identity, Elesin's Oyo bride remains mute throughout the play. Her encounter with Elesin takes her body from her, and turns it into a womb for pro-longing his iconic identity after he is gone. Both her significance as the body Elesin designates to carry his future, and her silence, are eloquent and provocative. If Jane signifies the feminine presence underscoring Pilkings' masculine power, the bride represents a silent body upon which the persistent will of a receding patriarchy boldly marks itself, literally denying her a voice.

Iyaloja, unlike Jane or Elesin's bride, controls the market place as a loca-tion for enunciating multiple subjectivities. Despite her authoritative presence, however, her matriarchal privilege serves to legitimate patriar-chal feudalism. She knows the significance of Elesin's choice of the market place as a site for his important performance and like a prepared "stage-manager," she aids the Praise Singer not only in managing Elesin's performance but also in focusing the crowd on the task at hand. Yet, when Elesin chooses for his bride a woman betrothed to her son, she relents. When the horseman fails to fulfill his calling for self-sacrifice, however, it is her power as a matriarch upon which Iyaloja draws to excoriate Elesin, closing the play with a plea to the bride: "Now forget the dead, forget even the living. Turn your mind to the unborn."

Through Iyaloja, Soyinka presents his thesis on agency in a neo-colonial setting. Elesin, Olunde, and the people of Oyo are not organized or conscious enough to resist the overlapping forces of oppression besieging their society. The mantle for action and change will now be the province of the unborn alone – of those not caught between the web of domination and subordination spun by the power structures of European colonial and traditional African societies. Thus, the play closes on a hopeful note expressed through Iyaloja's vision of communal action for the future, even as the precise nature or direction of such action is left undefined.

We are left with the question that framed this analysis of *Death and the King's Horseman* at its start. Namely, how does Soyinka use mythic tragedy to forge a language of active resistance and change, to describe a moment when postcolonial desire is born? Soyinka's dynamic perspective on mythology is built into his creation of mythic tradition as a theatre for struggles over signification. For the Oyo community, the custom of ritual sacrifice signified the continuity of their authentic identity in the midst of change. For Elesin Oba, his own part in the ceremony promised the fulfillment of his grand destiny, ordained from birth, yet one he proved reluctant to discharge. For Pilkings, the significance of the occasion lay in its timing – its coincidence with the visit of his royal overlord from England vested it with an attitude of political defiance to colonial mastery that had to be crushed. Olunde, "civilized" by colonial nationalism, saw his opportunity to redeem the family role in the performance of a ritual sacrifice as a way to register his inter-modernist alienation from the lessons of colonial modernity.

What of Soyinka? What does his treatment of the significations of Oyo's mythic tradition and the tragedy it wrought reveal about his reading of "the sign?" I have argued that for Soyinka, the chief merit of traditional usage lies, not in any "inherent" virtue, but rather its role in subverting colonialist epistemologies and in fostering consciousness for change. Soyinka's reliance on mythology as an epistemological resource for understanding cultural reality and determining agency, places him at odds with those who see mythology only as a site of assimilation, particularly into nativist symbolism. Soyinka boldly proclaims his faith in mythology as a formidable tool for understanding and politicizing social reality. Myth, as a social construct in the hands of dominant cultures, fixes and barricades the fluidity of identities in any community. It imposes a regulative order on culture's heteroglossia. Soyinka's thesis resists the fixing power of mythology by destabilizing the identities it constructs and de-centering the order within which it functions.

That seems to be the open direction of his play *Death and the King's Horseman*. Elesin, as a symbolic text is set up to be destabilized, just as the myth of the colonized native (Olunde) is set up for contradiction. Soyinka suggests that as a sign of knowing, myth is not only the sign of the dominant ideology of the times, but also a site for cultural struggle and agency. His genius lies in seducing his readers and spectators into the narrative structure of mythology with great fluency and dramatic persuasion before jettisoning the stable journey for a chaotic world begging for reformation and change. The dramatist's complexly creative action invites varieties of accents to coincide in any of the signs in the text. Therein lies the transformative and decolonizing potential of his works – that penchant for reversal, substitution, contradiction, re-inscription, and intervention. As Volosinov asserted in *Marxism and the Philosophy of Language*,[33] the symbolic nature of language makes it a useful location of struggle for meaning where varieties of accents coincide. As an organizing principle the symbolisms in language enable the simultaneous performances of assimilation and resistance. For Soyinka, mythic tragedy offers not simply a site for the uni-accentual assimilation into a dominant ideology and its symbolisms; rather, it provides an arena for the performance of multi-accentual energies that can propel social change. The myth Elesin

symbolizes and promises to enact in *Death and the King's Horseman* underscores Volosinov's theory of the radically alternative possibilities of mythology and other symbolic signs in language:

> The very same thing that makes the ideological sign vital and mutable
> is however that which makes it a refracting and distorting medium.
> The ruling class strives to impart a superclass, eternal character to
> the ideological sign, to extinguish or drive inward the struggle between
> social value judgments which occurs in it, to make the sign
> uniaccentual.[34]

Soyinka, like the Praise Singer in his play, seduces us into similar
symbolic signs through the exuberant presentation of Elesin's character
and his impending daring act. But as Stuart Hall opines, "there's no one,
final, absolute meaning – no ultimate signified, only the endlessly sliding
chain of signification."[35] More importantly, the play simultaneously sets up
and deconstructs political subjects and any illusions that they represent the
only subjects who can speak on behalf of the world-view they represent.
No world or character or symbol is given gratuitous stability, they are all
in the throes of regeneration through a fragmentation of the familiar. Myth
as Soyinka has used it, does not guarantee organic unity. Its fixity or
certainty is ideologically spurious.

The significance of myth, in the context of *Death and the King's Horseman*,
stems from its role in propelling tragedy – tragedy that fuels agency, implicitly defined as the determined will to rejuvenate social activism. Crucial to
this formulation of agency is its complex representation of self and community. Agency, as Soyinka's works imply, does not connote solipsistic action;
rather the individual becomes a signifier of communal consciousness and
correction. Solipsistic self, exemplified by Elesin as he interrupts the
communal event of a sacred death ritual to satisfy his personal desire for
a young bride, exists as a tyrannical signifier that must be subverted. Selfish
individualism implies self-destruction and a breeding ground for developing relations of domination and subordination, which for Soyinka's
dramaturgic strategies exist mainly to be debunked. How does Soyinka use
tragedy to put forth this notion of agency? Let us first examine the formal
attributes of Soyinka's concept of "African" or "Yoruba Tragedy" and see
how the play *Death and the King's Horseman* exemplifies such an esthetic paradigm.

A cultural construct enabling people and communities to define themselves as subjects of politically fluid societies is not only a necessity, but
also an urgent political strategy for developing agency in a heterogeneous
continent such as Africa. Soyinka's concept of tragedy seems to be a
response to the dynamics of Africa's histories and cultures. According to
him, tragedy should simultaneously express grief over alienation and spur
intense desires for change and perpetual becoming. Such a notion of

tragedy departs significantly from its Aristotelian counterpart, which sees tragic art as a vehicle to enable a cathartic process through which human flaws are purged to induce conformity to an established moral and political order. Soyinka's play *Death and the King's Horseman*, by contrast, simultaneously depicts the Oyo community's lamentation of turbulent change and its eventual desire, through defiance and resistance to internal and external tyrannies, to be the authors and subjects of such change rather than its objects. Soyinka's dramaturgy suggests that the kernel of agency is the constant ability to adapt to changing circumstances without losing focus of the transformative directions of such developments.

While the goal of Aristotelian tragedy is to produce a cathartic purgation of transgressive behavior, that of Soyinka is to stimulate communal consciousness of "The Fourth Stage" – the idea of transgressing and limiting tyranny so as to create democratic spaces. In *Death and the King's Horseman* the absence of what he called the "Promethean spark" is what initially led the community to its state of tragic anguish. During the major part of the play, the community failed to collectively grasp the "The Fourth Stage," leaving it paralyzed and unable to perform proactive agency. Iyaloja's penultimate words of advice to the bride suggested that it was only at the end, following the deaths of Olunde and Elesin, that the community achieved a sense of agency akin to what Homi Bhabha describes as a "translational" state: "where the construction of a political object that is new, neither the one nor the other, properly alienates our political expectations, and changes, as it must, the very forms of our recognition of the moments of politics."[36]

As a threnody, tragedy, according to Soyinka, provides the community a moment of opportunity to overhaul its mythology and moralities of being. From his location in the intersecting cultural spaces of Africa and the West, of colonialism followed by neo-colonialism, he resists canonizing mythology. Rather, he considers it a resource to promote inclusiveness and action, a resource the narrative of which does not explain the world as much as create a space for enunciative acts, just as the god Ogun did. In Soyinka's own words:

> Man re-affirms his indebtedness to earth, dedicates himself to the demands of continuity and invokes the energies of productivity. Reabsorbed within the communal psyche he provokes the resources of Nature, in turn he is replenished for the cyclic drain in his fragile individual potency.[37]

Unlike the fatalism implied in Aristotelian tragedy, Yoruba tragedy is described as a moment facilitating desires for self-reproduction without necessarily prescribing a specific program for change. Biodun Jeyifo stresses the mythic essence of Soyinka's tragedy by suggesting that the playwright uses his art "as a memory code in periods of social stress or disjunction, and as an antidote to moral complacency and spiritual stupor."[38]

For Soyinka, the destination of social action is secondary to the consciousness and courage to embark on the action itself.

What makes a tragic character in Yoruba or African tragedy, and what kind of identification does Soyinka prescribe for its reception? The tragic characters that Soyinka creates do not exist for themselves; rather they are community icons whose actions facilitate change and a communal sense of identity. They possess enormous will, pride, and the desire to pursue active citizenship. Because a creative and destructive dynamic represents the tragic moment in Soyinka's esthetic, the tragic character serves as the catalyst for regenerative action. The will and psyche of Soyinka's tragic character is defined by the consciousness and desire to facilitate creativity while destroying an insufficient order. In *Death and the King's Horseman*, the tragic character exists in more than one form. Elesin Oba and his son Olunde both have qualities of Soyinka's tragic character if they are looked at as a continuum. One symbolizes the local need for regeneration and the other localizes the global reach of such needs. At the beginning of the play Elesin Oba displays tragic will with arrogant pride while reassuring audiences and readers that the community's desire for becoming is encapsulated in his person. Olunde on the other hand displays his will with calculated understatement. But *Death and the King's Horseman* also cautions audiences that compensatory performances such as those of Elesin or Olunde may indeed highlight gaps between the aspirations of the community and those of the person acting in its behalf. Socially determined roles, democratic or tyrannical, do not necessarily diminish potential discrepancies between an individual's needs and the community's investments in his or her identity. As the plot illustrates, the dramatist invites identification with both characters – Elesin and Olunde – and the dynamics of their cultural contexts. The historical and cultural changes in Oyo turn the iconicity of Elesin's character into a floating signifier whose context of relevance had shifted significantly, while Olunde on the other hand achieves significance in the new environment. That this happens prior to their community's recognition of the fact, underscores the lamentation accompanying Elesin's failure and the apparent incoherence of his son's suicidal action. This strongly suggests that Soyinka demands more attention to the social context that gives characters their discursive depth rather than sole identification with them.

Soyinka insists that the language of a mythic tragedy be "invocational," "liturgical," and "myth embryonic."[39] Accordingly, from the outset, the language of *Death and the King's Horseman* invokes myth and the community's sense of tradition to fulfill narratives of its sense of being. Elesin's trance and exchange with the Praise Singer graphically illustrate the liturgical and mythological nature of the play's language as community members within the play, and readers and audiences outside it, are invited to the drama of a high ritual – one of renewal, where the old ways must forcefully give birth to a new way of accommodating to the dynamics of history. It is the musicality of the language as a vehicle for organizing and conveying the emotional tone of the ritual that Soyinka emphasizes. In his own words, the music of the play's language:

> undergoes transformation through myth into a secret (Masonic) correspondence with the symbolism of tragedy, a symbolic medium of spiritual emotions within the heart of a choric union. It transcends particularisation (of meaning) to tap the tragic source whence spring the familiar weird disruptive melodies. This Masonic union of sign and melody, the true tragic music, unearths cosmic uncertainties which pervade human existence, reveals the magnitude and power of creation, but above all creates a harrowing sense of omni-directional vastness where the creative intelligence resides and prompts the soul to futile exploration. The senses do not at such moments interpret myth in their particular concretions: we are left only with the emotional and spiritual values, the essential experience of cosmic reality.[40]

Thus, music is constitutive of the entire play's narrative structure and engenders identification and recognition. The playwright uses the tonal inflections of the language and music of his play to draw attention to "cosmic uncertainties which pervade human existence." The play's tragic trajectory "prompts the soul to futile explorations." Like his other metaphysical plays, the language of *Death and the King's Horseman* is an intense poetic statement whose imageries animate, thereby stimulating pathos, and offering colorful renditions of the inner thoughts and desires of individuals.

Soyinka goes as far as prescribing the most suitable structure for experiencing the "Masonic union of sign and melody" for a Yoruba tragedy such as *Death and the King's Horseman*. He suggests such a structure should mimic indigenous ritual plays where:

> Any individual within the "audience" knows better than to add his voice arbitrarily even to the most seductive passages of an invocatory song, or to contribute a refrain to the familiar sequence of liturgical exchanges among the protagonists. The moment for choric participation is well defined, but this does not imply that until such a moment, participation ceases. The so-called audience is itself an integral part of that arena of conflict; it contributes spiritual strength to the protagonist through its choric reality which must be conjured up and established, defining and investing the arena through offerings and incantations. The drama would be non-existent except within and against this symbolic representation of earth and cosmos, except within this communal compact whose choric essence supplies the collective energy for the challenger . . .[41]

This structure is implied in the narrative of *Death and the King's Horseman* and it seems that Soyinka conjures a climate of reception in which the audience moves from spot to spot, not in passive voyeurism, but as active participants in the music and dances integral to the presentation.

Overall, I think *Death and the King's Horseman* is a deliberate engagement with post-independence audiences particularly during moments of neo-colonial spiritual and political complacency. As the play illustrates, Soyinka's "The Fourth Stage" (and its emphasis on achieving states of liminality where identities fluctuate) refuses to privilege established modernist actors of social change such as "the oppressed," "colonized," "middle class," and "working class." Rather than romanticizing such easily defined instruments of change, the play describes instead, the conditions that shape a community's consciousness of marginalization and prompt struggles for resistance. Like Homi Bhabha's "Third Space," Soyinka's "The Fourth Stage" opens up "new forms of identification that may confuse the continuity of historical temporalities, confound ordering of cultural symbols, traumatize tradition."[42] This fluid vision of identity is consistent with the notion of non-formal citizenship, which I argue is most conducive to the enunciation of postcolonial desire.

Soyinka's insistence on the fluidity of identity formation and his refusal to allow his creative imagination to be hedged in by prescriptive models for interpreting social reality and history provoked a storm of criticism in Nigeria. In the 1970s, a cohort of ethnic nationalists devoted a large part of their book, *Towards the Decolonization of African Literature*[43] to defining the attributes of an authentic African writer. Led by Chinweizu, they concluded that Soyinka did not qualify as one. The writer's universalist vision, they complained, contradicted local notions of "self." Moreover, his use of English as the linguistic medium of choice elicited the charge that he wrote for European audiences. The irony of the ethnic nationalist critique lay in the fact that in the absence of an indigenous lingua franca, it was the colonial language of English that opened up Soyinka's work to the broadest possible audience in Nigeria itself. Above all, Soyinka's critics across a broad ideological spectrum – from the ethnic nationalists to the Marxists – denounced the dramatist's symbolic allusions to oppression and his refusal to embrace a well-defined direction for change. Soyinka's metaphoric language of resistance took no account of the materiality of tyranny, they charged.

The immediacy of the social and political problems generated by neo-colonialism left most Nigerian intellectuals impatient with seemingly symbolic solutions outside the realm of the social sciences. "Class struggle," "authentic African," "class suicide," "high culture" and "popular culture," "mysticism" and "materialism" – all became catch phrases for understanding the new global dispensation defining Nigeria's present and the local performance of marginality. Apocalyptic pronouncements on capitalism were made even as Nigerian society was violently reorganized by it.

In this intellectual climate, orthodoxies flourished. The decade of the 1970s did not offer an intellectual climate hospitable to Soyinka's conception of culture as a site of socialization, a theatre for the playing out of a dialectic between the symbolic and the social, the individual and community.

In Soyinka's defense, I would argue that identity, culture, and myth as resources for determining being, becoming, and belonging, are always tentative and formulated in difference. Notions of homogeneous groupings like the working class, the people, and the masses, do not provoke as much critical tension nor do they suggest the contiguity and unstable nature of identity and culture. Soyinka's boldness lies in presenting metaphors of the critical tensions between the individual and community and the resourcefulness of such tensions in bringing about social change. He uses his drama to affirm Stuart Hall's assertion that "what we call the self is constituted out of and by difference, and remains contradictory, and that cultural forms are similarly, in that way, never whole, never fully closed or 'sutured'."[44] Contrary to the assertions of his critics, Soyinka's conception of "The Fourth Stage" is a coda for engaging conditions of neo-coloniality. The scope of neo-colonialism is transnational – especially to the extent that it implicates multinationals in the sustenance of dictatorial regimes. In this context, the very flexibility of "The Fourth Stage" as a guideline to non-formal citizenship may embody the most effective mode of resistance, for it opens up the opportunity of coalition building across a spectrum of identities anchored in fixities of nation, region, ethnicity, and religion. Soyinka's vision of decolonization as a transformative, communal process that does not necessarily follow prescribed models of social organization, renders his work a formidable antithesis to the coloniality of power within and outside Africa.

2 Femi Osofisan

Theatre, nation, and the revolutionary ideal

In the field of drama, a recourse to ruse becomes de rigueur, if only because, in theatrical performance, the fate of several persons is involved, hence the artist must accept it as a primary obligation to proceed through such strategies of enlightened guile that will ensure that his or her collaborators do not become the careless victims of official thugs . . . properly deployed, the terror of the state can be confronted, demystified. But it has to be a conscious tactic of deployment, one that has also to be constantly re-tuned and re-honed to the particular moment, a covert and metamorphic system of maneuvering which, for want of a better term, I have summarized as "surreptitious insurrection".[1]

The tyrannical state which Nigeria's radical political dramatist Femi Osofisan seeks to demystify and challenge is a neo-colonial one. Its oppressive logic, however, mirrors colonialism's impact in draining those it dominates of their humanity, forcing them to ask, as Frantz Fanon puts it, "In reality, who am I?"[2] This fundamental existential question lies at the heart of communal and individual stirrings for citizenship in post-imperial Nigeria. It is one that has resonated in the richly metaphorical drama of Femi Osofisan and animated the responses of his primarily middle-class audiences in Africa since the 1970s.

After Wole Soyinka, Femi Osofisan is Nigeria's leading literary figure whose works occupy a hallowed place in high school and university syllabi and are widely performed by university and amateur theatre groups. Like Soyinka, Osofisan was born of Christian parents in a Yoruba town – Erunwon in the state of Ogun. His education, too, was cosmopolitan, embracing the University of Ibadan, Nigeria, the Universite Cheick Anta Diop in Dakar, Senegal, and Universite de Paris III in France. Unlike Soyinka, however, he entered the world as it stood poised on the threshold of decolonization – in 1946, which placed him in a younger generation of more programmatic radical dissidents often impatient with the seeming utopianism of their intellectual forebears. The Marxism and Negritudism he encountered in Paris would leave a lasting imprint on his approach to politically conscious art. His doctoral dissertation, a classic inter-modernist text bearing a hint of Negritudism entitled "The Origins of Drama in West Africa," traced the evolution of African drama from its ostensibly "traditional" roots to its "modern" incarnations in English and French. I met the playwright during his stint as a visiting professor at Ile-Ife which I entered as a student in 1979. I took part in a production of his play *Once Upon Four Robbers* – a celebrated work that I would go on to direct for the Nigerian University Theatre Festival a few years later. It was Osofisan who introduced me to the possibilities and pitfalls of an "indigenous" socialist dramatic tradition.

Most of Osofisan's plays appear to deliberately engage and often contest Soyinka's dramaturgy in an attempt to ignite the revolutionary consciousness of a placid middle class. If, as Soyinka has suggested, his was "a wasted generation," Osofisan indicts his own cohort as one incapable of self-awareness, let alone of conceptualizing agency in a world complicated by neo-colonialism and large-scale corruption. As he writes: "the educated class is at the core of development in any modern economy, and . . . the failure of Nigeria, and in other African countries, is to be traced to the lamentable decadence of that class."[3] He insists that his dramaturgy seeks primarily to forge a radical decolonizing culture and language for this most cosmopolitan of social groups by consistently questioning and challenging its collusion with the neo-colonial state:

> Almost all of my plays, since I became a self-conscious dramatist, have been passionately devoted to it, and dominated by it. In some works I am trying to expose this class failure and probe its causes. In others I am denouncing its corrosive agents, while in others I am ridiculing its antics. And in still others, I am trying to stir the class out of its customary apathy into combat, provoking it into anger and active resistance . . . I am constantly, ceaselessly pounding at the educated class, trying to lance, and heal from within, that abscess which Fanon so presciently identified long ago as our distorted consciousness, and which shows itself in collective amnesia and inertia, in cowardice, and an inordinate horror of insurrection.[4]

An earlier generation of the educated middle class which led Nigeria's nationalist struggle against English imperialism, harbored a hopeful vision of the nascent nation's destiny as Africa's beacon of democracy and prosperity. Such optimism, however, languished in a morass of post-independence corruption, military dictatorship, and poverty. The more thoughtful members of a cynical new cohort of Nigerian bourgeoisie found themselves asking incessantly that existential question, "who are we?" The incoherence of national belonging led inevitably to conflict among ethnic groups reorganized by English colonial policies and reinforced by neo-colonial nationalism into such categories as the Igbos, Hausas and Yorubas.

An offshoot of such rivalries led to the so-called "Biafra War" over Igbo secession in 1967, which killed over two million people. When that war ended in 1970 with the coerced return of the secessionists to the Nigerian federation, the country experienced another moment of collective, although fragile national identity, this time more complex than that produced by the movement for independence from England. The demand for crude oil in industrialized economies generated a great deal of material wealth unsupported, however, by a well-established political infrastructure. The large-scale importation of foreign goods, the construction of universi-ties, and the operation of factories that reproduced First World technology, offered the illusion of a viable nation in the making. The salaries of civil servants were indiscriminately increased and, by 1977, a pan-African Festival of Black Cultures breathed into Nigerian nationalism a sense of local and global significance. The cultural festival gave the Nigerian state a global stage to perform a sense of multiple, although organically coherent national culture concocted around the colonial paradigm of a nation based on a triple ethnicity (Yoruba, Igbo, and Hausa) and surrounded by errant minorities.

The euphoria of nationalism founded upon unity in diversity, did not, however, last too long, particularly for those elements of the middle class, who, hoping to benefit from the oil generated windfall, found themselves in a malaise of economic, political, and cultural paralysis instead. In a society stratified by class, ethnicity, and gender, a dominant sense of state nationalism buttressed by oil wealth asserted itself while other micro-nationalisms emerged to place a majority of Nigerians against the state. The universities provided a space for developing strategies to contest the unitary narrative of nationhood devised by an undemocratic governing elite. Femi Osofisan, like Wole Soyinka and other playwrights, taught and wrote for such disaffected constituencies seeking to challenge the official version of Nigerian national identity.

For Osofisan, theatre is a discursive practice consistently challenging systems within and without its cultural borders. Suffering a sense of betrayal at the hands of anti-colonial nationalists whose campaign for decoloniza-tion terminated with the achievement of a ceremonial and limited political independence, Osofisan persistently criticizes Nigeria's neo-colonial culture for its failure to empower the nation's citizenry at large. He belongs to a generation of Nigerians born amid the independence movement of the post-Second World War era, who came of age in what he called "the tragic period of coups d'état and of noisy military regimes." The world in which they grew up was defined by "unceasing anarchy."[5] As the voice of the new disenchanted and more pragmatic bourgeoisie of the 1970s and 1980s, Osofisan distances himself from the utopian ideals of the earlier generation of anti-colonial nationalists whose democratic aspirations had come to nought:

The older writers represented a watershed, in both the socio-historical and the purely esthetic aspects of artistic expression, and it was a watershed from which we had to depart in order to keep our rendezvous with history ... Muted now are the lyrical, clairvoyant cadences of Okigbo, the raw inchoate passions of Soyinka and his challenging esotericism; and muted also, Achebe's sedate, serious concern for the often-tragic mutations in social culture. These voices, together with their unending mythopoetic narcissism, had to be outgrown and left behind, because when all is said and done, behind their genuinely humane attitude there was always a plea for reactionary or simply impracticable idealist utopia, engaged in the false maze of a tragic cycle.[6]

Osofisan's plays engage and challenge the premises of works by Nigeria's first generation of writers such as John Pepper Clark and Wole Soyinka. Like Soyinka, Osofisan is concerned about the materiality and political dimension of culture and mythology in propelling postcolonial desire and agency. He deploys an art form "glamorously authentic, rooted in the indigenous soil, or at least in the playwright's imagination of it" to do battle against the twin forces of neo-colonialism and military dictatorship.[7] Unlike Soyinka, however, Marxism and revolutionary political philosophies and movements have heavily influenced him. As a result, his dramatic practice is inherently nationalistic, and framed by the rhetoric of European Modernist thinking about nation states and cultures. Indeed, Osofisan was an active member of a left-leaning critical establishment within Nigerian universities in the 1970s that attacked Soyinka for his alleged elitism, Eurocentrism, and reactionary cultural politics. Like his fellow Marxists, Osofisan held a deterministic view of class and cultural identities that left little room for Soyinka's insistence on the fluidity of identity formation. If, for Soyinka, the essence of postcolonial desire lay in communal consciousness of oppression and the aspiration for change, irrespective of the precise ideological direction of that change, for Osofisan such desire, in order to be effective, had to fructify in the establishment of a socialist political entity. It was in this ideological context that Osofisan's dramaturgy entered into an oppositional dialogue with that of his senior compatriot.

Yet in his deployment of creative strategies, Osofisan shared with Soyinka the common hybrid ground of inter-modernism. For, Yoruba mythology became in his hands, a tool not only for subverting the epistemology of European modernity, but also the means to craft an inter-modernist language of socialism – itself an anticolonial, counter-cultural tradition within European modernity. In other words, his plays "irrationally" brought together spirits and humans in order to prescribe a profoundly rational path to equity within European constructs of the nation state. Ultimately, the creative techniques of Osofisan and Soyinka – the parodic mimicry of history, the appropriation of Yoruba storytelling models where divine voices dialogue with humans and animal trickster figures tell parables – go a long way in bridging whatever ideological differences may exist between them.

The combination of a socialist perspective with Yoruba folklore runs like a politico-cultural refrain through much of Osofisan's body of work – from his earliest plays such as *The Chattering and the Song, Who is Afraid of Solarin, Farewell to a Cannibal Rage, Restless Run of Locusts, Once Upon Four Robbers, Eshu and the Vagabond Minstrel, Birthdays Are Not For Dying, Morountodun, Midnight Hotel,* through the more recent *Tegonni* and *Nkrumah-Ni, Africa-Ni.* Sandra Richards captures the ambiguity of his hybrid style when she calls Osofisan "the radical conservative."[8]

Thematically, Osofisan's plays describe Nigeria as a historically determined metaphysical chaos where protagonist characters must contest, re-order, and liberate their identities and the national structure that must accommodate them. Characters appear as artifacts and icons of social strife, in constant struggle as they seek self-definition in a condition of stasis produced by history. As polysemic signs, they are readily recognizable in popular Yoruba and Nigerian folklore, signifiers of the anger, cynicism, and frustrations of the social group they address. The conflicts in which they are embroiled do not constitute struggles among individuals, as much as contests between cultural and political spaces within which the antagonists enunciate agency. The ideological import of Osofisan's plays was especially attractive to university students and professors suffering a gradual but increasingly obvious decline in their economic fortunes since the 1970s. In university theatres, his plays remain the most frequently performed, not only because of their radical appeal but also for their highly innovative theatricality and entertainment value. Music in its residual and emergent mode, dances in their innovatory forms, and storytelling traditions steeped in Yoruba mythology define the esthetics of all his plays. During the annual university theatre arts festivals, it is common to see five or more of his plays presented in a twenty-play festival.

Osofisan's play *Once Upon Four Robbers* offers a particularly compelling illustration of the playwright's dramaturgy and popular appeal. It presents a poignant description of post-independence nationalism and its failure to forge any worthwhile sense of an inclusive national identity and agency. It is set in the historical context of popular disillusionment with the results of independence as Nigeria emerged from colonialism and stepped right into a civil war that lay bare the precarious foundation of Nigerian nationalism. The play targets the wealthy ruling elite which, after succeeding the imperial masters, showed scant regard for the anticolonial movement's promise of self-determination and social justice. Osofisan suggests that the unabashed exploitation of Nigeria's resources by the ruling elite prompted less privileged Nigerians to view their nation as a site of plunder by all. The play contends that only those who benefited from state nationalism projected Nigeria's image abroad as Africa's most remarkable success story and home to the continent's most fortunate citizens, while those marginalized by such nationalism turned to crime and mimicries of state brutality to achieve a sense of self-worth. *Once Upon Four Robbers* offers a vivid rendering of the raucous internal – intra-modernist – tensions that continue to sunder Nigeria's aspirations to a unified nationalism. At the same time, Osofisan's artistic techniques – particularly his use of Yoruba narrative patterns with their mixing of worldly and godly characters, and the interactive mode, blurred the ideological distance between himself and Soyinka. What follows is a detailed analysis of Osofisan's politicized esthetics through the prism of this celebrated play.

Once Upon Four Robbers

The play places at center stage, the issue of armed robbery, which was and still is a familiar malaise in Nigeria's most populous metropolises. Borrowing from Yoruba storytelling traditions, Osofisan offers an open-ended plot, soliciting the participation of his audience in resolving social conflict. The play is set in the city of Lagos and suggests an outdoor performance amid a carnivalesque ambience. The focus on singing and dancing demands a physically vigorous performance from the actors. The dramatist places us diegetically within a folkloric narrative as the vehicle through which we must journey into the city and the psyche of the characters who populate it.

The play is launched by a storyteller who, as in the traditional Yoruba storytelling format, offers to narrate a fable and solicits audience participation in its telling. Not willing to rely solely on the auditorium to bring forth volunteer storytellers, Osofisan plants actors in the audience to facilitate an enthusiastic response to the narrator's promise of a tale. Startled by such an invasion of its own space, the audience is motivated to join in the story as actors emerge from within the seated crowd, singing, walking on to the stage, picking up their costumes, and "casting" themselves in various roles. As narrator and actors begin to settle into their roles and calmness returns to the auditorium, the refrain "Alugbirin gbirin" from actors and audience alike sets the tone for the evening's entertainment. Aafa, the play's narrator proceeds:

An Ancient tale I will tell you
Tale ancient and modern
A tale of four armed robbers
Dangerous highwaymen
Freebooters, source of tears
Like kites, eaters of accursed sacrifice
Visitors who leave the house desolate
Dispatchers of lives to heaven.[9]

Osofisan draws from Yoruba folklore the familiar figure of the tortoise to frame his story. As he explains, his search for inspiration in the repertory of folk-tales yielded several stories concerned with robbery, but none as fascinating as the tale of the Tortoise and the Market Women:

> According to this story, our restless hero discovers the trick of mesmerizing the market people through the use of song. Repeatedly, he uses this trick to lure the traders to sleep, making away with their goods each time. All attempts to catch him fail, as all the guards the traders employ also prove vulnerable to this strange hypnosis.[10]

Osofisan adapts this ancient tale to a modern narrative of urban Nigeria, which despite its claims to modernization and social mobility remains a hotbed of everyday violence. In his opinion, because state nationalism seems to have set an example of pilfering as the dominant mode of effective citizenship, less privileged people take their cue from it to perform this perverse form of patriotism. They stalk the streets and rob the homes of those who have benefited from the new-found, oil-generated opulence.

The play's narrator is not merely a transmitter of its tale. Rather, he signifies other layers of knowledge and ways of knowing available to the audience. Called Aafa, he appears as an Islamic scholar and mystic, with the powers of clairvoyance and magic. Contemporary audiences unfamiliar with Yoruba tradition interpret these powers as conferring upon the character of Aafa the ability to weave, alter, and participate in the story. For the older generations and, indeed, all those familiar with Yoruba cosmology, however, Aafa represents the identity of the god Orunmila – the god of divination, who divines and invites Esu, the trickster god and supreme catalyst of action and agency, to initiate action. According to Yoruba mythology Esu is the complementary "other" of Orunmila through whom divinations about the past, present, and future are made. Sent to the world of human beings by the supreme deity Olodumare, Orunmila's task is to help humans develop knowledge of themselves and the deities with whom they share their cosmos. Endowed with the ability to speak any human language, Orunmila divines, while Esu facilitates the process of enacting action. These deities encode meanings that influence Osofisan's dramaturgy in significant ways.

The opening segment of the play happens in silhouette and silence as a robber is placed on a stake and executed by soldiers choreographed as puppets. Despite the timing of the execution at an early hour, a voyeuristic crowd congregates in a carnivalesque manner, bearing witness to the moment. As the crowd disperses, we end up with four characters on stage, three of them agitated and one sobbing. Central to their angst is the issue of the body – theirs and that of their executed leader, and most importantly, the space within which their bodies must enunciate agency. The characters we meet are Major, Hassan, Angola, and Alhaja and they are the robbers whose leader has just been executed. Furious, frustrated, and sad, they must make a decision. Should the group continue its "work" of protest through antisocial depredations, or simply disintegrate? Major, despite his reputation for valiance, does not wish to continue. This astounds and annoys his colleagues who accuse him of betrayal and cowardice. Challenged and rebuked by Angola and Hassan, Major reels off a catalog of his brave actions executed in impossible situations. As they ponder what next, a voice is heard, that of Aafa. Acting impulsively as demanded by their "profession," the robbers hide from what they believe to be a potential victim, who appears to be preparing to say his prayers. As they attempt to mug Aafa, he begins an incantation, casting a spell on Angola and Hassan who, like somnambulists, slap and bow to each other in a highly comic routine. The other two robbers, Alhaja and Major, come out of their hiding to plead with Aafa to release their colleagues from the spell. Aafa not only forgives them, but also offers them a redemptive opportunity. They must not rob from the poor again, nor kill or maim another person, and only rob three times more. He offers them a spell which when sung will plunge victims into senseless sleep, offering the robbers an opportunity to steal their possessions. To safeguard the spell from individual abuse, each robber has a verse and order with which he or she must entrance victims. Osofisan seems to allude to a metaphor of nationalism by assuming subjectivity can only be possible through a collective spine of identification.

The first test of the new power Aafa offers occurs in that most public of spaces portrayed in Yoruba folklore, namely the market place. The robbers invade this space, which is largely ruled by women, and sing their victims to sleep. The spell proves highly effective. When the women awaken to the realization that they have fallen prey to a grand theft, they enlist the help of soldiers led by a Sergeant. The banter between the soldiers and women indicates the soldiers' incredulity at the power of a mere song to seduce an entire market into insentience. Their doubt is, however, short-lived as the robbers strike again. Despite a successful heist, Major insists on calling it quits. As he backs out on his colleagues, the soldiers regain consciousness, engage the robbers in a shoot-out, and hurt and arrest Major while the others escape. Instead of giving back some of the recovered goods stolen from the women, the soldiers decide to keep them as booty. For the rest of the play, they build a platform for Major's execution.

As the soldiers labor toward the execution, Alhaja approaches them in the guise of a seductive street hawker whose charm disarms them. She succeeds temporarily in dissuading the soldiers from carrying out the execution. Using Hassan and Angola as ordinary bystanders opposed to the execution and willing to corroborate her story, Alhaja succeeds in persuading the soldiers that the robber scheduled for execution is the unfortunate son of a mother who died as a nationalist patriot during the country's civil war. Some soldiers however, smell a rat, arrest their wavering colleagues and decide to go ahead with the execution. As the renegade soldiers are arrested, the crowd, which includes the market women, recognizes the other robbers and immediately gets the soldiers to arrest them. An added twist to the story is that the Sergeant recognizes his twin brother among the robbers.

The playwright uses the opposing standpoints of the brothers to pose the play's ultimate nationalist question: Is family more important than the nation? Alternatively, should the individual's interest override a sense of collective identity? The ensuing dialogue between the brothers is easily resolved as the Sergeant insists his loyalty and identity are wedded to the neo-colonial nation his brother so callously wants to bring down. At that moment, the robbers chant their spellbinding song. As the soldiers and crowd begin to fall asleep, Aafa reappears to poll the audience on how the play should end in the aftermath of the preceding stalemate. As written, if the overwhelming majority insists that the execution must go on, the robbers will be killed. If, on the other hand, they vote for the robbers' release, the robbers will invade the auditorium and even rob audience members. The playwright's intention is to generate debate in the auditorium.

Osofisan has described in graphic terms, the audience's reaction to the participatory dramaturgy of *Once Upon Four Robbers*:

> Each night, as the audience disperses, it is in tumult. I mix into the crowd, unobtrusively, and I listen. The arguments are fierce. The government is vilified, then defended. There is a plurality of passionate voices. Positions are taken and then renounced, and then affirmed again. Those who voted "for" now wish to vote "against," and vice-versa. No one is at ease.[11]

Written with highly theatricalized songs and dances, the play departs from the literary conventions typifying Soyinka's drama. Borrowing from Yoruba Popular Theatre styles, Osofisan creates a performance text whose energy infects the auditorium with festivity, anticipation, and pathos. He not only contradicts the utopianism and nationalist idealism of previous generations of writers like Soyinka, but also develops a populist theatrical convention whose metaphorical codes are more accessible to audiences beyond the middle class. The play's populist approach lies not only in the interactive nature of the relationship it establishes between actors and audience, but also in its rendition in "Nigerian English" that in the late 1970s became the medium for developing a unique identity that simultaneously countered English culture and posed a non-elitist challenge to the neo-colonial nationalism of the period.

Once Upon Four Robbers weaves the theme of anticolonial nationalism with the retrieval of indigenous mythologies into a dramaturgical language and culture of decolonization. Embodying a hybrid approach that draws upon Yoruba folklore to champion socialism, this play induces a sense of political responsibility in its middle-class audiences wherever it plays. As indicated earlier, Osofisan privileges the mythological duo of Orunmila and Esu as sources for developing a political dramaturgy. While the former divines and offers strategies for agency, the latter catalyzes it. In *Once Upon Four Robbers*, Aafa and Major fit perfectly into those roles. Aafa divines for the robbers and audiences, while Major's recalcitrance facilitates action within the story, exposing moments of conflict – that between himself and the other robbers; the senior and lower ranks of the army; Hassan and his brother the Sergeant; and the audience's struggle to decide whether the robbers' unfortunate lot in life offers extenuating circumstances for exonerating them.

As if playing Orunmila himself, Osofisan uses every opportunity to divine Nigeria's problems from a socialist perspective by using characters and situations to diagnose and justify impending actions. For example, whenever they speak, the robbers offer audiences and readers alike a detailed class analysis of Nigeria's social reality. As Major declares:

> But Man is so fragile, so easy to kill. Especially if he robs and lies, if he wantonly breaks the law. Serg, today that law is on the side of those who have, and in abundance, who are fed and bulging, who can afford several concubines. But tomorrow, that law will change. The poor will seize it and twist its neck. The starving will smash the gates of the supermarkets, the homeless will no longer yield in fear to your bulldozers.[12]

Osofisan also uses the songs to offer us insight into the structure and ethos of the society that marginalizes the robbers. As custodians of the economy, the market women boast in song:

> The work of profit
> Brought us to this world
> This life that is a market
> Some sell with ease and flourish
> And some are clients
> Who pay their greed in gold

> The lure of profit
> Has conquered our souls
> And changed us into cannibals
> Oh praise the selfless British
> Who with the joyous sound
> Of minted coins and gold
> Brought us civilization[13]

As a dramatist concerned with subaltern agency, Osofisan proposes that marginalized elements be vested with formal citizenship rather than serve merely as objects of middle-class political discourses. Unlike Soyinka's "The Fourth Stage" where the ideological fuel that energizes democratic renewal does not name any definite destination, Osofisan's notion of agency points unambiguously in the direction of a socialist utopia. The characters of his plays, as symbolic representatives of Nigeria's social reality, aim to transform a society paralyzed by capitalism into a participatory democracy founded upon equity and social justice.

For Osofisan, the only way to contest the Euro-modernist framework of capitalism within which Nigeria is trapped, is to harness Yoruba mythology as a resource for shaping a counter-European and anticolonial esthetic. The resort to folklore serves other purposes in a military dictatorship whose authoritarian rulers have little use for change. Osofisan calls his technique of Yoruba revivalism "a covert and metamorphic system of maneuvering which, for want of a better term, I have summarized as 'surreptitious insurrection'."[14] The "surreptitious insurrection" of which he speaks allows him the creative latitude he needs to advance his politically subversive project without provoking reprisals from Nigeria's succession of military rulers. A cohort of critics and artists who continue to see Nigeria as a land caught in the binary landscape of a Eurocentric culture on the one hand, and a complicitous neo-colonial indigenous one on the other, participate fully in this "insurrection." The socialist nationalists who dominate Nigerian universities, perform their cultural politics by radically revising indigenous mythologies for the specific purpose of engaging Eurocentrism and its neo-colonial variant in the Nigerian nation state.

It is within this context that Osofisan selects the mythology of the ruled to fashion a more radical and socialist nationalism in his works. In his own words:

> History so far has been a record of the achievements of kings, warriors and so on. Now I believe that that is where a progressive artist, say, should take sides with those who are at the bottom . . . It is high time we began to interpret on behalf of the oppressed world."[15]

Relying on the nationalist impulse of his audience, Osofisan makes mythology a valuable repertory of signs that can simultaneously facilitate communication and collective political consciousness. He does not, however, take for granted the tensions that may exist between audiences and the politically committed dramatist. He cautions that most theatregoers seek entertainment and escape from the "agonizing realities of their life through momentary escape into the fabulous world of illusion." They may not welcome exhortations "to think," to wrest themselves away from the

seductive embrace of conventional wisdom on popular norms and practices. In order to be didactically effective, therefore, the playwright must
"package his play cleverly through the furtive tasks that art itself can
furnish," Osofisan insists.[16]

Through *Once Upon Four Robbers*, Osofisan draws our attention to issues
of dissonance between citizenship and postcolonial subjectivity. Citizenship implies a form of agency through which the state and its institutions
of governance and social organization recognize being and belonging.
If formal citizenship suggests acceptance into a national identity, and
informal citizenship underscores the limits of one's presence in that society,
it seems that agency has to be located elsewhere. For Soyinka, that "elsewhere" appears to be the non-fixable, regenerative destination and identity
that I have called non-formal citizenship. Osofisan, on the other hand,
locates it in the subaltern vanguard of a socialist revolution that will lead
the dispossessed to formal citizenship. Thus, formal citizenship and a fixed
identity, which Soyinka fears ultimately undermine the impulse for change,
represent for Osofisan the goal of political activism, provided they lead to
a more equitable organization of society. For Femi Osofisan, identity in a
postcolonial context must have a destination – a socialist one mixed with
strains of Negritudism. Most of the characters in *Once Upon Four Robbers*
are alienated victims of a state that can describe them at best, as informal
citizens. The political transformation of the characters demands that they
attain consciousness of their informality before they can progress to a
formal identity through action (in this case a violent one) without the state's
approval. It is to these conditions of citizenship that Major alludes when
he declares:

> We are the race victims are made of! We dream, we hug the gutters
> till we are plastered with slime. Then we begin to believe that slime
> is the only reality. We build it into a cult ... and others continue to
> lap the cream of the land.[17]

Osofisan expects audiences to vote for freeing the robbers rather than have
them executed. As the playwright sees it, the end represents a moment
that translates dissidence into the participatory democracy supposedly
promised by socialism.

Osofisan uses his play to suggest that European modernity of the capitalist variety confers an informal nation state, hence the neo-colonial nature
of the Nigerian nation. Because it has no subjective sense of being within
the modernity responsible for its emergence, Nigeria will, at best, cling
precariously to the margins of European modernity until it adopts an alternative vision of the world. He sees his dramaturgy as political activism that
seeks to inspire the construction of a different modernity whose frame of
reference is derived, at least partially, from African resources. By invoking

Yoruba mythology and deploying Orunmila and Esu as central metaphors in his plays (played by himself and the audience respectively), he invites his audiences to reconfigure the social space within which identity can be performed proactively. Osofisan's *Once Upon Four Robbers* illustrates the notion of "social reality" that Lewis Gordon attributes to Frantz Fanon: "social reality is an achievement, not a given reality. It is a function of action, itself a function of subjective and intersubjective encounter."[18] Osofisan's play depicts subaltern quests for a subjective presence while "intersubjective encounters" manifest themselves in the internecine conflicts among the lowly robbers and soldiers.

The inter-modernist tenor of Osofisan's dramaturgy emerges in his appropriation of European models to denounce Nigeria's domination – past and present – by the industrialized countries at the center of European modernity, illustrating the ways in which the inter-modernist language of resistance is often influenced by the process of domination itself. The reactive nationalism and mode of decolonization that he envisions are themselves steeped in the same Euro-modernist premises upon which European colonialism rested in Nigeria. Osofisan invests heavily in the notion of the nation state as a mode for organizing people. The very concept of a nation state is, however, as much a colonial construct as the nation of Nigeria is an English invention. Moreover, his prescription of Marxism as a resource for crafting an alternative modernity obviously draws upon a European paradigm as well, although one that represents a discourse of opposition to the dominant liberal tradition of Western modernity. Thus, Osofisan is arguably guilty of what Gayatri Spivak describes as rejecting "a structure, which we critique yet inhabit intimately."[19]

Nigeria's crisis of intra-modernism emerges in the act of omission that characterizes Osofisan's treatment of gender in the interstices of "intersubjective encounters" in his *Once Upon Four Robbers*. While producing a decolonizing rhetoric in his plays, Osofisan sometimes conflates sociality with collectivity. Sociality connotes a heterogeneous web of individuals embedded in hierarchical relations of power. Such an entity must take account of differences of gender and ethnicity in addition to those of class. In other words, it must recognize the multipositionality of individual identities. Collectivity on the other hand, connotes a homogeneous bloc defined by an overriding collective identity such as class. In *Once Upon Four Robbers*, a certain machismo describes both the dominant culture and the violent reactions to it. The only prominent female character in the play figures in different circumstances either as a wife, a metaphorical mother, or as an object of male desire. When we meet Alhaja, the consort of the robber chief in the play, she is sobbing and in mourning for her recently executed husband. Cast as a sort of "Mother Courage," she develops a maternal relationship with the other robbers, reminding them:

My husband brought you out of the slum. From the cold he put clothes on your back. From the rain, he found you shelter. He put your scattered life together, raised you into a man. He put the first gun in your hand, taught you to stand and fight, for justice.[20]

Alhaja's mothering role assumes a mythological dimension when, falling into a trance she declares:

> me, his mother, in my withering. I will shout, I will call my husband. But lost in the stream of being, Orunmila will not respond. And all alone I will swell with the terrible burden of unwanted seed, unwanted because condemned to die. I will swell, I will explode, bearing the laughter of new corpses.[21]

However significant in opening up spaces of postcolonial desire for an alternative society, Alhaja's role is nonetheless characterized by stasis even as the male characters seek mobility. She remains the mother, lover, or daughter whose story is incomplete without the men whose action facilitates hers. The market women do not fare much better. Perhaps Osofisan's intention is to show the hyper-masculinity of the national space within which identity and agency has to be forged. In doing so, however, he reproduces the very marginalizing frame – in this case for women – which he wants to demolish. This is an especially troublesome lapse for a writer so well known for casting women as protagonists in his plays.

In recent years, Osofisan has found himself in a role similar to the one in which he consistently cast Soyinka. Neither Marxism nor the critical nationalist discourse he has long championed appeals to a new generation of Nigerians who initially canonized Osofisan but now seek different and more dispersed sources of inspiration. Without first-hand experience of colonialism and the post-independence civil war, and confronted by a ruling class more tyrannical than ever, they have little faith in the promise of a coherent national identity. Skeptical of the nineteenth-century concept of nation states that must be consolidated with the help of an indigenous dominant culture, they embrace a transnational perspective instead. Their inclination for change and non-formality transcends national boundaries and nationalist ideologies.

Osofisan finds himself at odds with this latest outlook and the writing that represents it. He is bewildered by the artistic free-style and non-conformism of the late twentieth-century generation of Nigerian dramatists and writers. Nostalgia laces his recollection of the appeal of Marxism to his generation, several members of which had "risen from lowly peasant and working class backgrounds." For these Nigerians, Marxism offered the clearest path to bridging the "vicious gap" emerging between the rich and the poor, the panacea for underdevelopment, "the open sesame to the door of Utopia." Osofisan intended his drama to "bring the majority of our people to this triumphant reading of history, and do battle with our ruling classes."[22]

By contrast, the dramatist's successors have embraced what smacks of a more dispersed vision of their world, reminiscent of Soyinka's "The Fourth Stage." Ironically, the older playwright, whom Osofisan strove so hard to cast in the mantle of conservatism, appears more in synchronism with the cultural innovations and the social realities they represent in modern day Nigeria. The prescience of "The Fourth Stage" now haunts Osofisan as the new generation seeks a non-programmatic agenda for change. Initially, Osofisan greeted the advent of the new esthetic style allegedly characterized by "visual, sonorous and olfactory chaos"[23] with barely concealed disdain:

> Mythopoesy, fabulation, polyphony – or according to some cacophony – these are the narrative goals, and grammar . . . High preference is given to syntactic and semantic idiosyncrasies, such as the use of sudden phrasal inversions, verbal inflation, ideophones, eccentric punctuation and neologisms. The notion of time itself becomes arbitrary, and selective, freed of its moorings in calendar reality . . . Is what we are witnessing then the death of Utopia? Are these works the metaphoric mirror of the frustration of our dreams for a better society, of our authors' covert proclamation of defeat in our frustrated ambition to bring our countries to freedom and justice and economic progress?[24]

Osofisan "the rebel" suddenly finds himself in the role of a cultural conservative with the shifting of the context that once gave his works greater indexicality. More recently, however, the playwright himself is widely perceived as having moved in the direction of the style he once castigated as "African Absurdism." Harry Garuba noted in his compelling review of Osofisan's play *The Album of the Midnight Blackout*, that the dramatist's "love for pastiche and parody, the roguish delight in abrogating and appropriating the works of other writers and the bold foregrounding of these "thefts" within his own, speak of a postmodern consciousness even if perhaps, unconsciously deployed."[25] The review leaves the impression that Osofisan has employed his guile again and is parodying the esthetics he so vigorously denounced once. Or that he is taking steps, however tentative, toward knowing the new generation of writers and the audiences they write for, so that he can write with and for them.

Yet, as I have already argued, however focused the ideological direction of Osofisan's postcolonial desire, his creative style has always approached the indefinable "chaos" of Soyinka's mythopoesy. As *Once Upon Four Robbers* illustrates, Osofisan's resort to the metaphysical, trans-temporal tapestry of spirits and humans embedded in Yoruba storytelling traditions, and his parody of history, complicate the ideological nuances of his dramaturgy and place him in a hybrid inter-modernist interstice not unlike that which Soyinka occupies. It remains to be seen what direction Osofisan will pursue in the twenty-first century. Whatever that may be, there is no question that his drama has served as a point of departure for conceptualizing political change by textualizing the persistence of colonialism in post-colonial Nigeria. Whatever the final verdict on the efficacy of socialism, Nigeria's Marxist dramatist continues to share with his anticolonial fore-bears and post-imperial successors the vision of a revolutionary, egalitarian space where identities of effective citizenship – whether formal or non-formal – can reproduce themselves.

3 Tess Onwueme

Theatre, gender, and power

> OMU: Together we form this moon shape. Lie in ambush surrounding the throne as the men emerge. We together in this naked legion, will salute them in our natural state. Taunting their eyes with their own shame. This naked dance is a last resort women have had over the ages. If our men force us to the wall, we must use it as our final weapon. Unusual problems demand unusual solutions.[1]

In the Prologue to Tess Onwueme's play, *The Reign of Wazobia*, the matriarch Omu's proposed strategy of female insurrection against a male campaign to dethrone Anioma Kingdom's feminist sovereign Wazobia, represents a provocative semiotic subversion of patriarchy. An army of female bodies, objectified for ages as things of sex, transform *themselves* into political statements against the kingdom's conventional structure of male privilege. Men in Anioma Kingdom in the mid-western region of Ilaaa believe that "serious matters of state concern are too heavy for the brittle heads of women and children."[2] The women's collective defiance of such assumptions by the destabilization of that ultimate gendered signifier of tradition – the monarchy itself, sets the subversive tone of Onwueme's *The Reign of Wazobia*. First written and published in 1988, when "tradition," "ritual," and "mythology" had become key words informing Nigerian anti-colonial narratives in dramatic theory and practice, Onwueme's play sought to de-colonize the role of women within the nationalist project to establish a more democratic and pluralistic society.

Born half a generation after her mentor Femi Osofisan, Tess Onwueme attended the Universities of Ife and Benin before moving to the United States, where she occupies an endowed chair at the University of Wisconsin, Eau Claire. Her dramaturgy, as illustrated in such works as *Then She Said It*, *Shakara: The Dance Hall Queen*, *The Missing Face*, *Tell It To Women*, *Riot in Heaven*, *Parable for a Season*, *Legacies*, *Mirror for Campus*, *Ban Empty Barn*, *The Desert Encroaches*, *The Broken Calabash*, and *A Hen Too Soon*, persistently interrogates modes of representing women as subjects of history and anti-colonial modernity. Like Wole Soyinka and Femi Osofisan, Tess Onwueme

Plate 3.1 Nigerian actress Clarion Chukwurah playing the lead role in the film version of *Wazobia* – directed by Awam Amkpa. Photograph by Waka Photos.

explores the attraction of "mythology" and "traditionalism" to the emergent middle class craving indigenous values with which to empower their inter-modernist identities in Nigeria. As Biodun Jeyifo has observed, however, "mythology" and "traditions" proved unsafe in the hands of dramatists like Soyinka and Osofisan. Onwueme treads their path in developing what Jeyifo termed a "mythoclastic" attitude to the cultural cravings of educated audiences seeking rootedness in indigenous modernity.[3] If Yoruba mythology served as a medium for Osofisan's imaginings of a socialist utopia, Igbo usages have provided Onwueme with a treasure trove of metaphors for the subversion of male prerogative. If Osofisan's plays draw upon Yoruba folkloric resources to make existential queries like "who are we?" "what class do we belong to?" and "how do we deal with the dialectic between individuality and collectivity?" within anticolonial nationalism, Onwueme's works invert Igbo traditions to infuse these issues of identity and subjectivity with the politics of gender. She seems to wonder with R. Radakrishnan, "Why is it that the advent of the politics of nationalism signals the subordination if not the demise of women's politics?"[4]

From her location as a woman in an inter-modernist landscape, Onwueme injects the social significance of her sex into discourses of postcolonial desire by highlighting an intra-modernist crisis over gender roles and expectations in post-imperial Nigeria. Her dramatic rewrites of political history skillfully indict her audience's relative lack of interest in foreign and indigenous forms of patriarchy, emphasizing the futility of any project of empowerment that fails to reverse the traditional marginalization of Nigeria's voiceless female majority. Onwueme's plays *The Broken Calabash* and *A Hen Too Soon* challenge the "normative structures" governing relationships between men and women, among them the institution of marriage. They confront marriage as a social contract predicated upon politics that inherently deprive women of agency.

Her play *The Reign of Wazobia* goes even further in visualizing a paradigmatic shift within the cultural revivalist politics of dissent against neo-colonial nationalism. It imagines women's transition from the "informal" citizenship to which they were relegated by indigenous and foreign traditions, to the rights and responsibilities of "formal citizenship" within a democratic framework. The open-ended conclusion of the play implicitly suggests that the achievement of such "formal" citizenship, in turn, leads to limitless possibilities for universalizing the egalitarian goals of postcolonial desire through "non-formal" citizenship. *The Reign of Wazobia* makes a plea for what Onwueme recently called "internal reparations" (for women)[5] as a complement to the compensation for trans-Atlantic slavery demanded by members of the Africa diaspora from contemporary centers of Euro-American modernity.

Although my association with Tess Onwueme dates back to our college days in Ile-Ife, it was *The Reign of Wazobia* that did more to broaden and complicate my conception of postcolonial desire than any of her other plays. Two years ago I collaborated with the playwright to produce and direct a feature film based on this work and here offer a reading of it as a feminist interpretation of postcolonial desire.

The Reign of Wazobia

The incorporation of the word "Wazobia" in the play's title is as deeply seductive as it is fraught with subversive innuendo. "Wazobia" denotes "come" but implies "come together." It is derived from the three primary languages promoted by English colonialism in Nigeria – Yoruba, Hausa, and Igbo. Coined by nationalists who believed that the unity of these three ethnic groups guaranteed nationhood, the word continues to be perpetuated by neo-colonial nationalists, who also link the preservation of the national union to harmony among the colonially derived ethnic entities. The title "Wazobia" then prompts the question whether the play is yet another call to national unity. If so, why would a politically sophisticated writer like Tess Onwueme lend her voice to the facile nationalism purveyed by contemporary Nigeria's neo-colonial dictators? Before long, it becomes apparent that she has done nothing of the sort. She has, instead, subverted a neologism with a post-independence currency, by adapting it to her own call for unity among women fragmented by patriarchy and class. *The Reign of Wazobia* portrays the vision of a monolithic political collectivity as a utopian ideal – momentary and fragmentary, untenable as long as internal inequities remain.

Structured in six Movements and a Prologue, the play opens and ends with a confrontation between the men and women of post-imperial Anioma. At the center of the conflict is Wazobia the protagonist, an incongruous, if overloaded, cultural sign within the social context of the play. Onwueme later explains how and why Wazobia came to be "King" of her realm. The Prologue begins with a dramatic effect. Dancing women burst into a magical setting, described by the playwright in the following words: "It is night, but the moon slowly tears through the clouds, perforating the sky to expose the bare beauty and essence of this pastoral kingdom."[6] The women are dancing as a gesture of defiance in support of their female king Wazobia. As their movement and the accompanying music approach a climax, a masquerade appears. It plunges itself into the dance and slowly reverses the choreographic sequence, very much to the women's excitement.

Wazobia, seemingly confused by the direction of events, hesitates as the women invite her into the dance. She joins the "reverse choreography," only to withdraw, bringing the dance to a halt. The masquerade walks off staring accusingly at Wazobia. The moment presents a metaphor of the tensions between the individual and the collective that bedevil the community of women in Anioma, as it does societies of men everywhere. It presages further conflicts between Wazobia and other women as the saga unfolds. Meanwhile, Wazobia's hesitation on the dance floor demoralizes her supporters into lying supine on the ground. The "King" is then galvanized into action. She implores the women to resume their dance of protest against the men's battle against her reign. If the men of Ilaaa thought the installation of a woman on the throne was only a symbolic gesture that would serve as a stand-in for a patriarchal monarchy, Wazobia's call to the women is a deliberate disorientation of such symbolism:

> WAZOBIA: Arise women!
> They say your feet are feeble, Show them those feet carry the burden of the womb.
> They say your hands are frail,
> Show them those hands have claws . . .
> With your claws hook them.[7]

The spectacle that ensues shatters, in unexpected fashion, what I term the "gyno-spectatorial"[8] prism through which the women are seen in their community. As the sounds of the invading men pervade the auditorium, the women strip naked and slowly transform their metaphoric dance of protest into quasi-military positions of defense around the palace. The men arrive, bringing with them a steaming pot of herbs, which in Igbo tradition signifies a loss of confidence in the monarch by the Council of chiefs. The women counter this signal of Wazobia's impending ouster by breaking the pot – thereby demystifying the chiefs' received authority over kingship and the male power it traditionally implies.

Onwueme takes us from a Prologue saturated with female and male bodies in physical conflict to a quieter moment in Movement One. Wazobia is engaged in a soliloquy that reflects upon her new sense of power and its promise of feminist reform: "I Wazobia, have come with these feminine fingers . . . To knit your world together."[9] Summoning her drummer to duty she divulges, "I have tasted power and will not go," thus reminding the spectators that the representation of power is the source of the play's conflict. At this point, a series of flashbacks traces the course of events that culminated in the unprecedented elevation of a woman – Wazobia – to the suzerainty of Anioma.

The audience learns that when the old king died without an obvious heir to the throne, a priest of Anioma set up a ritual consultation with the gods about filling the power vacuum until a suitable permanent successor could be found. In the kingdom of Anioma, as in most African societies, the world of the gods overlaps with that of humans and divine guidance is sought during vital decision-making moments through the medium of oracles. The priest's reading of the oracles, was, however, interrupted by a prominent character in the play – Omu. Described as the most powerful woman in Anioma appointed to administer women's affairs in the kingdom in the service of patriarchy, she was slighted by her exclusion from the ritual. The priest's immediate response exposes the patriarchal gaze with which Omu and all women are perceived in the kingdom:

> PRIEST: Since when have women become the pillar of the state?
>   This is a night of vigil,
>   It is a time of silence, of peace . . .
>   What we men strive
>   To sew, to put together
>   That lobe which threatens ever
>   To split apart
>   Women like hens pecking for worms
>   Always set apart the spheres.[10]

Ironically enough, the oracles prescribed a mode of choosing a temporary successor to the throne that would turn out to challenge the priest's assumptions about women's place. As the priest informed the populace of Anioma, a temporary king had to be drawn from the general population and crowned for three agricultural seasons while the men decided who the next king would be. To that end, the community – male and female – was summoned to the market square to participate in a communal festival. The merrymaking climaxed with the moment of the new king's selection. The priest sprayed a white clay powder known as "nzu," and threw his staff of office into the air. The crowd waited with bated breath to see upon whom it would land for it would be he who would be king. Lo and behold! It landed not upon a male member of the community as expected, but rather on a comely young woman named Wazobia. Anioma's women were jubilant, and re-enacted the scene during Wazobia's coronation. The men were less happy. Most resentful of all was Iyase, the senior-most chief of the king's council.

In Movement Two, Onwueme takes us into the world of royal women whose identities Wazobia's choice immediately complicates. As wives to the previous king, would each of them be a wife to the female king? Here Onwueme muddies the heterosexual paradigm of relationships between husbands and wives. Does her ascension to the monarchy symbolically transmute her into a male, and if so, will she also become a "husband" to the widowed queens? The wives Anehe, Wa, Zo, and Bia all wonder what the new dispensation brings. The throne is male but is now represented by a female. What implications does this incongruity carry for their status? Is the "king" their new husband? As they all jockey for favorable positions with the "king," Wazobia reveals her mission to the women:

> WAZOBIA: It is not time to kneel but a time to stand
> It is no time to succumb but to stand, my women.
> It is no time to gloat on praises, women.
> The task ahead calls for abstinence and sacrifice.[11]

At this point, Omu – assigned by Anioma custom the role of matriarchal custodian of the patriarchal order – arrives to restore the traditional place of women in the newly minted context. She reminds the queens that "Tradition . . . handed down from generation to generation" forbade the women to resume normal life until funeral rites for the dead king – their husband – were completed. Moreover, the widows were required by custom to dance in public spaces with their heads shaven to mourn the passing of their lord and master. Here Onwueme uses two women as contestatory signifiers locked in a conflict of values that carry profound implications for the way people in Anioma understand their identity and exercise agency. As Omu – preserver and translator of patriarchal traditions to the female population – seeks to re-align the women to the status quo despite the gendered political upheaval of the day, Wazobia defies the inequity embedded in Anioma tradition by retorting, "my women will not dance." Onwueme performs what Bill Ashcroft has called "the most effective revolt" by denying "the system its power over representation."[12] Her formulation of Wazobia as king achieves this effect by destabilizing the paramount signifier of male domination – the monarchy. Moreover, the playwright introduces disorder in the sociocultural context that historically normalized the discourse of patriotism by placing the women in the community in a state of joyous rebellion in support of the she-king.

Onwueme extends her strokes of destabilization by introducing a domestic conflict between a palm-wine taper and his wife as a microcosm of
the play's larger crisis of gender identity and prerogative. The man, a wife
beater, chases his victim into the palace. Onwueme stresses the depth of
men's objectification of female bodies in the ensuing conflict. This palm-
wine taper, not unlike his social superiors, declares his right to abuse his
wife because she is a "mere woman that I paid to get with my own hard-
earned money" who had dared to "challenge me in my house ... Does
she think I carry these balls between my thighs for nothing?"

Such bold assertions of male prerogative provoke the new sovereign's
intervention. She announces an open meeting of all her subjects the
following day to resolve the question of domestic relations. At this point,
the Third Movement begins with attempts by the chiefs to curtail
Wazobia's juridical powers by arguing for the exclusion of women from
proceedings involving grave matters of the state. The "king" counters
forcefully that women must have "equal representation in rulership." In
open court the following day, she decrees an end to domestic abuse and
the equality of the sexes within marriage. But when Wazobia asks the
wife-beating man to publicly apologize to the woman he violated, he not
only refuses but defies both the essence of the newly established ethic of
inter-sex relationships, as well as its female architect by baring his buttocks
to Wazobia. He then divorces his wife to the amazement and amusement
of many onlookers. The women celebrate while the men walk off the stage
in protest. Wazobia uses this moment of triumph to persuade Omu to
make common cause with the feminist insurrection under way. The
Movement ends with Omu's decision to join the women in their quest for
their own voices.

Movement Four begins more sedately at the home of one of the chiefs –
Idehen. Idehen and the prominent Iyase each hope to ascend the throne in
the event that a more permanent heir is not immediately available. This is
the first time Onwueme shows the men overtly plotting to usurp Wazobia's
position and the power she represents. The playwright uses this short
Movement to capture the anxiety of men caught in the vortex of a political
turmoil occasioned by a cosmic betrayal – an ominous turn of events that
threatens to strip them of their historic privileges perhaps forever. That the
gods and their oracles would select a woman to the throne represents as
much of an unexpected threat as the chosen one's ability to mobilize the
women against the very foundations of male supremacy. In a burst of frustration at his own sense of impotence, Idehen ponders:

> What use am I? ... A chief they call me who can stand on two toes
> and allow a woman, a mere woman, to clear her rotten throat and
> spit the phlegm at my face? As night overtakes day, we sit in com-
> placency, while Wazobia ... Wazobia wears the crown and stands
> between us.[13]

The throne the chiefs revere so greatly and the position with which they conjugate their identities, is now held by a *"mere woman"* who uses that position to reinterpret her gender identity in such a way as to castrate Idehen's sense of self.

Onwueme also uses this Movement to expose the gendered underpinnings of anticolonial nationalism. Chief Idehen blames European colonial modernity for infecting women with the contagion of equality and freedom. Ironically enough, imperialism, as portrayed by the post-imperial "native" custodians and beneficiaries of patriarchy, emerges as an impediment to the structures of internal colonization in Anioma:

> IDEHEN: We are failures to our ancestors. Were we not here when the missionaries came in to us and began to inoculate the so-called Christianity with its extended family of education and equality? Now the toxic effect takes hold of our ranks. The osu, the social outcasts, and the poor were the first to drink from the contagious water of the white men. The outcasts were the first to be curdled in the embrace of the white body. Now we are all locked in the leprous grip of freedom.

Here, Idehen castigates the Europeans' use of the rhetoric of equality to mask their designs for proselytizing social outcasts within a colonial context that was itself a bastion of inequality. For chiefs like Idehen, freedom and agency in any form outside the mandate of indigenous patriarchy signified foreignness, and thus posed a colonizing threat. Translating Wazobia's transgressions as a possible repeat of the foreign incursions that once marginalized their local power, the chiefs devise a strategy and rhetoric of opposition cloaked in the usages of Igbo tradition calculated to appeal to a broad section of the male population. According to custom, priests used a boiling pot of herbs to convey to a ruling monarch the masculinized community's loss of confidence in his reign. The chiefs now plan to take recourse to this ancient usage to limit the discursive reach of Wazobia's power. Convinced their mission would restore order to a world slowly sliding away from patriarchal control, Iyase declares the maxim with which the she-king would be resisted:

> IYASE: Wazobia has stayed beyond her limit. She is only a regent
> And tradition stipulates
> That a regent can reign for only three seasons
> The chiefs know this,
> The men know this,
> It is a very easy argument, persuading them to force
> Wazobia down from the throne.
> Men will depose Wazobia, that fattened cow, must crumble.
> All the chiefs and men of Ilaaa.

The black goat must be chased in to roost early, lest it
   stray into night,
Damaging valuable goods.[14]

Onwueme begins Movement Five with a dramatic illustration of Idehen's personal aspirations for kingship underpinning larger concerns for the survival of existing sexual hierarchies. He tiptoes into the throne room looking jealously at the much-coveted crown. Wazobia walks in as Idehen stretches out to feel the crown. What follows is an embarrassing and humiliating scene for Idehen. For decorum demands that he not do offense to the office of the king by seeming to want to usurp it, however resentful he may be of its present occupant. In a desperate attempt to deflect Wazobia's displeasure from his misconduct, he falsely declares deep love for the king and explains that his presence in the throne room is prompted by his sense of responsibility to inform her of a male plot led by Iyase to depose her.

As Idehen retreats from the scene, Bia, one of the widowed queens, enters to warn Wazobia about Idehen's part in the male conspiracy. As a thoughtful Wazobia retreats into her bedroom, Zo, another of the dead king's wives, appears to inquire of Bia the reasons for Wazobia's state of perturbation. As the two women converse, they hear footsteps, and quickly conceal themselves behind the curtains of the throne room. From their hiding places, they listen in on Iyase scheming to poison the new king. Iyase's collaborator in this conspiracy is the late king's eldest wife Anehe – a woman convinced that Wazobia's accession will bode ill for the former monarch's widowed consorts. When the conspirators leave, Bia and Zo set off to seek out Omu to help lead the women against the men.

Movement Six adds momentum to the impending war of the sexes by portraying the expansion of the male dissidents' campaign against the *idea* represented by Wazobia. Onwueme skillfully weaves metaphor and proverb to capture the chiefs' sense that Wazobia embodied an addictive habit that if allowed to infect the general populace would subvert the *natural* order of the universe by placing women above men:

IYASE: Wa-zo-bia. The new wine that intoxicates, sending our women running Amok on the streets, throwing their dignity behind. No matter what happens, women are women. Like children, an overdose of this new wine, baptized as freedom by Wazobia, is bound to turn them giddy. That we may keep our balance, this new tail or wing by women must be clipped. Lest they take to flight and soar above us. Water can never flow from the foot to the head. We are the head, women can never rule us.[15]

Iyase and Idehen invoke a castrating narrative steeped in sexual imagery to persuade their fellow chieftains that women's subjectivity is incompatible with the preservation of feminine virtue, sexual subservience, and masculine honor in Anioma. Wazobia's rise spells nothing short of the emasculation of the kingdom's males and the disruption of the "rational" civilization devised by men:

> With what mouth will it be said that we sons of Ilaaa lost our manhood with a sweep of a woman's hand? That what we men strive to put together women in their natural state set apart with their thighs setting the world ablaze in naked flame?"[16]

As this comment suggests, the chiefs' rhetoric of castration conflates women's political power with their sexual dominance in an awful specter of nature run riot. An earlier public exchange between Iyase and Idehen underscores this point. Iyase asks mockingly whether women were seeking emancipation from "the kitchen," to which Idehen responds, "Emancipation from lying below to lying on top." In other words, a female king with the temerity to decree equal rights for women created precedents for a revolution in the very structure of the existing order in all its manifestations – from the political to the deeply personal.

Such rhetoric sets the stage for a traditionally masculine response to an alien invasion. Conscripting the priests into their movement, the men march on the palace chanting war songs, only to encounter an army of naked female adversaries. At this point the circular narrative of the play reverts to the scene that constituted the Prologue. As the women fan out from the palace to enclose the men, their action spawns an interesting climax. According to Onwueme's stage directions: "Led by the Omu, they advance, naked and in unison, form an arc behind Wazobia. The men are so shocked that they retreat, stagger and freeze in their stupefaction."[17] To a male advance guard imbued with the notion of the feminine as supine and passive bodies eminently governable by men, the women warriors' psychosexual stance, their feminized politico-military onslaught, is shockingly unexpected. For the women take over the narration of their bodies simultaneously with their appropriation of a political space hitherto reserved for the enunciation of patriarchy. The outcome of the battle remains unresolved. What is more certain is the performance of a collective postcolonial desire for self-determination, this time overtly and unabashedly gendered.

Onwueme's portrayal of post-imperial Nigeria's intra-modernist crisis over gender exposes the often insidious marriage of anticolonial nationalism with male supremacy. The *Reign of Wazobia* directly engages the question of women's place in the new nation. Male freedom fighters against English colonialism imagined an independent Nigeria as a national "home" in which women would occupy procreative, maternal, and domestic managerial roles, illustrating Ania Loomba's claim that "despite their other differences, and despite their contests over native women, colonial and indigenous patriarchies often collaborated to keep women 'in their place.'"[18] In Onwueme's depiction, Omu, before her conversion to Wazobia's cause, represents this feminine ideal domesticated to help manage patriarchy by enforcing conformity among women. The former king's wives, too, signify normative female identities in the context of traditional Ilaaa.

In Wazobia, however, Onwueme creates a perfect foil to traditional Anioma womanhood – a character who refuses to accommodate her postcolonial desires within the constricting boundaries that define the roles of "mother," submissive "lover," or "daughter" as the binary "Other" stabilizing patriarchal order. Her reign represents a conflicting signifier with which men and women struggle to assert their subjectivities. In the struggle that ensues, Wazobia's male adversaries conflate the she-king's impulse for equal rights for women with the alien influence of their colonial invaders, placing the allegedly emasculating impact of the women's campaign on a par with the "native" emasculation occasioned by imperialism. This connection imbues Anioma Kingdom's male conception of anticolonial nationalism with a reflexive support of indigenous patriarchy. What emerges is a contest between the sexes over the very meaning of independence and postcolonial reconstruction. For women in Wazobia's camp, the preservation of "native" patriarchy is not only not essential, but also rather inimical to the true promise of post-imperial self-determination.

In this context, the very Igbo traditions that may serve as engines of male oppression also turn out to have the potential to undermine that oppression. Onwueme's iconoclastic imagination turns the divine oracles of traditional Ilaaa into revolutionary instruments that facilitate imaginings of alternative universes in which women have their own voices. Thus, Afam Ebogu was right to suggest:

> Onwueme argues that traditional political and socio-cultural institutions, essentially erected by men as mythic structures of domination, have built in mechanisms for subverting their very effectiveness, and that the time has come for women to identify these traditions and institutional structures and use them to liberate themselves.[19]

For Onwueme then, indigenous traditions and mythologies assume significance not for the intrinsic value of their supposed authenticity, but rather for their dynamism as vehicles of reform.

Nevertheless, Wazobia as crafted by Onwueme, is neither a stable sign nor do her actions drive audiences to a specific social destination. Rather, her reign represents a momentary coalescence of social actions, movements, and desires for subjectivity. Like the neologism from which her name is derived, Wazobia may be interpreted as a state of consciousness, a transitory mode and an act of "knowing." The play ends inconclusively, with the outcome of the battle between the sexes remaining undefined.

Plate 3.2 Wazobia and one of her chiefs played by Acho Ugeyin in the film version of *Wazobia*. Photograph by Waka Photos.

Thus, not unlike Soyinka, Onwueme stresses chaos and fragmentation of stable social fabrics as necessary dynamos for the evolution of culture and identities. Beginning the play with its end, she offers a richly textured portrait of a society in transition – from an ontological oppressive state to an indefinable future in which people develop a metaphorical sense of "non-formality."

The language of the play is deceptively simple and marked by a vocabulary that is in essence a Nigerian English usually spoken and written by Onwueme's intended homeland audiences. Nigerian English signifies a linguistic vortex of translations by polyglot peoples. Embellished with proverbs and gnomic sayings, the language shifts seamlessly from one idiom to another. For instance Wazobia proclaims, "I, Wazobia,/Will show them/That women bear elephant tusks/Over their shoulders."[20] Or another character Wa: "Must we beg the ground to walk on it? Must we cut our necks just because we do not belong?"[21] Or, indeed, the strident Idehen: "You must know that when a child dances by the footpath, its drummer must be playing in a nearby bush."[22]

Using a folkloric narrative style to tell a simple but poetic story, Onwueme, like her mentors Soyinka and Osofisan, fashions the resources of history into a feminist re-reading of power, identity, and space. She challenges her inter-modernist middle-class, usually educated audiences to acknowledge, even celebrate the use of mythology and tradition as signifiers with which to re-invent themselves and their lesser compatriots.

Onwueme's critics have charged that the historical context in which *The Reign of Wazobia* is placed is not nuanced enough to address the neo-colonial dictatorial frame within which the men of Anioma seek to recuperate their "manhood" by recourse to tradition. They have pointed out that the institution of monarchy came to Ilaaa through its internal colonization by the Bini Empire, suggesting the region's multilayered imperial legacy which Onwueme does little to capture.[23] In the playwright's defense, however, it may be argued that *The Reign of Wazobia* represents an incomplete text. Onwueme emphasizes the unfinished nature of dramatic representations, which in her case accounts for the hanging signifiers that litter her play. A deliberate inventiveness permeates the loose, non-linear structure of the play as well as its populist tenor. The play's lack of resolution of the issues it raises implicitly privileges the *process* of transformation over its destination, although Onwueme certainly moves further in the direction of defining its direction than Soyinka did in "The Fourth Stage." Nonetheless, the chaotic note on which the curtain goes down in *Wazobia* hints at Onwueme's endorsement of a Soyinka-like conception of non-formal citizenship as the most effective mode for realizing the universalist potential of postcolonial desire.

As the audience for Tess Onwueme's works broadens to include diasporic communities outside Africa, the playwright will be challenged by new generations of playwrights in Nigeria and in Africa at large, who care less about the nation as a space for performing subjectivity, and whose linguistic demands are more complicated. This cohort is less invested in mythology and traditions than in the quest for an expansive cosmopolitanism within which to signify their local and global identities. Perhaps, like her mentors, Onwueme will also be writing with and for future generations about the complexity of feminist representations. In our recent film adaptation of the play, Onwueme provokes her audiences more intensely by problematizing not simply the overt political relationship between men and women, but their sexual relationships as well. In this version of the story, Wazobia translates her new-found power into romantic and sexual encounters with other women, thus defying the heterosexual underpinnings of Nigeria's traditional patriarchy, as well as its prime symbol, the monarchy.[24] What reaction this elicits from Nigerian audiences, remains to be seen.

4 The Yoruba Traveling Theatres

Popular theatre and desires for postcolonial subjectivity

> Yoruba Traveling Theatre ... is at its greatest scale of availability to the "common man," to the popular masses, in this region of the continent. Moreover, it is a theatre which goes to the people rather than waiting for the people to come to it.[1]

Yoruba Traveling Theatre "came to me" over thirty years ago, when as a young schoolboy, I was invited to a birthday party at the Obanta Hotel in Kano, a northern Nigerian town far away from the birthplace of this peripatetic dramatic tradition. The party's honoree was a friend whose Yoruba parents owned the hotel and regularly hosted itinerant Yoruba Traveling Theatre companies. My first experience of the carnivalesque style of Yoruba performance left me entranced. A sequence of dance skits, a solo, and a chorus response made up the "opening glee" as the story unfolded. The protagonist stated his cause and identified likely antagonists. Songs interspersed every act, sometimes commenting on the story and at other times simply providing melodic continuity to highly physical performances that ended in a "closing glee" that summarized and underscored the play's ideological significance. Highly interactive in approach, the show invited a willing audience to join the actors in swaying and dancing to the tune of the music, and to engage the moral conundrums of its plot.

That I first encountered Yoruba cultural practice in a predominantly non-Yoruba, far northern Islamic city, was not unusual. Indeed, Yoruba Traveling Theatre constituted a major medium of interaction between the diverse and hybrid populations of the Yorubas and other ethnic groups in cities and towns throughout Nigeria. The Kano of my childhood was, like much of urban Nigeria, a postcolonial entrepôt of cosmopolitan culture, a quintessential laboratory of what I call the "overlapping identities" defining Nigerians in their post-independence era. Resplendent in the melody and choreography of its dramatic resurrections of indigenous tales, and its participatory mode, Yoruba Traveling Theatre opened up a process of desiring, in which acts of remembering and memorializing native traditions, reinventing cultural reality, and weaving discourses of anticolonial nationalism gave people a collective sense of selfhood independent of England's colonial order. Yet, the postcolonial modernity thus wrought by the wandering artists of Yoruba drama was irrevocably intertwined with the assumptions, ethnic constructions, and even stylistic elements of the very colonial modernity the shackles of which they appeared to want so much to shake off.

It is to the ambiguous yearning for unified postcolonial nationhood embodied in Yoruba Traveling Theatre (YTT) that I turn in this chapter. I argue that as the most developed and enduring non-literary theatrical tradition defining tropes of alternative political and cultural identities in Nigeria, Yoruba Traveling Theatre not only produced vibrant anticolonial representations at significant historical moments, but also complicated them by imbuing them with a Yoruba regional exceptionalism originating at least partly in regional and ethnic reorganizations crafted by Nigeria's colonial master, England. The YTT's use of indigenous themes and symbols within the framework of a multi-ethnic montage of Yorubas, Ibos, Hausas, and others constructed by the English, made them celebrated practitioners of the most populist dramaturgy Nigeria ever experienced. Their indigenous themes and symbols were products of cross-cultural global and local contacts between the Yorubas and others with whom they crossed paths in the realms of trade, military engagement, and cultural exchange even before the colonial era, while their acceptance of English categories of ethnic organization, as also their adaptation of European and American concert styles represented their incorporation into the vortex of Euro-modernity. The pioneering works of the late Hubert Ogunde illustrate the general esthetic tendencies and political content of Yoruba Traveling Theatres better than most other artists, and I will for that reason, devote part of this chapter to an analysis of Ogunde's place in the complex worlds embedded in Yoruba drama.

West Africa's Yoruba Traveling Theatre traditions reflect and knit together a mosaic of cultures spawned by what Nigerian historian Akin Mabogunje describes as the region's "long story of human movements, incursions, displacements, intermixtures or successions of peoples, and of the impact of these on the beliefs, attitudes and social organization of the various peoples who today inhabit this great area."[2] In general, the YTT's presentations thematize, romanticize, and sometimes mythologize the encounters within and between concepts of Yorubaness and citizenship in locations traversed by people representing an immense variety of ethnicities. They occur in public spaces such as streets, makeshift tents, soccer stadiums, and church or school halls for all manner of audiences. These communal locales lent the traveling theatre tradition a populism and accessibility that also made it one of the most viable commercial enterprises in West Africa. According to Biodun Jeyifo, a leading commentator on the subject, the Traveling Theatre performance which developed before the rise of permanent theatre structures, while "physically homeless," is "solidly socially rooted" by virtue of having drawn audiences from all social classes.[3]

By 1990, no less than two hundred and thirty-two theatre companies claimed allegiance to this vibrant Yoruba tradition. Spontaneous and eclectic, their repertory and shows borrow willfully and unapologetically from other ethnic groups in Africa, as well as from external sources located in Europe and America. Some have even adapted Gilbert and Sullivan music-hall conventions and minstrelsy styles from the United States to forge a strain called the "concert party" tradition, channeling these cross-continental influences into the populist project of reflecting and gauging the political and social temperament of audiences drawn from a variety of social backgrounds. Their engagement with audiences typically begins several hours before the actual play opens. According to Biodun Jeyifo:

> the height of pre-production enticement of the audience takes the form of a roistering campaign around town or village in the company's bus or "mummy-wagon," with loudspeakers blaring forth the evening's performance to the accompaniment of vocal and instrumental music played by the company's orchestra. This somewhat mandatory mobile show of the Traveling Theatre troupes has become . . . an entertainment form in its own right, with each troupe trying to best its competitors in the profession by the distinctiveness and tone of its own campaign show.[4]

Three decades ago these tactics took my young heart by storm. I followed up my experience at the Obanta Hotel with a visit to a comedy show by Baba Sala the same year. Although I belonged to a non-Hausa and non-Yoruba Christian family in a predominantly Islamic city, I spoke Yoruba fluently a result of my upbringing in the cosmopolitan "Sabon Gari" section of the city, home to a cross-section of Nigerians including Yorubas, Ibos, and other ethnic groups from across Nigeria. The YTT plays, however, were accessible even to those without fluency in Yoruba, because they were sometimes rendered in "pidgin English" and were spectacular enough to communicate their simple story lines to non-Yoruba speaking audiences. Before long, I became a devoted fan of the famed comedian Jagua who was based in the northern town of Kaduna.

Over time, my role as observer and voyeur yielded to one of active participation in YTT-related dramatic productions. The Department of Dramatic Arts at the University of Ife (now re-named Obafemi Awolowo University) in Ile-Ife where I was a student, recruited Yoruba Traveling Theatre performers in an attempt to develop a hybrid program based on a combination of traditional and literary theatre conventions. The actors belonged to an outfit called the "UNIFE Theatre"[5] under the direction of Wole Soyinka. I joined them, performing in such productions as Amos

Tutuola's *Palmwine Drinkerd*, Ola Rotimi's *Kurunmi*, Guillarme Oyono-Mbia's *Three Suitors, One Husband*, and Wole Soyinka's *Requiem for A Futurologist* with such versatile artists as Peter Fatomilola, Kola Oyewo, Laide Adewale, Femi Ojeyemi, and Gboyega Ajayi. In addition, I served a graduate directing apprenticeship with the company, holding daily improvisational sessions and directing plays that represented some of the most intense creative moments of my career. The actors I worked with had an unusual ability to manipulate language whether Yoruba, standard English, or pidgin English. Hybridizing the traditions of Yoruba Traveling Theatre with modern literary drama, the productions that resulted offered their largely university audiences a fascinating and lyrical experience. This hands-on tangential experience with YTT activities heightened my curiosity about the origins and adaptability of the Yoruba dramatic tradition.

My investigations into these issues revealed that Yoruba Traveling Theatre stemmed from two traditions of dissent in Nigeria.[6] One was associated with the social and esthetic activities of rebel members of the Oyo royal court in southwestern Nigeria about 1593.[7] The other originated in the movement of Nigerian Christians for an Africanized Church during Nigeria's nationalist struggle.[8]

The Oyo dissenters embraced the cult of *Egungun*[9] ancestor worship, which according to many scholars gave rise to the Alarinjo (literally meaning the traveling performers) among the Yorubas on the Atlantic coast. Commentators such as Joel Adedeji, Ebun Clark, and Oyekan Owomoyela,[10] maintain that the itinerant nature of ancient Alarinjo theatre and its interactive performance style suggest a close link to contemporary Yoruba Traveling Theatre practice. The Alarinjo performance tradition grew out of a plot hatched by Alapini, a member of the royal court of Oyo (known as the Oyo Mesi) to thwart the king Alafin Ogbolu's plan to move his capital to its original site at Katunga. Threatened by the Nupe Empire in the northern flanks of its territory, the imperialistic Oyo Empire had been forced to shift its headquarters south of Katunga. There, it flourished as a military and mercantile power, participating actively in the Atlantic slave trade.[11]

Thus, when the king – Alafin Ogbolu (also known as Abipa), initiated a proposal to return the capital to its original location at Oyo-Ile or Katunga, he met with resistance from chieftains belonging to his court. Led by Alapini and other members of the Egungun performance cult, these dissenters devised a strategy to foil the king's designs. Knowing that the king would send emissaries to the proposed site, they set up a group of masquerades impersonating six stock characters associated in Oyo mythology with creative mishaps. According to Joel Adedeji,[12] the characters – the hunchback, the albino, the leper, the prognathus, the cripple, and the dwarf – mimicked the councilors in the Oyo-Mesi. The "performance" achieved its objective by frightening the king's emissaries. The king then sent another batch of inspectors, this time with famous hunters to investigate these ghostly figures. Alapini's plot was discovered and from then onwards the Alafin was nicknamed "Oba Moro" meaning "the king who caught ghosts." He retained the impersonators in his court as entertainers, appointing their chief as the head of the troupe.

The diaries of two English explorers Hugh Clapperton and Richard Lander[13] suggest that as guests of the Alafin on February 22, 1826, they were enterained by Alarinjo performers. Estimates of the date when the court artists became public and itinerant remain speculative owing to conflicting oral and written records. What is more certain is that after the collapse of the Oyo Empire, the Alarinjo tradition mutated into street performances that ritualized the exploits of the ghost-catching king, and fostered the creation of a professional guild to safeguard the interests of the traveling actors. Meanwhile, the emergence of vibrant urban cultures in Lagos and elsewhere by the 1820s – shaped in part by the advent of cosmopolitan immigrant populations of freed slaves from North and South America[14] – gave traveling theatres a new lease of life. As casualties of European modernity, African refugee communities produced a cultural landscape based on the revival of African performance traditions hybridized by familiar European conventions. Cities like Lagos – so named by the Portuguese – brought newcomers from the Atlantic world into contact with elites from the hinterland. Together they created a cosmopolis replete with a vibrant nationalist press, educational facilities, and Africanized Christian churches. Adopting names such as the "United Progressive Society" and "The Brazilian Dramatic Company," organizations built by these heterogeneous leaders stood poised to assert an anticolonial self-definition as the English established themselves as Nigeria's imperial masters. In that context, it was the Yoruba Traveling Theatre's pervasive anticolonial nationalist responses to English colonial modernity that gave this tradition so deeply steeped in ancient Yoruba cultures, its greatest contemporary relevance.

Twenty-nine years after the imperialistic dissection of Africa by various European powers at the infamous Berlin conference of 1884,[15] England transformed its trading networks in West Africa into tools of direct political domination. By 1914, various regions tapped into intricate webs of commerce by the Royal Niger Trading Company, had been amalgamated into a colonial nation called Nigeria. The English strategy of developing a colonial nationalism based on the promotion of African acculturation to the English language and culture evoked fierce resistance by those forcibly conscripted into the new nation and its global framework. In the struggle to define an oppositional sense of self, various ethnic groups, including the Yorubas, embarked upon movements of cultural revivalism in the context of which Yoruba Traveling Theatre assumed great significance.

As part of their project to incorporate Nigerians into English colonial modernity, the imperial masters sought to consolidate Christian values by outlawing indigenous performance traditions that partook of any element of ancestral and spirit worship, including traveling performers affiliated with the Alarinjo. Rather than disappearing entirely, however, such traditions became residual forms of entertainment for alienated Christian converts whose identity crisis took the form of nostalgia for the native arts.[16] Christianized Nigerians' agitation for "Africanist" churches spurred the founding of the *United African Methodist, Cherubim and Seraphim*, and the *Aladura* whose modes of worship included outlawed dances, and singing and performance traditions rooted in ancestral worship, adapted to Christian practice. Eventually, the performances left the churches for community halls, where, tailored to contemporary urban cultures, they were transmuted into "new" dramatic traditions such as Yoruba Traveling Theatres.

The cultural appeal of performance traditions such as the YTT soared as African anticolonial activism gained momentum in the aftermath of the Second World War. Conscious of their part in achieving the Allied triumph, and galvanized by an economic boom which followed the war, colonized nations across Africa sought more democratic relationships with their imperial masters. Palm oil from the east, cocoa from the west, peanuts from the north, and sorghum, maize, and guinea corn from the middle belt, forged a lucrative new market economy, the spoils of which Africans wanted to share. In particular, the educated elite and emergent working classes in various urban centers, their expectations whetted by the economic possibilities of the post-war boom, served as the vanguard of a nationalist movement that drew inspiration from indigenous cultural traditions.[17] In the 1940s and 1950s, they even sported native costumes, defiantly spoke indigenous languages in public spaces, and danced to hybrids of African music such as "highlife" and "juju."[18]

The Yoruba Traveling Theatres addressed the aspirations of these groups by actively cultivating and sustaining the anticolonial nationalism of their audiences while tapping into their economic power to afford a commercial theatre.[19] Yet, while they overtly produced symbolic means of cultural revival that spoke to a colonized people's nostalgia for its denigrated roots, they simultaneously crafted a pan-Yoruba ethno-nationalism with which the Yorubas could negotiate identity and power in an anticipated postcolonial Nigeria. Between 1920 and the1960s, the political thrust of their work was broadly anticolonial, appealing to audiences regardless of their ethnic affiliation. Their focus on Yoruba ethno-nationalism on the other hand, became more pronounced in the post-independence period, particularly after the Nigeria/Biafra civil war of 1967–1970. Defying the promise of postcolonial unity, regional conflicts over oil resources culminated in fratricidal struggle which took nearly two million lives. In its aftermath, Nigeria entered an era of neo-colonial military dictatorships that sold the country out to foreign oil interests, attempting at the same time to consolidate its power behind a new nationalist culture that downplayed regional differences. The YTT responded to the challenges of the times by intensifying their pan-Yoruba nationalism while pitching their support for "one Nigeria." Their plays began to focus on mystic themes, fantasies, and stories of a spiritual world in what Biodun Jeyifo characterized as a "nationalistic cultural assertion" against the challenge of foreign cultural assaults, and at the same time a celebration of "an ethno-national Yoruba identity within the pluralistic setting of the Nigerian nation state."[20]

Ironically enough, this dual pronged cultural nationalism mirrored the principles of ethnic and regional reorganization upon which British Nigeria was based, so that the colonial administration itself set the terms within which colonialism could be contested. The Richards and McPherson Constitutions of 1946 and 1951 constructed a colonial state united by its allegiance to a foreign potentate, but fractured along primarily four regional and ethnic lines. In the face of imminent political independence in the 1950s, diverse cultural groups amalgamated by the English into a colonized nation state began to define their political identities in ethnic and regional terms, fueling a torrent of violent ethno-nationalistic strife. As Barber, Collins, and Ricard have pointed out, Nigerian politics, which had hitherto been national and to some extent pan-African, yielded to widespread ethnicization in the 1950s, largely in response to the Richards and McPherson Constitutions of 1946 and 1951, which set up the Nigerian state along regional and ethnic lines.[21] Such ethnicization was institutionalized in organizations like the Ibo Union in eastern Nigeria, the "Egbe Omo Oduduwa" in the west, the "Jami'yyar Mutanen Arewa" in the north, and the Tiv Progressive Union representing the middle sections of the country. These regional combinations took the form of political parties in the 1960s and 1970s, the intra- and inter-group conflicts of which shaped the political terrain of the post-independence period.

The YTT's expression of Yoruba cultural distinctiveness within a pan-Nigerian framework subscribed to the colonial vision of Nigerian pluralism (a vision originally governed at least in part by the imperial strategy of "divide and rule"), even as it critiqued the discord inflamed by the narrow dictates of ethnic chauvinism. YTT companies articulated an anticolonial nation state while at the same time reinforcing a Yoruba distinctiveness. Hence, their practices are simultaneously intensely local and global. Moreover, the traditionalism of their themes notwithstanding, mainstream Yoruba Traveling Theatre companies began to adapt European and American performance conventions once rejected by anticolonial nationalists of the pre-independence years, thereby underscoring their new cosmopolitanism. Music hall, big band, and other Euro-American performance conventions were grafted onto native cultures to formulate a composite national cultural identity that was simultaneously local and global. This cosmopolitan flavor appealed to their elite audiences – themselves the occasional butt of satire in YTT productions. I will later on contextualize such a phenomenon within the modernist framework of my thesis by suggesting that YTTs clearly illustrate what I term inter-modernist and intra-modernist identities within Nigeria as a postcolonial state. While the former alludes to its contest against colonial modernity, the latter suggests the tensions and conflicts such a modernity generated within ideas and notions of Yorubaness and Nigerianess.

These concessions to external influences – whether colonial or post-imperial Western – are clearly evident in the life and works of one of the Yoruba genre's most distinguished practitioners – Herbert Ogunde. No commentary on the Yoruba Traveling Theatres would be quite complete without some attention to Ogunde for no single figure illustrates the style, content, and political significance of the Yoruba Traveling Theatres, or the paradoxes embedded in its epistemological vision, than he. It is to this former colonial policeman and school teacher-turned dramatist and his signature play *Strike and Hunger* that I devote the following section.

Hubert Ogunde (1916–1990) and innovations in Yoruba Traveling Theatre traditions

> Foreigners depict Africans as buffoons and social degenerates who have no culture, music, dance, and way of life, but are mere loyal imitators of their masters. Africans shall be most guilty if they fail to prove to the world by practical demonstrations, that their detractors have been guilty of gross mis-interpretations by presenting on our own stage and if possible on theirs too, African culture and way of life and those melodies and graceful dances that are purely of African origin.[22]

These words sounded Hubert Ogunde's battle cry when he stormed Nigeria's theatre scene in 1947. Before he was done, forty-three years later, he had done much indeed to defy the stereotype of African cultural sterility. Ogunde taught school and served in the police force before he entered the tumultuous realm of African professional theatre. According to his biographer Ebun Clark,[23] Ogunde produced his first amateur play – a religious piece titled *The Garden of Eden and the Throne of God* – on commission by the Afrocentric church known as the Cherubim and Seraphim Movement in 1944. The play's outstanding success among the new Christian converts eager to find a place for indigenous traditions within the modern imperatives of their urban life-styles in such settings as Lagos, encouraged Ogunde to become a full-time dramatist. In 1947, he inaugurated a theatre company called "African Music Research Party" and opened his first touring show titled *Tiger's Empire*. The play was a satirical attack on English colonial rule. The formation of the company and the temper of its first play attracted enormous enthusiasm and appreciation from the nationalist press and various anticolonial organizations. A nationalist reviewer in the *Daily Service* exulted:

The African has got a potential talent in stage-craft, and if given the opportunity could compete with any other race and even outshine them. The last three years, at least, have brought into light Africans with great creative resources who have won admiration of both natives and aliens for their originality, foresight and organizing ability on the stage.[24]

Ogunde went on to write other plays such as *Darkness and Light* and *Mr Devil's Money*, both of which reflected Christian morality tinged with native cultural revivalism. These works belonged to what Ebun Clark calls Ogunde's "Operatic phase" between 1944 and 1949, in which he performed within a genre called "Native Air Operas" developed in Africanized churches Ogunde himself patronized and worked for. By adopting once proscribed indigenous performance styles, African churches thus struck a note of anticolonial nationalism. The artistic merit of productions like *Mr Devil's Money* also won praise – however patronizing in tenor – from such English expatriates as one Major Anthony Syer who observed in the *Daily Service*:

> Since my arrival in this country, I have seen many African plays and operas . . . but I had the greatest surprise of my life when I attended the rehearsal of the African Music Research Party, written, composed and produced by Hubert Ogunde, a young native producer . . . The theme is based on an old African story depicting the "here and after" of a man who signed a pact with an evil spirit in order to be wealthy. To see the cast rehearsing the Opera, dances, to hear the cheap native drums supplying the music with precision without any mechanical aid, the clapping of hands, and the high standards of discipline maintained throughout is to think one is back at a London theatre. The singing is excellent. Dance formations, lighting and the stage settings are concrete proof that the African is no more behind as many people think.[25]

What Major Syer failed to note was that *Mr Devil's Money* chastised Nigerians for contributing to their own colonial subordination by signing dirty pacts with the English – a chastisement in synchronism with emerging nationalist sentiments of the day. Indeed, the enthusiastic reception of Ogunde's works by the indigenous elite paved the way for the flowering of the Yoruba Traveling Theatres. Building on the foundations laid by the Alarinjo performers, Ogunde took his plays not only across southwestern Nigeria where the majority of the Yorubas lived, but also to the north of the country where other ethnic groups were beginning to identify with the nationalist discourse informing his plays.

In this context, the landmark *Strike and Hunger* established Ogunde's reputation as a foremost anticolonial dramatist of his time. Influenced by the development of trade unionism and working-class political activism in 1940s' Nigeria, especially the General Strike of 1945, *Strike and Hunger* offered a romantic perspective on the resilience of workers and their demands for a fair and equitable society. The play entered the spotlight of national attention when the colonial administration interrupted its performance during a tour in Jos,[26] and then banned it in the northern province. Ogunde was instantly transformed from a Yoruba hero into a national figure.[27]

Strike and Hunger is set in a fictional feudal world where a king of foreign origin usurps the throne, represses the citizens' claims to subjectivity, and coerces them to labor hard for meager returns. King Yejide's oppressive presence and miserly distribution of wealth plunges the land into a famine. The monarch's action is said to have wronged even nature's principle of balance and coexistence aptly symbolized by the metaphorical raging sea at the end of the story. Yet, the alien potentate is not beyond redemption. When the people rebel by organizing labor unrest to destabilize the economy, he changes course and abjures his dictatorial behavior.

This tale of citizenship denied and restored, represented not only a direct indictment of English rule, but also a recognition of its potential to spur radical rebellion. It excoriated the clerks and armed men serving as King Yejide's vehicle of oppression, in what constituted a direct reference to the indigenous collaborators of the colonial regime. After the fashion of most of Ogunde's plays, the characters were defined by a simple Manichean binary and did not display any detailed psychological depth. The plot summed up iconic functions designating their personalities. Names like "clerks" (akowe), "messenger" (ojise), "one strong man" (Okunrin Alagbara Kan), "people" (awon enian), "dancers" (awon onijo), were used to indicate the primacy of the plot over identification with specific characters. Apart from Oba Yejide, the other character endowed with a name different from his function was the workers' leader Ayinde, who served as a foil to the king. The play's major themes – Oba Yejide's origin, lack of respect for and understanding of his subjects, the tyrannical nature of his rule, and nature's apocalyptic warning that the rebellion was a precursor of worse things to come, – are all revealed to the audience in the musical "Opening glee":

> Come people of the world, rally round to fight hunger
> Descend O Angels, grant us audience
> Angels, behold the people of the world
> Deprived of the good things of life
> See the obverse of the world
> . . .
>
> Yejide the king, power of life,
> Is reigning as if the leopard is reigning

Over the fishes in the lagoon
Eh! The lord Almighty that created you
Created us
And he does not create us
To become slaves
God Almighty shall judge, the dead shall judge
The Head of our fathers in the sky that died
Shall fight the murderers
We are hungry, we that feed in agony
Old people die of hunger
In the house of the poor
Their pregnant women give birth in suffering
They are giving birth at the market of hunger
God Almighty shall judge
The dead shall judge.[28]

The king's name suggests that he hails from beyond the seas, as his arrogance is melodramatically underscored:

You old ones, all of you people
You servants and messengers
Slaves of my father
I am glorified by nature and good deeds
I reign on earth and above
Tremble, people
Fear, fear and tremble![29]

As the people protest and organize, the plot's tempo and music peak with the dance structuring their dissent:

We workers do not have money to feed
And we do not have clothes, nor garments
We walk "naked like monkeys"
Yejide the king is eating, Yejide the King is drinking
He forgets that the day of recompensation is coming
God Almighty shall judge
The Dead shall judge
The head of our fathers that die
Shall fight the murderers.[30]

Questions of citizenship and nationhood lay at the heart of the play's concerns. Yejide's subjects found themselves in a context they resented and sustained at the same time. When they welcomed the new king from abroad, they thought they were broadening their horizon beyond those of their surrounding neighbors. Their embrace of a foreign sovereign symbolized the community's desire for cultural diversity and cosmopolitanism. The ruler's introduction of new farming methods, trains and the railways, and other technologies reassured the people that their choice would pave the path to modernization. Yet when the king's suzerainty degenerated into autocracy, the governed did not fail to assert their voices in organized resistance. They forced the king to recognize his folly and make amends by increasing workers' wages and promising to promote their welfare.

In itself, the play did not offer any programmatic anticolonial thesis. Moreover, the promise it offered was one of the amelioration rather than the abolition of colonial government. In *Strike and Hunger*, the people neither overthrew the king nor changed the political structure that enabled his dictatorship. Rather, Ogunde appeared to be saying that the preservation of tranquility rested upon recognizing the people's right to share in the wealth they helped create. The play revealed its architect's ambivalence toward the European presence in Nigeria. Far from regarding all white men as inherently bad, Ogunde appreciated those of them that appeared to him to exhibit a moral conscience. In this category, for instance, he placed the crusaders against the slave trade. Indeed, Ogunde's humanistic plea for social justice sprang from a combination of his Christian values with a mature nationalist consciousness and apparently discounted the near impossibility of achieving equity within colonialism.[31] Frantz Fanon comments on the typicality of Ogunde's ambivalent thesis when, in his analysis of the colonized, he opines, "The natives' challenge to the colonial world is not a rational confrontation of points of view. It is not a treatise on the universal, but the untidy affirmation of an original idea propounded as an absolute."[32] That idea, in Ogunde's case, is a vehement disclaimer on domination and an act of refusal.

Yet, however moderate the logic of Ogunde's anticolonialist discourse, its subversive significance stemmed from the temporal moment of its creation and performance. The alarm with which the colonial authority received the play must be viewed in the context of emergent anti-imperialism following the Second World War, channeled four months before the play opened in October 1945, especially through the activism of organized labor. The national labor union – itself created by the English as a way of socializing the "natives" into a colonial labor discourse – launched a general strike, halting work on the railways and the civil service. Trade unions complained bitterly about the failure of their wages to keep pace with rising living costs, and England's lack of investment in its colony.[33] Especially alarming to the English was the potential regional reach of the strike. The south, a traditional bastion of anticolonial activism, was expected to fall under the influence of the dissenting laborers. The north, on the other hand, had historically been a more secure stronghold of colonial rule. There, the English pursued an indirect strategy of colonial domination, taking care not to interfere with the hegemony of the Islamic Hausa/Fulani Emirates. By the mid-1940s, they had persuaded these emirs of their need to achieve the cosmopolitanism enjoyed by the south through Western education to be provided by the colonial masters. Englishmen's pursuit of different policies with regard to Christianization and the spread of Western education in Nigeria's diverse regions fostered regional rivalries that militated against the emergence of a unified anticolonial movement. Thus, northern leaders like Abubakar Tafawa Balewa, who was to become the first prime minister of post-independence Nigeria, were decidedly unreceptive to the nationalist call for political independence.[34]

The colonial administration's decision to ban Ogunde's play in the northern city of Jos – home to many English officers by virtue of its relatively mild climate – must be understood in the context of the regional diversity of the anticolonial response. Against the background of the 1945 strike, which helped nationalize resentment against the English, the performance of *Strike and Hunger*, if allowed to go through, might convert hitherto compliant northerners into confirmed pro-independence nationalists. Hence, the alacrity with which the colonial administration forced the curtain to go down on Ogunde's drama soon after it debuted.

Undeterred by official repression, Ogunde's company went on to create other works which continued to sound the refrain of labor militancy and anticolonial activism. *Bread and Bullet* told the story of rebellious miners who went on a strike in 1949 at the Enugu Colliery and were fired upon by the colonial police. Several demonstrators were killed, provoking national outrage and support for the miners. Premiered in 1950, the play became a popular political statement particularly after its interruption by the police during a performance in Kano, and a subsequent ban on future shows of Ogunde's theatre company throughout the northern region.

Ogunde's work, however nationalist in political tenor, was, however, evolving stylistically into a cosmopolitan genre in keeping with the hybrid sense of nationhood poised to take hold of West Africa in the 1950s and early 1960s. During a visit to England to study its popular theatrical traditions, Ogunde noted the popularity of music hall and variety entertainment, strains of which he had experienced in the cities of Ghana. In Ghana, a syncretic performance tradition called "Concert Party"[35] had taken off in most of the coastal cities. Similar to the fare offered by Lagos and other cities in Nigeria, "Concert Party" fused European, American, and traditional Ghanaian comic and musical forms to create a genre suited to the tastes of the emergent social classes in post-independence Ghana. On his return to Nigeria, Ogunde's company was re-named "Ogunde's Concert Party" and his performance style vigorously adapted to providing his audiences with more cutting edge and cosmopolitan theatre. He introduced saxophones, elaborate chorus line performances, and European costumes in plays created from 1950 to 1964. Blending the Alarinjo, music hall revues, slapstick comedy, songs, and dance, Ogunde developed a performance structure made of "the opening glee," "drama," and "closing glee." This style reflected the mood of many cities in southwestern Nigeria and neighboring countries, in which an increasingly cosmopolitan elite's exuberant tastes for hybrid cultural trends set the tone for social reality and sense of belonging.

With the advent of political independence, Ogunde's practices became more entertainment revues that gave Nigerians a break from the militant anticolonialism of yore. Tragically enough, even as his celebratory *Song of Unity*, produced on a government commission in 1960, projected the hope of a new and unified nation, Nigeria's socio-political fabric stood poised on the verge of disintegration – sundered by regional animosities that deepened after 1964. The tentative and fragile homology of anticolonial discourses yielded to regionalist politics. As the various regions formulated by the colonizing process negotiated their places in the emergent nation state, conflicts between and within these entities ensued on a grand scale. According to Nkemdirim:

> The unevenness of development or modernization in the society as a whole gave the power struggle a more or less regional bias. The main ethnic clusters pitted against each other, the Hausa against the Yoruba, the Yoruba against the Ibo and the Northerners against the Southerners as a whole.[36]

Regional ethnic clusters in the form of the Ibo Union in the east, the Egbe Omo Oduduwa in the west, the Jami'yyar Mutanen Arewa in the north, and the Tiv Progressive Union in the mid-region, sourced the new post-independence political parties. The Action Group represented the interests of the west, the National Council of Nigeria and Citizens, the east, Northern People's Congress, the north, and the United Middle Belt Congress that of central Nigeria. The intensity of ethnic power rivalries consuming these groups is reflected in post-independence parliamentary records. For instance, Chief Obafemi Awolowo of the Action Group declared: "It seemed clear to me that Azikiwe's policy was to corrode the self-respect of the Yoruba people as a group: to build up the Ibo nation as a 'master race.'"

This allegation was fueled by comments such as the following by Dr Nnamdi Azikiwe of the National Council of Nigeria and Citizens:

> It would appear that the God of Africa has created the Ibo nation to lead the children of Africa from the bondage of the ages ... The martial prowess of the Ibo nation at all stages of human history has enabled them not only to conquer others but also to adapt themselves

to the role of preserver . . . The Ibo nation cannot shrink its responsibility from its manifest destiny.

Malam Abubakar Tafawa Balewa of the Northern Peoples Congress abandoned all pretenses of living in "one nation" by asserting: "Many Nigerians
deceive themselves by thinking that Nigeria is one . . . particularly some
of the press people . . . This is wrong. I am sorry to say that this presence
of unity is artificial."[37] The regional political parties were not, however,
monolithic entities. In the western region where the majority of Ogunde's
audiences lived, internal rifts in the main political party split a once unified
front into two contestatory voices. Disagreements between Obafemi
Awolowo and his deputy Oladoke Akintola split the Action Group and
weakened the region's political capital in negotiations within the emergent
nation state.

Keeping the critical language of its pre-independence practices,
Ogunde's company responded with *Yoruba Ronu!* (Yoruba Think!). The play
was a scathing attack against the disunity, bickering, and opportunism displayed by the political leaders of the region. The plot presented a kingdom,
the legitimate king of which was betrayed and imprisoned by his deputy to
the detriment of the stability and rights of its citizens. The parallels with
political intrigues within the Action Group were clear. The leader of that
party, Awolowo, was deposed and imprisoned by his deputy Akintola, in
collaboration with extra-regional allies in the central government. Accounts
of the command performance state that the chief minister-by-usurpation
banned the play and proscribed Ogunde's theatre company. Effected in a
part of the country where his largest audiences lived, the ban devastated
Ogunde's company economically and pushed it to the verge of bankruptcy.

The repression may have had its desired effect. Between the late 1960s
and 1970s, Ogunde's plays lost their antagonistic and critical tone. As
Nigeria entered a phase of military dictatorships fortified by oil revenues,
the playwright became something of an establishment figure. He devoted
himself to developing a more commercially oriented theatre whose main
themes proposed a more stable Nigerian society despite the obvious political misadventures perpetrated by the military and civilian governments.
Plays produced then included *Keep Nigeria One* (1968), *Muritala* (1976), and
Nigeria (1977). During the 1980s he became a prominent supporter of the
military governments, producing "safe" plays. As a cultural ambassador he
embarked on regular government-funded tours within and outside Nigeria.
Before his death in 1990, he was tipped to head the newly formed National
Theatre Troupe.

Ogunde's cooptation by Nigeria's repressive oil boom regimes coincided
with a waning in the popularity of Yoruba Traveling Theatres. In the late
1970s, urban centers became increasingly dangerous places for their
middle-class clients. A violent socio-economic malaise followed close on

the heels of the Nigerian civil war and oil boom, jeopardizing the social act of watching cultural performances in theatres or community halls. Mass migration to the urban cities, general unemployment and underemployment, and the absence of a social safety net induced a systematic criminalization of a new postcolonial "underclass." Armed robberies in public spaces kept audiences away from the theatre, prompting the Yoruba companies to shift their performance sites to television, photoplay magazines, music records, and videotapes. Asserting their usual power of adaptation, they not only reoriented their works to these diverse modes of entertainment, but also went on to pioneer indigenous filmmaking.

Ogunde's impact on the practices and directions of Yoruba Traveling Theatre were enormous. He succeeded in developing an "imagined community" through the medium of nationalist discourses in pre- and post-independent Nigeria. His practices satisfied the textual expectations of his audience by assuming an insidious populism, and defining a national symbolic community run by anticolonial Nigerians. Yet, Ogunde's focus on Yoruba cultural identity within the framework of "One Nigeria" implicitly subscribed to the paradigm of ethnic organization constituted by English colonialism. Unfortunately, by the 1970s, his vision of social justice and national unity amid cultural pluralism gave way to a conservative cultural practice that legitimized neo-colonial nationalism within which Yoruba ethno-nationalism occupied an important if precarious position. As an illustration of Yoruba Traveling Theatres, Ogunde's practices draw attention to the ephemerality and historical specificity of anti-establishment discourses. They show how companies once engaged in cultivating the discursive fields of radical issues might end up redundant when the communities they once served outgrow their discourses.

As proposed earlier, though Yoruba Traveling Theatres contributed to anticolonial nationalism, they produced a complicated regional or pan-Yoruba nationalism. For, what constitutes the "Yoruba" nation is a diverse, sometimes violent history of being. As it provided counter-memory and anticolonial images and narrations of nationhood, the offer of texts of a homogeneous stable coexistence is more a political desire than historical reality. Nevertheless, it offered a textual system for a people who refused to be overpowered by European imperialism despite a complicated and sometimes complicitous relationship to that history.[38]

I suggest that the activities and practices of Yoruba Traveling Theatre have participated in developing a system of representation wherein issues of overlapping colonial archeologies are articulated. Their vast repertory of plays illustrates how they simultaneously define the inter-modernist and intra-modernist frames that defined Nigeria as a modern country. A fundamental historical point is how these works represent the contact and incorporation of Yoruba cultures into Euro-modernity. Most of the Yoruba empires achieved their prominence through contact, incursions, and domination by the expansions of Euro-modernity to Africa. Such contact manifested itself through slavery, dispersal, and relocation of its peoples across wide expanses produced by Euro-modernity's imperial histories. The YTT practices also reveal contacts between Yoruba nations and other neighboring nations and empires before their incorporation into Nigeria, hence underscoring their inter-modernist identity. The intra-modernist dimensions of their practices manifest themselves in the different plays attentive to the desires of the individual ethnicities constituting the pan-Yoruba identity. Plays drawing folkloric inspirations from Egba, Ijebu, Oyo, and Ibadan cultural backgrounds are cases in point. The subjectivities these plays display are heterogeneous, sometimes complementary and at other times conflicting with self-definition in the contemporary Nigeria into which they are colonially conscripted and which they post-colonially navigate.

Together, the Yoruba Traveling Theatre traditions point to an indigenous modernity that developed itself as a frontier of interaction and resistance to others such as European modernity. As the Yoruba global structures overlap with those of other African groups as well as the British global and colonial culture, Yoruba popular theatre traditions offer a nexus through which people and groups cross these overlapping modernities. Yoruba Traveling Theatres reflect the voices and desires of those caught in the interstices of global systems jockeying for hegemonic positions in the complicated cultural landscape called Nigeria. The practices of Hubert Ogunde, Duro Ladipo, Kola Ogunmola, Lere Paimo, Ade Folayan, and an army of other smaller-scale groups have contributed significantly to memories and memorials of what it is to be Yoruba in relation to other ethnicities and nations. Beyond offering deep historical insight with their metaphorical readings of history, they have continued to invite audiences to negotiate identity, location, and agency through their dexterous performances. Biodun Jeyifo has observed:

> The dominant image of Yoruba Traveling Theatre movement . . . is that of *change, process and evolution* . . . it is . . . apparent that new forces, new structures of perceiving and feeling are contending with the old in the world of the Traveling Theatre troupes. The basic animist, supernaturalist aspects of the world-view of the troupes, in their recourse to indigenous pre-colonial folkloric traditions and belief systems, is necessarily having to contend with another outlook which derives from the secular forces of commodity production, the market economy, and an ever increasing social division of labor.[39]

I add that such practices, whether residual or active, are faced with renewed enactments of nationalism in a Nigeria still struggling to redefine itself to people caught in and outside its boundaries. As the rest of the world welcomes the twenty-first century, it remains to be seen if the discourses of Euro-modernity which mapped and consigned Africa to its margins, will be successfully dethroned, the continent's maps redrawn and national identities reframed by cultural practices such as Yoruba Traveling Theatres. If this happens, Nigeria as a nation state will have to fundamentally reorganize itself, and the practices put forth by Yoruba Traveling Theatre might re-surface again to participate in offering a counter-identity to not only the singular identity known as "Yorubas," but also to that of the nation state as we know it. The Traveling Theatre traditions may even inspire new practices struggling to construct a more hybrid notion of "self" and a wider field of achieving subjective significance.

Many years after that first encounter with these practices, I remember how desperate I was for images of residual Africa in my Catholic secondary school. Though I am not of the pre-independence generation, the significance of those moments of defiance, re-inscription, and disrupting the dominating discourse of colonialism and its neo-colonial variant still animates me. As I ponder if the practitioners ever thought of the historicity of their works, Homi Bhabha's opinion sounds even louder in my ears: "The power of the postcolonial translation of modernity rests in its *performative, deformative* structure that does not simply revalue the contents of a cultural tradition, or transpose values cross-culturally."[40] Remembering Baba Sala's over-sized wooden bow tie, Jagua's linguistic caricature of the "whiteman" or his black surrogate, or the lady Funmilayo Ranco Baby's boxing and wrestling antics, makes me nod in affirmation that they have, in their own ways, performed resistance, despite the challenges posed by discourses of colonialism and its neo-colonial progeny.

5   Theatre, democracy, and community development

Ahmadu Bello University and the Nigerian Popular Theatre Alliance

> Drama and Theatre for Development and change ... [aims to bring] to the most oppressed in these local communities more confidence in themselves, especially in their own epistemologies and powers of learning; and ... to give them access to a wider social and political analysis. [This wider analysis might be both national and international.][1]

It was a balmy northern Nigerian evening during the rainy season of 1984. A troupe of student actors playing drums, gongs, and flutes, strolled through the shantytown of Samaru opposite the carefully landscaped campus of Ahmadu Bello University in the city of Zaria. Accompanied by young onlookers who grew into an animated audience of adults as well as children before long, the actors set up stage with a tarpaulin canvas on a Samaru street cordoned off for dramatic performances. As the play opened amid songs and dances in Hausa and pidgin English, the two main narrator-protagonists Dauda and Sauna, invited passersby and members of the audience to mediate a fierce internecine dispute over the lack of water in the community. Before the end of the event, no witness to the show was left in any doubt as to the overtly political purpose of the play – which was not simply to dramatize the unsanitary living conditions of Samaru's inhabitants, but also to galvanize the local community to seek redress through social and political activism.

Samaru's Story, as the play was called, embodied the mission of a broad movement in Nigeria to empower local communities through theatre. This movement, known as Theatre for Development (TFD), had, by 1980, emerged as a formidable counterpoint to neo-colonial cultural politics. Originating in Zaria's Ahmadu Bello University (ABU), the activist TFD evolved from the tradition of community theatre. In developing nations relegated to the margins of European modernity, TFD has made conscious use of the performing arts to achieve what the Canadian theatre animator Ross Kidd has described as "a process of social change; changes in self-concept, attitude, awareness, skill, or behavior."[2] Its art has gone beyond metaphorical representations of under-development to facilitate action on social problems. In this context, theatre becomes a forum for organizing communities into decolonizing discourses that give them a voice as well as the organizational means to negotiate the cultural and political terms of their own social progress. Theatre for Development reconceptualizes the very notion of development in postcolonial Africa to mean not simply the provision of water, hospitals, and shelter for under-privileged communities but, more broadly, to encompass a complex process that uses culture to enact and sustain strategies for full and effective participation in society. This vision of development through culture was institutionalized in Nigeria in 1988 when various local TFD groups throughout the country launched a nation-wide organization called the Nigerian Popular Theatre Alliance (NPTA).

As a theatre student at Ahmadu Bello University, I played Dauda in Samaru that balmy night in 1984. In the present chapter, I tell the larger story of which Dauda was an optimistic symbol – the story of postcolonial aspirations for freedom and social justice as they unfolded through the activities of the NPTA. Unlike the Yoruba Traveling Theatres, the professional artists of which cultivated a simultaneously ethno-nationalist and pan-Africanist prism for contesting colonial modernity, TFD brought together amateur and professional actors, social workers, and health functionaries in a broader movement to help communities help themselves. Forty-two years after independence from English rule, a large section of the Nigerian population still suffers from poverty and a structurally induced paralysis of agency. If, as suggested earlier in this book, colonial modernity networked Nigeria into a global entity by giving it a uniquely dependent identity, neo-colonial modernity perpetuates Nigeria's continued subservience to imperialist economies while signifying a quasi-independent national reality within and against which citizenship is negotiated. Two competing tropes of modernity animate the internal struggles of postcolonial Nigeria. An undemocratic neo-colonial nationalism has long been locked in combat with a resilient culture of decolonization with which individuals and groups critique, resist, and refuse a neo-colonial belonging. The practices of Theatre for Development are located in this oppositional culture of decolonization.

Theatre for Development originated in the 1970s in the Drama department of Ahmadu Bello University (ABU) in the northern Nigerian city of Zaria. It was born in a climate of radical political activism when ideologies such as Marxism, pan-Africanism and a spectrum of anticolonial nationalisms were providing postcolonial universities a framework for resisting the colonial epistemologies underpinning existing scholarship.[3] A cohort of staff and students belonging to ABU's Drama department including Michael Etherton, Oga Abah, Saddique Balewa, Salihu Bappa, Tunde Lakoju, and Egwugwu Illah, pioneered the Nigerian variant of Theatre for Development. The community-based ABU Drama program aimed to build relationships with less privileged sections of the society surrounding the university. It recognized theatre as a system of signification that could facilitate the transformation of groups of people into proactive communities willing to transcend their differences as they worked to improve their lot in the nation. That faith in the transforming power of the arts at ABU lives on. Fifteen years after I left the university's Drama department, one of its resident NPTA stalwarts known as Oga Abah autographed for me a copy of his book entitled *Performing Life: Case Studies in the Practice of Theatre for Development* with the inscription: "The place still stimulates!"[4]

Insisting that transformative education could not be achieved through formal institutions alone, the ABU program embraced a pedagogy combining formal learning with "informal" and non-formal epistemologies. "Informal" education referred to experiences accumulated through everyday social interactions with family, friends, and peers. "Non-formal" education, on the other hand, stemmed from social organizations seeking to foster critical awareness of the identities and environments of individuals and groups in a complex, pluralistic, but hierarchical society. Inspired by examples set by developing world educators like the Brazilians Paulo Freire and Augusto Boal, and the French engineer Charles Maguerez,[5] the ABU drama program integrated non-formal cultural practices with a formal curriculum distinctly anticolonial in tenor. As the sole source of social mobility in countries like Nigeria, formal education alienated those it endowed with cultural and political capital, from the vast populace excluded from its institutions. Validating non-formal and informal pedagogical modes as appropriate sites for education and socialization made the drama program at the university a forum for developing activist strategies for students as well as for the communities with which they were affiliated.

Although it was originally viewed as a good model of "town and gown" associations, by the late 1970s, the ABU group started attracting derision from university administrators who felt that its grass-root activism was too political and could potentially undermine the elitist power of university degrees. Consequently, by 1978, the university authorities had scaled down its status to the "Drama Section" of the Department of English, with the expectation that it would treat drama merely as a sub-discipline of English and literary studies. Rather than deter the group however, these restrictions stimulated its community activism. ABU dramaturges used the situation to develop a broader critical context for studying literary drama, drawing attention to textuality, contextual politics, and the politics of readership and spectatorship. They also began to forge partnerships with "base groups" drawn from local communities designed to galvanize those communities to activism from within.

By 1980, the ABU group had established more stable outreach structures such as its now famous Samaru Street Theatre and Community

Drama projects in Hayin Dogo, Palladan, and Bomo. Over the next eight years, it developed an organization called the Zaria Popular Theatre Alliance (ZAPTA) which, in turn, became the foundation and model for a national organization of community-based theatre artists called the Nigerian Popular Theatre Alliance (NPTA). ZAPTA addressed the issues of health, poverty, class, gender, and ethnicity in the lives of socially marginalized Nigerians. More significantly, its large-scale community work drew national attention to ABU's drama program, legitimating the practice of "Theatre for Development" as an academic discipline and a forum for activist theatre training.

The ABU group did not rely on any fixed or institutionally derived methodology. Rather, its methods were project specific, and geared toward developmental goals. Rejecting "top down" models of development, the group shifted the meaning of "development" from a traditional social science paradigm and made it, instead, a cultural statement enabling marginalized people and communities to represent their histories in their own voices, and participate as full citizens in local, national, and global worlds. They attempted to answer questions such as: what is education and how does it enable effective citizenship? What factors shape the disparate experiences of different social groups? Can one group claim to be "developed" when a large majority of its fellow citizens has no access to basic resources – whether material, social, or political? How can cultural practices like theatre nurture the growth of marginal agency and social activism "from below"?

These questions provided the framework for a microanalysis of the students' identities in relation to the wider Nigerian society of which they were a part. Students were set apart from the masses of their compatriots by the privileges expected to flow from their university degrees. As such they were cautioned to guard against assuming a patronizing posture toward the communities they purported to help and to appreciate the process of mutual leaning that resulted from community theatre. As a founding member of the ABU group observed:

> In wanting to help others who are clearly perceived to be less fortunate than ourselves, we find it very difficult to see how they can *materially* help us. We recognize that we may achieve humility, or self-lessness, but we do not see how the very poor can improve our own material living standards. At best, all we acknowledge is that we may need to lower our own standards of living. *Determining in advance how our consciousness may be raised, we actually preclude it happening.*[6]

Diligent research on the performance traditions of target communities helped the students create performance texts they could then take back to the communities; texts that provided a forum for inter-group dialogue between the students and the townspeople outside the university. In this context, the notion of *development* entailed an act of self-discovery and identity definition for both groups. The parties to the dialogue then moved on to analyze the global contexts of their work by examining international case studies as well as the work of cultural theorists such as Augusto Boal, Paulo Freire, and Renato Constantino.[7]

Free of fixed spatial moorings, Theatre for Development in ABU could happen anywhere – in courtyards and back alleys, on the streets and in market places. The open-endedness of these performances provided ideological and presentational flexibility for both performers and their audiences.[8]

The following pages describe case studies of ABU-affiliated Theatre for Development projects in which I participated two decades ago after training with Wole Soyinka in literary and guerrilla theatre. These case studies highlight the theatrical and historical relevance of community theatre to the broad issue of decolonization.

The Samaru project 1984[9]

Samaru is a relatively new "shantytown" – a sort of Nigerian ghetto spawned by the rise of Ahmadu Bello University. It is separated from the sanitized campus of ABU by a major highway that leads on to the Islamic city of Sokoto. Populated by people of diverse ethnic origins, almost every household in Samaru has a relative or dependant working or studying at the university. It affords poorer students and semi-skilled, low-income university workers the only affordable place to live. Despite the presence of middle-class enclaves, the town is, for the most part, notorious for its poor sanitary conditions, bad housing, and disorganized road plans all of which stand out in especially sharp relief against the privileged state of the neighboring ABU. Prostitution, petty crimes, and high rates of alcoholism are endemic in Samaru.

In 1984, twenty-three first year undergraduates and three MA students (including myself),[10] were assigned the task of creating and performing a street play dealing with Samaru's civic problems. The first part of the exercise consisted in visiting the shantytown in groups of three and four students in an attempt to identify the most glaring inequities in resource distribution between the town and its prosperous neighbor across the highway. A week of interaction with the Samaru community yielded the consensus that poor sanitation and the lack of drinkable water constituted one of its most serious crises. Thus, we decided to craft a play drawing attention to the perennial shortage of water in Samaru. Students and community members discussed a host of issues in this regard, centering primarily on the discriminatory effects of poor urban planning and the resource gap that prevailed between Samaru and the ABU community.

Moreover, the play's architects undertook "participant observation" cultural tours of the town to learn about its storytelling traditions as they were enacted in beer parlors, on the streets, and during local festivals. There followed preliminary improvisation exercises aimed at constituting an ensemble based on vignettes, tableaus, "story circles" gathered in the case of this research. The final outcome was a Hausa-language play entitled *The Story of Samaru* or *Wasan Samaru*.

Enacted on the streets of Samaru on an improvised stage made of tarpaulin, *The Story of Samaru* unfolded through the antics and narratives of two stock characters named Dauda (whom I played) and Sauna (played by Jenkeri Okwori). Inseparable friends yet unable to agree on almost anything, comical ne'er do wells apt to drink and gamble their lives away, they tantalized the gathering crowd of onlookers into stepping into their internecine arguments with humor and the highly physicalized gestures that characterized street theatre. The debate between the short, slow and wiry Sauna and the taller, more intellectually pretentious Dauda revolved around Samaru's crisis of water shortage. This crisis unfolded through the protagonists' representation of the stories of two local farmers whose world the audience was invited to enter and mediate. We met the farmers Malam Usman and Malam Nuhu as they made their way to their respective farms, lamenting the failure of the rains and the impossibility of trapping enough rainwater for domestic use.

Usman returned home to find that his wife Binta had not cooked dinner for lack of water. Upset, he bullied every member of his household to go out in search of the precious resource, threatening to evict anyone who disobeyed his dictum. An obvious subtext of this scene consisted of an indictment of the domestic violence endemic in Samaru. At this stage, Dauda and Sauna interrupted the narrative soliciting the audience's response to violence against women in the community. The performance came to a temporary halt as various audience members expressed their opinions on that fractious subject. It picked up again with another scene set in the household of the other farmer, Malam Nuhu.

A perfect foil for the Usman character, Nuhu was a calm and supportive husband who resolved to accompany his wife in her quest for water and possibly beg his neighbors for help if they could afford any. His wife Maryam informed him the neighbors had already refused her entreaties and suggested the university as a likely source of water. Judging by its lush gardens, numerous storage tanks, and a man-made dam, it was surely in a position to alleviate the needs of its drought-ridden neighbors. Nuhu demurred. Had Maryam not taken note of the high security on the campus, enforced by ferocious guard dogs to ward off non-residents? The only option left was to go to a natural spring located in the farm of a wealthy but wicked man in the vicinity of Samaru. As Nuhu and Maryam made their way to the natural spring, they met Usman's wife and daughter, whom they persuaded to come along, hoping a larger group would appeal to the charitable instincts of the rich farmer, who was, after all, once a peasant just like them.

To their pleasant surprise, they found the spring unfortified by its traditional ambushing security system. They got their water, not realizing that the owner had contaminated the source of the spring with a dangerous detergent. Usman fell ill from drinking the adulterated water and accused his wife of attempting to poison him because he had earlier indicated a desire to marry a second wife. Dauda and Sauna appeared in the scene to stop Usman from physically assaulting his wife and invited the audience to resolve the issues raised by the play. A lively debate ensued as the onlookers probed the roots of their community's sufferings. Some of them implicated the students as active participants in the structures oppressing the Samaru community, especially for reporting Samaru residents to the security department whenever they came to the university for water. The accusations climaxed with the identification of one of the students present as one who had physically assaulted a woman who came to the male hostel in search of water. This outpouring of grievances was underpinned by class tensions – the Samaru townspeople felt that upon graduation, these same students would join the ranks of forces blamed for their underdevelopment. During rehearsals and performance, the irony of self-parody became apparent to the students as they recognized their complicity in the social crisis they had set out to study and deconstruct.

Out of these recriminations however, flowed constructive proposals of self-help. Someone suggested the formation of a cooperative that would levy a cash contribution upon its constituent households according to their means, the proceeds to be invested in digging boreholes in strategic parts of the town. The play's subtext of domestic violence generated more heated debate as the community was forced to confront this contentious issue in public for the first time.

The student group emerged from this experience awed by the over-whelming magnitude of the problems they had touched. They had learned not only the means to analyze inequities in social structures through the theatre process, but had also acquired the cultural tools – local perform-ance traditions – with which to develop customized performance texts geared to specific audiences. Materials derived from the project proved invaluable to a Community Drama course that I taught at the university the following year. My collaborative work with Jenkeri Okwori who played Sauna was further developed in our weekly television comedy *This is Our Life* and a national and international production tour of the anti-apartheid play *Woza Albert!*

A year after the Samaru project was crafted, ABU's Drama department was invited to press theatre into the service of an infinitely more chal-lenging social problem – leprosy.

The leprosy project 1985[11]

In June 1985, the director of a World Health Organization (WHO)-funded leprosarium approached the then head of the drama section (Brian Crow) with a formidable request. Unlike leprosy hospitals in other parts of the country and the rest of the developing world, the one located on the fringes of Zaria City was faced with an abundant supply of unused preventative and curative drugs. The hospital attributed this state of affairs to cultural factors that prevented people with symptoms of leprosy from turning up for diagnosis and treatment. The social stigma attached to the disease also hindered the successful rehabilitation of cured patients, leading to a high rate of relapse and death in extreme cases. Indeed, so taboo was the subject of leprosy that some clinics were converted into storage barns for harvested corn and straw.

The mandate of the theatre project prompted by the leprosarium was to draw attention to the causes and symptoms of leprosy and to fight the cultural stigma that impeded the diagnosis and cure of the disease. The project was to involve not just the students and staff of the drama section but also health and social workers. Before long, the Drama department faced its first and most frustrating obstacle: the total lack of interest among the students and some of the designated social workers who were themselves caught up in reproducing the same taboos and stigmas about leprosy that afflicted the larger community. It took two weeks of lectures, demonstrations, and clinical visits to "educate" the core group of students and social workers. Vital medical information given the group included the fact that anyone could contract the airborne and moisture-seeking virus; that all the virus needed to penetrate the human body was a skin laceration or bruise; that like all viruses, normal antibodies in human beings were enough to ward them off as long as the people ate averagely balanced meals; that the disease when contracted produced two main kinds of symptoms – a thick wax-like skin rash or an eczema-like skin rash; and that when detected early the disease was completely curable without traces of its symptoms and degenerative conditions.

It turned out that there were no base groups willing to join the project. The social workers had to rely on their own less successful network to create a small base group. The other problem concerned language, as many members of the theatre class spoke little Hausa, the predominant language of the surrounding region. One option was to use speakers of the language as well as the health and social workers in performance roles and non-speakers in the research and poster making processes.

Armed with essential medical information and the participation of medical staff, a project group was constituted. After planning a "participant-observation" strategy, and assurances of support from local village heads, the group went into seven communities known to have a high incidence of leprosy. The initial visit was "invasive" as the group burst into those communities in Land Rovers and trucks. On arrival, the group broke into dances and songs about health and sanitation. They displayed posters and handed out graphic leaflets describing the dreaded disease. As crowds built up, the group divided into smaller units each of which addressed portions of the community about the project. This first encounter developed an initial network complementing that of the social workers. Subsequent groups identified community members with whom they would collaborate as the project evolved further, and established base groups. This preparation culminated in the creation of two short plays, one of which demonstrated the ways in which leprosy manifests itself, the other depicting the predicaments of rehabilitation.

The first sketch vested the stigmatized disease in the body of a wealthy "Alhaji."[12] Blessed with four wives, several cattle, and an electrically powered home, this man enjoyed a great deal of influence in his community, his vanity amply indulged by the poor peasants dependent on seasonal employment on his estates. Yet, the arrogance of his public demeanor belied a private trauma. He stopped sleeping with his wives, curtailed the scale of his usually lavish entertainment sprees, and became a recluse. Rumors about his mental state spread through the village and its neighboring communities. It turned out that enormous patches of dry waxy skin on his body had prompted his withdrawal from society. In the beginning, he tried to cover these patches with make-up and creams as well as by wearing more elaborate ceremonial clothing to the most insignificant of events. Concerned by this new behavior, his wives ambushed him one day as he stepped out of his bathroom. He eventually revealed his fears that he may have contracted leprosy, but proved reluctant to seek medical attention. His wives, however, immediately contacted the local dispensary. A health worker visited his home, proffered a diagnosis and started the patient on a course of treatment. A few weeks later, the symptoms of the disease disappeared, leaving the Alhaji free to resume his normal life. In fulfillment of a promise made to the health worker, the cured man then shared his experience with leprosy with the public, paving the way for greater awareness of, and organization against, this and other diseases brought on by a poorly managed environment.

The narrative was interspersed with songs, with a chorus offering insight into the issues of poverty, health, and activism. The play was performed in various communities, occasionally giving rise to some remarkable instances of audience identification with the subject at hand. Some ascended the stage offering the "health worker" amid the actors their bodies for examination or to consult him about suspicious symptoms displayed by family and friends. These unexpected situations generated a plot structure, which replaced the student actor in the role of the health worker with a trained professional, thereby turning the play's end into an open clinic. The theatre group eventually set up mobile booths attended by doctors and nurses. Subsequent performances ended with clinics, which recorded data on various communicable skin diseases and followed up those related to leprosy.

The second play that emerged from the leprosy project confronted the social prejudices associated with the disease head on. It narrated the tale of Habiba, who, when she displayed what appeared to be the symptoms of an advanced stage of leprosy, was promptly ostracized by her family and community. The virus had damaged nerves in her hands and feet and distorted her facial features. In desperation, she took shelter in the local leprosarium that welcomed her and undertook to treat her condition. Habiba recovered, but without the option to return to her community, she settled as a vegetable farmer in a village adjacent to her original home. With help from the local village head, she gradually emerged as a celebrated vegetable farmer in the region. As her fame spread, she revealed to her admiring customers the true cause of her "disability" – the neurological damage to her feet that leprosy had wrought. Encouraged by her story of survival, women in her adopted community started a farming co-op, inviting Habiba to head the organization. When news of the former leper's newfound success reached her former family and community, they came to her, sought her forgiveness, and organized a big ceremony to welcome her home. During the ceremony, Habiba chided the community for its prejudice and encouraged others suffering from leprosy to seek help.

In performance, this play evoked great empathy from its audiences, particularly the women. The two plays that resulted from the leprosy project became potent tools to develop critical consciousness of the tyranny of tradition and to engender desires for communal subjectivity. The interactive nature of these projects was manifested in audience members' quest for direct medical attention at the end of the performances as well as in the sometimes-poignant ideological debates about poverty and disease that followed. I recall a particularly difficult conversation about the "fact" that the poor cannot really have the right antibodies to ward off diseases. Unlike the Samaru theatre project, which lasted ten weeks, the leprosy project stretched into twenty weeks, with social workers integrating its lessons into their training, and local communities taking over their production. The plays were eventually broadcast on the state radio. The leprosarium used the success of the project to launch more health campaigns across the state. Overall, the leprosy project influenced the policies of the Ministry of Health and its international affiliate – the World Health Organization.

Although the patients themselves did not act in the leprosy plays, their personal stories breathed life into, and lent an air of authenticity to the dramatic performances and gave the despised victims of the disease a sense of social validation. The students on the other hand, not only empowered marginalized groups by their work, but also themselves matured in the course of their dramaturgical experiences. They graduated from states of fear and ignorance into their roles as agents of positive social change. Thus, the community theatre projects at ABU held out the promise of accomplishing a collective subjectivity that transformed the activist as much as the "beneficiary" of activism by weaving a diversity of lived experiences into a pluralistic language of citizenship. The cultural texts resulting from the students' interactions with local communities became points of convergence between identities originally set upon a collision course by colonial and neo-colonial histories. Commentators on Theatre for Development have often portrayed community projects as a one-way process of acculturation in which a politically conscious and ideologically well-formed middle class, serving as "facilitators," "animators," "catalysts," or "conscientizers" co-opts the oppressed "other" into its activist world as passive objects of social activism. In such renditions of popular theatre, the "subaltern" frequently fails to find his or her voice, while the bourgeois activists themselves remain more or less unchanged by their activist theatre experience. My work in Community Theatre, however, suggests that community building is an open-ended process characterized by the mutual evolution of the various parties involved. The process of "becoming" and achieving subjectivity goes beyond the assimilation of one group into the other's reality. Projects like those associated with Samaru and leprosy established fresh contexts for negotiating political and cultural identities and facilitated new sutures of difference. In other words, the ABU's theatre work provided the building blocks for crafting ever shifting communities rather than assume any "a priori" community.

In the course of the 1980s, the ABU group broadened the scope of its community building by entering into alliances with non-institution-based groups rooted in local communities across the region of Zaria. By 1987, six groups including the *ABU* collective, *Muna Fata* from Palladan, *So Dangi* from Hayin Dogo, *Haske* from Samaru, and the drama wing of the feminist group *Women in Nigeria*, had banded together to form the Zaria Popular Theatre Alliance (ZAPTA). Monthly workshops were held in the various localities where the constituent groups were based. The workshops entailed training and researching performance and cultural traditions of the local communities as well as identifying key regional social and developmental issues. For the ABU community, membership in the Alliance was optional for students although mandatory for tutors teaching the Popular Theatre and Community Theatre courses. As a member of the latter group, I bore first-hand witness to the transformation of one non-university local youth organization into a typical member of the Zaria Popular Theatre Alliance. The next section is devoted to a discussion of that process of transformation.

So Dangi Community Development Club

Literally meaning "love thy neighbor," *So Dangi* was inaugurated as a youth club in Hayin Dogo in 1977. Located three miles away from the university,

Hayin Dogo is primarily a farming community with some "blue collar" residents employed at the university. *So Dangi*'s ideological and cultural agenda was always mediated by interest groups outside its own communities, particularly by political parties who occasionally lured members of the youth group into their own camps by means of a variety of unfulfilled promises.

Initially, the club concentrated on providing welfare services and staging social events for the Hayin Dogo community. It raised funds for various "self-help" projects, built roads, and dug wells. In 1987 the club decided that it needed a broader base for its activities and thus chose to affiliate with the ABU community theatre program.

The first joint training workshop, involving *So Dangi* members as well as ABU students and faculty, paved the way to a play that migrated from the streets of Samaru to no less a forum than the British Broadcasting Corporation's World Service, in part through the mediation of a British Theatre for Development enthusiast by the name of Nick Owen. For the club, drama became not only a site for socialization and a means to explore a range of social issues, but also a major instrument of public relations. Thus, for instance, their work attracted the patronage of local village leaders who invited them to public ceremonies. A member of the club who played an extraordinary clown was subsequently recommended to the Emir of Zaria, who appointed him as his court jester. This singular recognition immediately drew national attention to the activities of the club. As its relationship with ABU gained publicity, rival clubs began vying for an association with the ZAPTA.

The dynamics of Nigerian national politics, however, complicated the sustenance of coalitions such as that between *So Dangi* and the ABU group. The promise of a viable political and cultural alliance in the Zaria region was squashed by the renewal of social crisis in 1987, this time having to do with the outbreak of religious hostilities between Muslims and Christians. Churches were set ablaze, Christian homes and non-Hausa families attacked. A set of revenge attacks against Islamic families followed. The university community found itself embroiled in the conflagration, spurring my departure from Nigeria. For my colleagues who dared to remain, the conflict became a catalyst for an even more ambitious community theatre collective. The Nigerian Popular Theatre Alliance rose from the ashes of communal strife in northern Nigeria.

Nigerian Popular Theatre Alliance

Theatre for Development enthusiasts at ABU channeled their unfulfilled aspirations arising out of the ZAPTA experience into an even broader alliance of community theatre groups known as the Nigerian Popular Theatre Alliance (NPTA). Inspired by the return of Oga Abah from England, and Jenkeri Okwori's extraordinary energy and optimism, other groups and organizations around the country closed ranks behind the new entity in the late 1980s. With members spread across the country, the Alliance is organized in four zones – (the northwest, northeast, southwest and southeast). According to its original mission statement, the NPTA is a:

> non-profit alliance of theatre artists, performers, cultural and development workers who are interested in using Theatre for Development purposes. Its emphasis is communication and development through alternative means for empowerment and general welfare of the rural and urban populace.[13]

Members congregate quarterly. They run a series of workshops, lectures and seminars, exchanging notes on their activities and initiating development projects wherever they meet. As each group works in a locality, it develops tangential relationships with others in its zone, then nationally through the NPTA network. Because the structural transformation of society for equity is the Alliance's primary objective, it views theatre as a developmental communication process, which encourages "people to question and challenge the structures . . . it encourages people's own analysis, self confidence, and fighting spirit."[14]

This activist vision of art as a political vocabulary questioning conditions of being and negotiating desires for proactive belonging, is labeled "popular theatre." The diverse ways in which such a vision is fulfilled has given rise to multiple forms of popular theatre. For instance, the NPTA's "Traveling Theatre" unit consists of politicized groups which take their message to target communities and audiences. Its "Community Theatre" program on the other hand, calls upon members of a community to use performance to understand their own marginalization as well as to contest it. Other approaches to popular theatre such as "Theatre for Integrated Rural Development" (THIRD), and "Community Theatre for Integrated Rural Development" (CTHIRD), focus their development agendas on specific issues ranging from women's health and Aids awareness, to problems of sanitation and water. Figure 5.1 represents the multiple facets of popular theatre. The NPTA has sometimes attracted government support as well as funding from such international agencies as Canadian University Services Overseas, Canadian International Development Agency, MacArthur Foundation, Ford Foundation, and the British Council.

The canalization of the ABU group's work into the NPTA has lessened its subjugation to the university's bureaucratic demands by consolidating the collective's practice in non-formal settings. Moreover, in promoting its political and developmental mission, the NPTA has found a valuable ally in the realm of Nigeria's professional theatre. Based in the vibrant city of Lagos, the "Performance Studio Workshop (PSW) aims to serve as a catalyst for the uplift of the Nigerian Society"[15] by using entertainment to

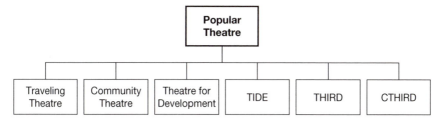

Figure 5.1 NPTA description of its activities.

Note: TIDE stands for Theatre for Integrated Development; THIRD stands for Theatre for Integrated Rural Development; CTHIRD stands for Community Theatre for Integrated Rural Development.[16]

empower communities for self help. Its alliance with the NPTA illustrates the diversity and range of Nigeria's Theatre for Development movement and, for that reason, merits separate analysis.

The Performance Studio Workshop

Chuck Mike, who as a student had assisted Wole Soyinka in various political theatre projects including his Guerrilla theatre work in the 1980s, pioneered the Performance Studio Workshop (PSW). Unlike amateur groups such as *So Dangi*, PSW is a collective of professional artists which trains actors to use their art as a tool of "interpretation and communication for the service of mankind [*sic*]."[17] One of the Workshop's reports declared:

> It is pertinent to note that each and every member of the Company should be armed with some technical knowledge of the material to be translated into the creative product beyond its dramaturgical purpose. This is largely because their contact with the people for whom they perform is intimate and persuasive. As such, audiences are physically attracted to the player's post performance and questions usually arise which they should be able to field intelligibly if the exercise of "edutainment" is to be thorough.[18]

The PSW's projects are shaped by its community outreach work addressing such issues as drug abuse, environmental and communal health, and the status of women. Figure 5.2 charts the scope of its work and the complex nature of their outreach program.

The chart suggests an intense focus on audience development whereby stories are created out of well-documented ethnographic researches into issues of social justice and equity in particular communities. A close examination of one of the PSW's most ambitious projects entitled "Project Sister Help" offers us insight into the libratory trope of its practices. "SISTER

HELP" is an acronym for "Synergizing Information Systems Towards Enhancing Reproductive Health and Eradicating Ligature Practices." Initiated in 1995, it was designed to raise awareness of the phenomenon of female genital mutilation, its impact upon women's health, and its social consequences, and to spur a public policy of intervention and eradication.

From its beginnings in Lagos, the project gradually spread to Ibadan and Benin. It was grounded in a year's worth of research involving interviews with both the victims and perpetrators of female circumcision as well as the study of cultural contexts where the practice is legitimized as tradition. The result was a highly provocative play entitled *Ikpiko* which

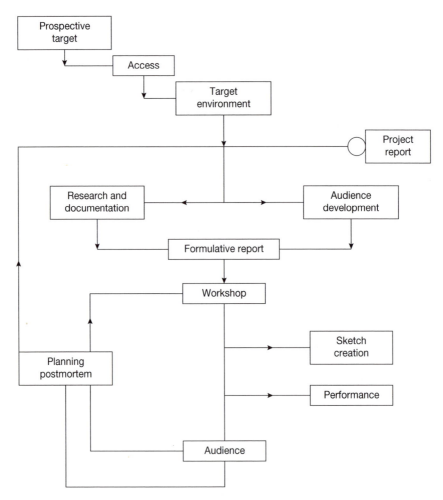

Figure 5.2 Performance Studio Workshop – theatre outreach chart.[19]

in the Edo language dominant in mid-western Nigeria means "outcast" signifying uncircumcised young women. A draft of the play summarizes three of its scenes as follows:

Play opens with LIGHTS

Scene 1: A seven year old child ties her clitoris and takes a blade to cut her genitals because she can no longer bear being ostracized by her mates who are circumcised.

Scene 2: A mother to be at seven months laid bare and her vaginal "hood" removed because it is believed that being uncircumcised poses a threat to the unborn infant.

Scene 3: A newly wed is diagnosed as manic depressive. She fears the act of sex because of the pain induced during intercourse as a result of genital mutilation.

Play ends with BLACKOUT[20]

This dramatic format, according to the PSW, offers numerous advantages in drawing attention to social problems such as female circumcision. It depersonalizes, and thus facilitates dialogue on controversial issues. It renders information about health and the oppressive aspects of religion and tradition palatable and accessible. The immediacy of interaction through the mode of interactive entertainment offers opportunities to clarify misapprehensions about little-discussed issues on the spot. Moreover, the performers are able to convey their political messages in multiple languages outside the spoken word such as mime, song, and dance. Familiar as these media of communication are to African cultures, they reinforce the play's persuasive appeal. In this context, the personal, interactive, informal nature of the PSW's format broadens its reach to include the vast majority of Nigerians cut off from the pale of public discussion by the lack of electricity, electronic media, and print literature.

Financially supported by its professional activities as well as by funding from international organizations like USAID, Ford Foundation, MacArthur Foundation, and the British Council, the PSW has collaborated with various women's groups, developed Theatre for Development "cells" in secondary schools and rural communities, and established liaisons with government and non-government agencies. The PSW's rhetoric of empowerment, participatory politics, and subjectivity parallels from the work of the ABU group and the NPTA. The interface among these groups has hybridized and enriched them all.

The experience of Nigeria's Theatre for Development offers the promise of formulating what the theatre scholar Guarav Desai has described as a theory of African popular theatre.[21] As Nigeria continues to cling to a neo-colonial identity on the margins of European modernity, groups such as

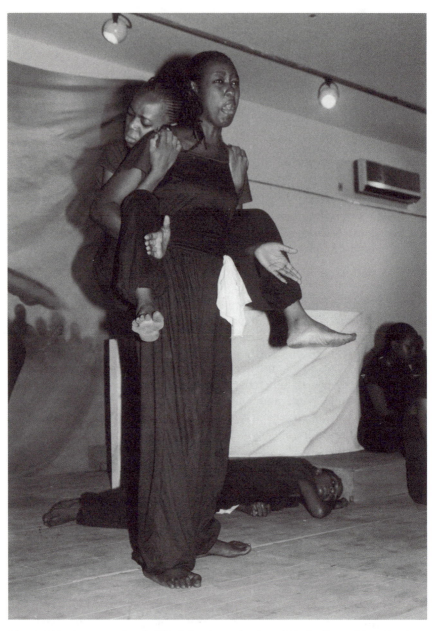

Plate 5.1 Performance Studio Workshop's production of *Ikpiko* directed by Chuck
Mike. Photograph from PSW archives.

Plate 5.2 Performance Studio Workshop's production of *Ikpiko* directed by Chuck
Mike. Photograph from PSW archives.

the ABU drama collective engage the contradictions posed by the new
nationalism championed by a pseudo-democratic elite.

Within the university, they deliberately instituted, beginning in the
1970s, a counter-modernist and counter-neo-colonialist pedagogy by
exposing the limitations of formal education as the sole avenue to social
mobility and agency. Although they borrowed from the works of such theorists and activists as Paulo Freire, Frantz Fanon, and Augusto Boal, the
motifs, symbols, and modes of their engagement with the issues of agency
and citizenship remained distinctly original, hybrid, and inter-modernist.

The language of decolonization developed by TFD practitioners in
collaboration with local communities consciously refuses assimilation into
both the colonizing Eurocentrism of formal education as well as the neo-
colonial nationalism that glosses over the inequities arising therefrom.
Its emphasis upon "informal" and "non-formal" epistemologies forged on
the streets of shantytowns and through interactions with marginalized
local communities undermines the stability of what it means to be "neo-
colonially modern" and deliberately disrupts accepted notions of what
constitutes a "modern university education." The ABU group's resistance
consists not only in questioning the primacy of Eurocentric discourses in
literary drama, but also in excavating indigenous performance traditions
pre-dating contact with Europe. Dozens of Masters of Arts theses at ABU

reflect this intra-modernist energy. Tunde Lakoju, Oga Abah, Salihu Bappa, Egwugwu Illah, Jenkeri Okwori, Jummai Ewu, and several others have written theses exploring the potential of indigenous traditions to produce and sustain a decolonizing culture with which to contest the authoritarianism of neo-colonialism. For them, these traditions signify an alternative modernity, a space in between the neo-colonial state and the imperialist modernity from which it enunciates senses of being and belonging. Theatre for Development by non-institution-based members of the NPTA also engages the inequities of a statist neo-colonial modernity even as it highlights the colonizing tendencies of oppressive indigenous traditions like female genital mutilation that are permitted to co-exist with contemporary culture. In the process, TFD challenges those who believe that indigenous traditions offer a comfortable binary opposition to neo-colonialism and presents a vision of humanist activism willing to critique structures of oppression wherever they may arise.

A broad conception of "development" anchored in the theory and prac-tice of participatory democracy lies at the very heart of the decolonization agenda of Nigerian popular theatres. Such a conception enlists the active participation of local communities in uplift projects that seek to improve public health and sanitation, redistribute material resources, and raise the status of women in society. The cultural texts that result from this inter-active approach to development-oriented dramaturgy as well as the audience responses they elicit reveal the *reciprocal* impact of different social groups upon each other. What unfolds is an alternative community in the making – pluralistic, often uncertain of its collective subjectivity to be sure, but nonetheless a community willing to take tentative steps toward real-izing its postcolonial dreams of genuine freedom.

Part 2
England

6 John Arden

Dramatizing the colonial nation

Kicking one another to the floor
(Year of 1974)
Neither Heath nor Wilson dares to understand
Green fields of Britain were always someone else's land.
Eat the flesh of Irishman

And Welsh and Scot (and Englishman):
Remain eternally unsatisfied
Though for each dinner-time of power yet one more living creature died
Hold up your extreme hands in moderation,
Usurpers of the imperium of this nation:
Read us your weekly lecture how the blood you spill
Is running only from the wounds of those who were the first to kill
Soft voices are not heard and never were:

Noise must be drowned down with fire and fear:
Attention, yes, is paid to those who shout aloud –
Tear out their tongues, therefore, lest they attract a crowd.

Drive them out of doors
Ease their feet onto the street
Distort them, if they are women, into hysterical wild whores –
Even your own fury, Generals, Lieutenants, by contrast is
Orderly, reasonable, patrician, sweet . . .[1]

John Arden's provocative preface to his iconoclastic play *The Island of the Mighty*, when I first read it during my undergraduate days at Ife, shattered forever my naïve conception of One Imperial Nation under the "Union Jack." Arden, like other counter-cultural dramatists, companies, and movements featured in the course offering on Alternative British Drama at my Nigerian university, introduced my post-imperial cohort to a political dramaturgy with deep resonance in the contradictions of our own neo-colonial world. The coloniality of English power and culture within Great Britain that these works depicted so stirringly, recalled our own struggles with thorny questions of national identity, class tensions, and ethno-regional particularisms.

I went on to choose Arden's play *Sergeant Musgrave's Dance* as my final year "directing" project in part because that play's insights into class colonization within England appeared especially relevant to the legacy of the brutal civil war over Igbo secession that Nigeria had just survived. That legacy came home to me, quite literally, when my parents, after retiring from the civil service, relocated to a new neighborhood in Kano largely populated by soldiers discharged from the Nigerian army after the Biafra War of 1967–1972. The military men in our neighborhood displayed anarchic impulses, extreme forms of despair, alienation, and alcoholism that shocked our middle-class civilian sensibilities. They constantly reminded us that the nationalist war for which they had sacrificed life and limb represented but an illusory construction of honor that brought them few rewards other than physical disability, mental illness, and unemployment.

Defying the usual expectations to produce a Nigerian play, I had chosen John Arden's play *Sergeant Musgrave's Dance* as a drama from far away England to pose before my audience the same questions I had asked my parents and older siblings about the soldiers and their role in implementing a unitary vision of nationalism. Why are the play's protagonists disenchanted with the national cause when, as soldiers, their very identity depends upon defending the nation? What implications does their anarchic logic carry for the definition of postcolonial desire, if any? Arden was attractive to me, not only for his political iconoclasm, but also because his apparent defiance of acceptable and institutionalized conventions of theatrical representation made it difficult for critics to compartmentalize him within familiar genres. If I choose to begin the English section of this comparative work with a postcolonial reading of Arden's attitude toward political theatre and resistant discourses in *Sergeant Musgrave's Dance*, it is because this play more than any other, launched my consciousness of the bridge that continues to link the peoples of contemporary Nigeria with those of its former imperial ruler – the bridge I call postcolonial desire.

Born in Barnsley in 1930, John Arden became a whimsical artistic icon in a post-Second World War England confronted with the rapid erosion of its once mighty empire. He spoke for a generation of bourgeoisie expanded and diversified in its social and provincial origins by the democratization of education in England beginning in the 1940s. Disenchanted with their imperial past, and troubled by the social inequities in their midst, a segment of this constituency embraced radical political causes and unconventional esthetics that reflected their alienation from the dominant institutions of their culture. These audiences embraced dramatic conventions that represented oppositional ideas about Western modernity in relation to issues of identity, subjectivity, and citizenship. As the new middle class took over governance, however, such opposition opened the way for insertion and inclusion that was subsequently stabilized and stylized into genres like Naturalism and Realism. Naturalism, performed within the citadels of dominant European cultures, sketched the world from the perspective of metropolitan centers. Realism, on the other hand, existed as its binary "Other," simultaneously belonging to the dominant while seeking a more critical "way of seeing." Refusing Naturalism became an act of rejecting subjugation to the mainstream. "The angry playwrights" of the 1950s like John Osborne in *Look Back in Anger*, channeled the anxieties and neurosis of England's new bourgeoisie through the medium of Realism – a theatrical mode that diluted the essence of their outrage.

In this context, John Arden was a dissident realist – a socialist – who stubbornly refused to create within conventions like Naturalism, which he believed to have been co-opted by the very violent dominant culture he was seeking to destabilize. He conceptualized this authoritarian culture as a colonial one which not only subjugated lower classes, women, and other ethnicities within and outside England, but also repressed and excluded from its cultural institutions alternative forms of representing "otherness." The ruling conventions of English theatre, according to him, refracted modernity through a colonial and imperialist prism, hence their thematic obsession with the loss of national glory within the geo-politics of the modern world. Unlike the "angry playwrights," Arden articulates his political esthetics allegorically, rather than presenting them as overt expressions of alienation. The ludic tenor of his style stems from its visualization of drama as a dialogical cultural practice rather than a well-made philosophical statement eloquently delivered to the audience. This dialogical approach, in turn, transforms his art into an opportunity for:

> bringing men [*sic*] together in a kind of secular Eucharist, so that they can leave the building feeling that they are a society, not just a collection of odds and sods who have been coincidentally killing time for a couple of hours on a wet evening.[2]

Arden privileged community theatre over commercial drama. Working in collaboration with his companion, Margaretta D'Arcy,[3] he sought not simply to illustrate history, but to apply its insights to a thesis of revolutionary change in the direction of socialism. Not content to merely describe the accession of the middle class to cultural dominance, he excoriated the violent conditions of *being* and *becoming* provided by the modern state, as well as the cultural means by which audiences are duped into political quiescence. He executed through his art, a form of political and cultural activism that problematized the ways of representing counter-hegemonic discourses by borrowing from popular forms of entertainment rejected by high culture. Poetry, ballads, communal dances, and songs became the raw materials with which he forged his politically charged stories. Such resources, he maintained:

can carry any strength of content from tragedy through satire to straight forward comedy, and neither be drowned in it nor seem too portentous. Social criticism, for example, tends in the theatre to be dangerously ephemeral and therefore disappointing ... but if it is expressed within the framework of the traditional poetic truths it can have a weight and an impact derived from something more than documentary facility.[4]

Arden's mode of deliberate experimentation has continued to alienate mainstream critics who are consistently frustrated by the playwright's departure from stable ways of telling stories in what they assume to be England's modern theatre. What follows is a postcolonial interpretation of *Sergeant Musgrave's Dance* as a socialist realist approach to resistant dramaturgy.

Sergeant Musgrave's Dance

Written and first performed in 1959, the play offers a window to the multiple and overlapping layers of England's imperial legacy. Ironically sub-titled "An unhistorical parable in three acts," it takes as its temporal setting, a historical benchmark – the high holy days of English imperialism between 1860 and 1880. Lord Frederick Lugard, Governor-General of Nigeria, later memorialized this moment as marking England's discharge of a noble mandate inherited from its own Roman civilizers:

> As Roman imperialism laid the foundations of modern civilization, and led the wild barbarians of these islands along the paths of progress, so in Africa today we are repaying the debt, and bringing to the dark places of the earth, the abode of barbarism and cruelty, the torch of progress, while ministering to the material needs of our own civilization ... We hold these countries because it is the genius of our race to colonize, to trade, and to govern.[5]

In light of the incontrovertible historical importance of Arden's chosen period for the setting of his play, the understatement embodied in its sub-title imparted to the work a ludic quality that seduced the audience into its plot. The paradoxical signification conveyed by the words "unhistorical parable" was further underscored by the timing of the play's publication. The year 1959, when it first appeared, marked the threshold of independence from imperialism for many parts of West Africa, especially Nigeria. Thus, for post-imperial subjects such as myself, reading *Sergeant Musgrave's Dance* a couple of decades after its birth, the play's dual temporal significance – both in terms of content as well as the date of its first appearance – reinforced its power as a postcolonial text. It problematized the issue of colonial nationalism, the legacy of which we were ourselves grappling with as we protested dictators beholden to foreign oil companies.

The play opens in a canal wharf. Four soldiers and a barge driver are negotiating the terms of a journey to a northern English town, whose access roads and rivulets are frozen by an exceptional winter. As the passengers wait for a thaw in the river that they might continue on their way the audience learns more about these protagonists. The Bargee, a seasoned navigator who had often taken all manner of wares to and from the town in question, turns out to play a crucial role in the play's final resolution. The soldiers consist of middle aged Attercliffe, handsome Hurst, and young and restless Sparky, led by the redoubtable Sergeant Musgrave. These men are seasoned combatants who have seen action in England's distant and violent colonial theatres. Now they appear armed with rifles, a Gatling gun, ammunition, and a trunk later revealed to be bearing the skeleton of their mate Billy Hicks who perished overseas fighting for England's empire. It is to Hick's town – a town in mourning – that Musgrave's men are traveling.

The protagonists finally arrive in Billy Hick's native town, only to be greeted by turmoil. The coal miners there have struck for higher wages and better working conditions. Led by Walsh and others, the coal miners have chosen the winter season as the most opportune moment to press their demands, placing themselves on a collision course against the Mayor, who also happens to own some of the mines. We are introduced to the dynamics of this strife in the town's main social hub run by a matronly landlady – Mrs Hitchcock's pub. There we meet the Parson, a man who combines religious authority and judicial management to uphold the town's political stability. We also meet Annie who works for Mrs Hitchcock; the local constable, whose function it was to uphold law and order; and some of the miners. As symbols of authority, the Parson, the Constable, and the Mayor are caricatures, that Arden describes as "silhouettes":

> What I have done is take a character – if you like, a nineteenth-century coal-mine owner who's also the mayor of a small town, and simply drawn him in very simple lines so that only the parts of his character that are important to the play are seen . . . I've purely emphasized in the Mayor those aspects of the man's character that deal with his attitude to the coal industry and his attitude to the military.[6]

These "silhouettes" authorize the coloniality of state power, which manifests itself on the bodies, and minds of citizens like the coal miners, Mrs Hitchcock, and Annie.

The soldiers' presence in the community generates diverse interpretations of their intentions. The miners regard them suspiciously as the government's agents of labor repression. The Mayor, on the other hand, recognizes an excellent opportunity to persuade the Sergeant to recruit troublesome strike leaders into the army and whisk them away to foreign parts. The soldiers divulge nothing about their true mission. The mystique surrounding their strange advent in the community persists.

As the plot progresses, it becomes apparent Musgrave and his men are deserters from the Imperial army, renegades who parted company with the imperial cause in protest against the brutal reprisals inflicted on colonized civilians to avenge the death of Billy Hicks. They are in the fallen's own hometown on a self-assigned military mission to atone for the atrocities committed abroad by alerting the townspeople to the violent follies of colonialism, to perform a dance of death in rejection of imperial nationalism. The soldiers' disillusionment is shaped not simply by their experience on the battlefield but by their social location on the periphery of the imperial nation. As the historian Ranajit Guha[7] has observed, because subaltern groups are created by their exclusion from the benefits of nationalism, their behavior always tends to threaten and oppose the ruling elite. Disgruntled by their marginalization within the social context of their own nation, and violated by deeds committed in colonial massacres, Sergeant Musgrave's men have come to inflict a communal catharsis they hope will draw attention to the violence and repressive coloniality of English nationalism.

After ordering his men to make a reconnaissance tour of the town, Musgrave has them congregate at the cemetery for a briefing where they re-dedicate themselves to their mission. When left alone by his men, the Sergeant reveals:

> God, my Lord God. Have You or have You not delivered this town into my hands? All my life a soldier I've made You prayers and made them straight, I've reared my one true axe against the timber and I've launched it true. *My regiment was my duty, and I called Death honest, killing by the book – but it all got scrawled and mucked about and I could not think clear … Now I have my duties different. I'm in this town to change all soldiers' duties. My prayer is: keep my mind clear so I can weigh Judgement against Mercy and Judgement against the Blood, and make this Dance as terrible as You have put into my brain.* The Word alone is terrible: the Deed must be worse. But I know it is Your Logic and You will provide.[8]

This soliloquy, with its invocation of God, reconfigures the relationship between divine mandate, the imperialist mission, and the call of duty with no small irony. Nineteenth-century English nationalism, forged in the crucible of an industrial revolution and the formation of a mercantile–manufacturing bourgeoisie, nonetheless drew on the language of Christianity to buttress the moral authority of its civilizing mission. England's new secular state narrated nationalism through aristocratic and religious metaphors that became signifiers of the country's heritage. For Musgrave and his men, however, the ostensible symmetry among Church, State, and citizens does not automatically lead to the logic of an imperialistic mandate. For Musgrave believes that God-fearing states must not mutilate and violently reorganize other people's reality, and should refrain from using their own less privileged citizens to do so. His "logic," then, contradicts the nationalistic discourse of the Imperial State, even as it assumes that God is on his side. After the fashion of a Puritan soldier with a Cromwellian resolve, he states: "we've had to leave behind us a colonial war that is a war of sin and unjust blood."[9] Thus, the project of colonization appears as incoherent to some of its foot soldiers charged with the duty of enforcing its regime, as it does to the "native" subjects of colonization.

Not all of Musgrave's men, however, rationalize their mission in terms of religious conscience. Hurst, for instance, sees the men's central mission as the promotion of the message of pacifism:

> When I met you I thought we had the same motives. To get out, get shut o' the Army with its "treat-you-like-dirt-but-you-do-the-dirty-work" – "kill him, kill them, they are all bloody rebels, State of Emergency, high standard turnout, military bearin'" – so I thought up some killing, I said I'll get me own in. I thought o' the Rights of Man. The Rights of Rebels: that's me! Then I went. And here's a sergeant on the road, he's took two men, he's deserted same as me, he's got money, he can bribe a civvy skipper to carry us to England . . . It's nowt to do wi' God. I don't understand all that about God, why d'you bring God into it! You've come here to tell the people and then there'd be no war.[10]

Hurst's outburst also betrays the class resentment of the subaltern dispatched to execute Imperialism's work of repression. However, Attercliffe in no uncertain terms, debunks the notion of honor embedded in the ostensibly civilizing mission of colonial violence:

> All wars, Sergeant Musgrave. They have got to turn against all wars. Colonial war, do we say, no war of honor? I'm a private soldier, I never had no honor, I went killing for the Queen, I did it for my wages, that wor my life. But I've got a new life. There was one night's work, and I said: no more killing.[11]

As a working-class man, Attercliffe had gained little from his nation's imperial adventures, and lost much. He had lost his wife to an ugly grocer because he was so busy trying to make ends meet. For all four men, their disaffection is united allegorically in a *dance*, of which Musgrave pleads, "make this Dance as terrible as You have put into my brain." The dance is designed as a public performance of defiance against the coloniality of nationhood and its manifestations in class and moral conflicts.

As the men settle into their new abode, we encounter Annie, the lover of the late Billy Hicks. Although Sparky is attracted to her, she is interested in the better-looking Hurst who rebuffs her advances. She later settles for Sparky and succeeds in persuading him to run away with her. This precipitates a conflict among the soldiers, culminating in Sparky's death at the end of a bayonet. Despite this distraction, Musgrave persists in staying the course and goes on with his "recruitment drive." He is determined to see the performance of anticolonial subjectivity through to its end, no matter what the impediments. Indeed, Musgrave judges Sparky's body to be catalytic to the ultimate "dance."

This final, terrible dance unfolds in the midst of ordinariness. The Sergeant supposedly conscripts the leaders of the miners' strike, as the Mayor had hoped. The Mayor summons the Dragoons based a few towns away to help keep the miners in line. Then, at a climactic moment, Musgrave displays Billy Hick's skeleton dressed in his scarlet uniform. He tells the shocked crowd that he and Attercliffe killed five innocent people overseas to avenge Billy's death. They will now atone for their misdeed by exacting five-fold that number in Billy's own town. Directing the Gatling gun at the crowd, he insists 25 people must be killed as a recompense for the colonial violence into which the soldiers were conscripted. Raising Billy's skeleton, Musgrave performs a ritual dance of atonement. The threatened massacre is, however, averted when the Dragoons arrive, shoot Hurst dead, and with the Bargee's help, arrest Attercliffe and Musgrave. What started out as Musgrave and his men's cleansing ritual becomes the town's own purification dance ridding its community of the renegade soldiers. Quelling the rebellion retains the oppressive status quo, rather than prompting a major shift in the community.

Mrs Hitchcock, the innkeeper, hints at the root of Musgrave's failure: his conflation of solipsistic action with collective agency. As she nurses Musgrave through his incarceration awaiting hanging, she admonishes him:

> use your Logic – if you can. Look at it this road: here we are, and we'd got life and love. Then you came in and you did your scribbling where nobody asked you. Aye, it's arsy-versy to what you said, but it's still an anarchy, isn't it? And it's all your work.[12]

It is also through the medium of Mrs Hitchcock that Arden finally delivers his central message about senseless heroism and the pitfalls of attempting reform within the same structural framework devised by the oppressor: "you can't cure the pox by further whoring."[13]

Critics greeted *Sergeant Musgrave's Men* with less than unreserved enthusiasm. The reaction of Harold Hobson of the *Sunday Times* was representative of a swathe of critical opinion: "Another frightful ordeal. It is time someone reminded our advanced dramatists that the principal function of the theatre is to give pleasure . . . It is the duty of the theatre, not to make men better, but to render them harmlessly happy."[14] Ronald Bryden went further by observing: "What's wrong with the play is a technical gamble in construction ... It's a weakness of *Musgrave* that what commences with the power and sureness of a legend or ballad peters out in discussion."[15] Eric Keown was even less flattering:

> Why was this piece put on? A play that was anti-Empire and anti-Army would conceivably have its appeal in Sloane Square, but surely not one that was eighty years out of date? If a tract was wanted on those lines it could have been written more persuasively by an intelligent child ... there might have been some felicities of dialogue to leaven this lump of absurdity, but I failed to detect them.[16]

Yet, we students in Nigeria in the early 1980s saw more in *Sergeant Musgrave's Dance* than a "lump of absurdity." We read it as a dramatic imagining of postcolonial desire not dissimilar to our own aspirations for a counter-cultural universe untainted by the inequities of neo-colonialism. Arden's pacifist, anti-imperialist vision carried multilayered lessons for the project of postcolonial reconstruction. It is true that on an immediate level, the cathartic ritual of Sergeant Musgrave's dance prescribed no explicitly programmatic solution to the hegemony of imperialistic nationalism. The soldiers' political activism had little direction or coherence beyond its obvious oppositional tendency, illustrating perhaps elements of Stuart Hall's insights into the operation of counter-hegemony in the English context:

> *Negotiation, resistance, struggle*: the relation between a subordinate and a dominant cultural formation, wherever they fall in this spectrum, are always intensely active, always oppositional in a structural sense (even when this "opposition" is latent, or experienced simply as the normal state of affairs) Their outcome is not given but made. The subordinate class brings to this theatre of struggle a repertoire of strategies and responses – ways of coping as well as ways of resisting. Each strategy in the repertoire mobilizes certain material, social and symbolic elements: it constructs these into the supports of the different ways the class lives, negotiates, and resists its continuing subordination. Not all the strategies are of equal weight; not all are potentially counter-hegemonic.[17]

Yet, the implications of Musgrave's ultimate failure carried immense import. Mrs Hitchcock's insight that "you can't cure the pox by further whoring" meant for us, not simply the literal truth that violence cannot cure violence but, rather, pointed to the inadvisability of accepting colonizing paradigms and epistemological structures as frameworks for reform. Musgrave and his men had sought to promote their message against colonial brutality by re-enacting a ritual of colonial brutality. Their failure underscored the necessity of changing the very scaffold upon which to inscribe a program of reform rather than simply inverting the colonizer's message within a conceptual and material context erected by the colonizer himself. To young radicals such as ourselves, this message of structural transformation pointed clearly in the direction of not simply non-violence, but of socialism as well – a destination in which the postcolonial desires of our own resistant dramaturges like Osofisan culminated.

On an immediate and explicit level, Arden's anti-imperialistic text exposed the incoherence of colonial nationalism – the failure of its hegemonic mission even within the metropolitan center. The ostensibly symbiotic relationship of God, Queen, honor, and Empire corresponded little to the reality of the colonial soldiers' own perceptions of their role or their lived experience. For one soldier, the allegiance to God undermined, rather than buttressed the imperial mandate to transform and civilize the "Other," while another saw little nobility in his own prescribed part as a foot soldier of repression in the colonial project. A deep class-consciousness of their own exploitation in advancement of the imperial project accentuated their disenchantment with that project. The very act of atonement devised by the Sergeant and his men, signifying the dramatic extent of their remorse at the killing of innocent "natives," combined with their consciousness of the marginal, informal nature of their own citizenship within the imperial nation, hinted at the soldiers' sense of identity with the colonized "Other." The boundaries of colonialism, then, transcended the geographical and cultural spaces of external, Afro-Asian colonies to encompass sections of the English populace at home and abroad. It was this conception of internal or intra-English colonialism, this implicit sense of identity of some working-class Englishmen with the foreign-born colonized that would establish the conceptual framework for imagining a hybrid English nation.

Yet, *Sergeant Musgrave's Dance* also revealed the heterogeneity of subaltern groupings. The subordinate are neither monolithic, nor is their sense of unity guaranteed. Indeed, the play portrays as many paths to anticolonial resistance – broadly defined – as there are internally colonized groups. From the onset, Arden refused to invest the entire narrative in Musgrave or any particular individual. Rather, he produced a story of evolving groups and communities seeking to transmute themselves from coerced entities into voluntary communities in deliberate search of collective senses of being and belonging. In the process, they sometimes collide with each other – as in the case of the miners and the soldiers. The miners are a voluntary community with the clear goal of protecting the interests of their members against mine owners and exploitative government policies. Such a union is never stable but always ritually reorganized for coherence. Arden stresses the fragments of difference, and their historical moments of communion, while exposing fissures as potential sources of fragmentation. Such characterization produces a persuasive archeology of deviance against dominance. Once again, Stuart Hall's notion of *articulation* in social struggle comes to mind when we try to understand Arden's construction of social signs in search of agency. According to Hall, *articulation* is:

> the form of the connection that can make a unity of two different elements, under certain conditions. It is a linkage which is not necessary, determined, absolute and essential for all time. You have to ask, under what circumstances can a connection be forged or made? The so-called "unity" of a discourse is really the articulation of different, distinct elements which can be rearticulated in different ways because they have no necessary "belongingness". The "unity" which matters is a linkage between the articulated discourse and the social forces with which it can, under certain historical conditions, but need not necessarily be connected.[18]

Arden uses such notions of social groupings and their potential political efficacy with poetic guile. Without necessarily romanticizing the miners' rebellion or their collective struggle, he displays a dramaturgy instructing audiences on both the futility of solipsism and contradictoriness of collective action. Musgrave's intense individuation of a collective action at various moments threatens the "articulation" uniting his men in a pacifist anticolonial discourse. Their grouping and the rationality of their "Logic" – based on a mimicry of colonial violence as a statement against that violence – did not, due to contextual reasons, lead to a broader "articulation" that might have united the miners' cause with that of the soldiers and the town. Using "Dance" as a signifier for celebrating those moments where articulation occurs, Arden gives us two main types of it – Musgrave's and that which the Mayor, with the help of the Dragoons, forces the town to undertake as a form of triumph over external aggression. Overall, his play suggests that all the characters, including those seemingly more authoritative such as the Mayor and Parson, are social pawns in the big nationalist and imperialist picture and rhetoric. They constitute what Robert Tressell in his classic proletarian novel calls "ragged trousered philanthropists" as their quest for social agency produces a crisis that hegemonic forces need for dominating people and limiting their subjectivity. The local relations of domination and subordination, and apparent identity crisis of the subordinated, are microcosmic of the larger nation the Dragoons emerge to secure.

Stylistically, Arden's use of the dance metaphor played out in a public space such as a market square, recalled postcolonial dramatists' use of ritual to articulate issues of communal consciousness and performances of subjectivity. As a mode of relating individuality to a group, a ritual solicits collective clarity of purpose. By their nature, rituals are forums for consolidating faith and they require a public site where their performances, through symbolic vectors, achieve a sense of collective identity and agency.

They solicit, caution, and enable connections between solipsistic and communal selves. In this context, Musgrave and his men see themselves as high priests of the ritual calculated to initiate the community into a state of anticolonial subjectivity. They believe that the meaning of the symbolic act of presenting Billy Hick's skeleton would unite the community in the political and symbolic discourse of anti-imperialism. Like Wole Soyinka's Elesin Oba and Osofisan's Major,[19] however, Musgrave grossly miscalculates. His sign or "logic" has lost its indexicality due to the social turmoil in Billy Hick's hometown. The residents have already coalesced into antagonistic social groups at war with each other – the miners versus the Mayor, for instance – so that the message of pacifism was likely to carry little weight. Thus, the catharsis that transpired cleansed not the community of war and violence, but of the antiwar dissenters.

Due to a seemingly low investment in psychological depth, the structure of the play is episodic. Songs, dances, and ballads aid the dramatic action by commenting on what had happened previously or what is about to happen. In other instances, they frame a character's commentary on the social context. From the Bargee's:

> The Empire wars are far away
> For duty's sake we sail away
> Me arms and legs is shot away
> And all for the wink of a shilling
> and a drink . . .[20]

to Mrs Hitchcock's parody of the Mayor:

> I am a proud coalowner
> And in scarlet here I stand
> Who shall come or shall go
> Through all of my coal-black land?[21]

Arden's episodic style embellished by "highly diversified spatial-temporal as well as agential structures," shifting situations, and a spectrum of relationships capturing the "plurality of social existence and experience" suggests the playwright's concern with limiting conventional modes of representation. It is, however, his political vision – the textuality of power illustrated by his works, and their internal and external configurations of coloniality that lend them enduring relevance for students of post-colonialism.

7 David Edgar

The nation's theatre and its anticolonial scribe

The best review I've ever had was when Michael Billington said that, like Balzac, David Edgar seems to be a secretary for our times. And that defined, rather more precisely than I'd ever defined before, what I'd like to be. I'd like to be a secretary for the times through which I am living.[1]

The play begins in the dark, literally. A sonorous voiceover announces an act of becoming. A postcolonial nation is about to happen. A people stand on the verge of transition from colonial objectification to the achievement of postcolonial subjectivity:

> VOICE: Long years ago, we made a tryst with destiny, and now the time comes when we shall redeem our pledge, not wholly or in full measure, but very substantially. A moment comes, which comes but rarely in history, when we step out from the old to the new, when an age ends, and when the soul of a nation, long oppressed finds utterance. At the stroke of the midnight hour, when the world sleeps, India will awake to life and freedom.[2]

In the original broadcast, the voice belonged to India's nationalist leader and first Prime Minister Jawaharlal Nehru. His historic pronouncement made in the Indian province of Punjab in 1947 traumatized the colonizer's psyche and prompted a struggle to redefine England's post-imperial sense of self. Nehru's words furnish an unusual opening for a play concerned primarily with a colonial culture convulsed by internal crisis and the retreat of its imperial past. As the play proceeds to an enactment of homecoming by English soldiers and administrators, the playwright hints at the imminence of a postcolonial crisis of identity in England.

As a theatre student in postcolonial Nigeria, I found the English dramatist David Edgar's play, aptly titled *Destiny*, intensely provocative. Its discourse extends postcolonial theory by looking at the impact of anticolonial agitations for subjectivity on definitions of English national culture. Rather than simply focusing on the effects of English colonialism in India, the playwright uses England's imperialist legacy to define the foundations of English nationalism in the 1970s. Underscoring Gayatari Spivak's assertion "that imperialism, understood as England's social mission, was a crucial part of the cultural representation of England to the English,"[3] David Edgar's *Destiny* firmed up what John Arden sought to do in his *Sergeant Musgrave's Dance* by creating an English archeology of identity, relationships, and cultures undergoing an existential crisis as the British Empire eroded.

As John Arden's dramaturgy built a gateway to my knowledge of the political underpinnings of English theatre, so the stylistic innovations and radical politics of the author of *Destiny* heightened my curiosity about the impact of postcoloniality, if any, on the colonizer's sense of self. If John Arden helped inaugurate socialist realism as a cultural practice that named, limited, and subverted the theatre of England's dominant culture, David Edgar actualized that practice by presenting it in a variety of incarnations both within and outside the institutions of the cultural establishment. While avant-garde and other counter-cultural attitudes provided a politically enabling landscape for John Arden's works in the 1960s, the 1970s and 1980s witnessed a far more urgent search for effective means to understand and overthrow a conservative culture that had trickled down to the organized working class.

David Edgar's dramaturgy belongs in an esthetic movement that is historically counter-hegemonic. Arden generated an esthetic ideology defying fixity and institutionalization. Edgar, on the other hand, sought to institutionalize radical political themes and styles in such places as universities, and national and regional theatres. While Arden posed questions about socialist alternatives to mainstream English politics, Edgar provided strategies for inaugurating a socialist culture within it. He did this by problematizing and connecting England's imperial and colonial past to the inequities of its post-imperial present. But changes in socialist states across the world and internal reconfigurations within the English Left, left Edgar with a new conundrum: what kind of cultural context and texts can generate a society that enables the full and effective democratic operation of local and global citizenships? His play *Pentecost* addressed this question in some depth. As I show in this chapter, Edgar's consciousness shifted from the exuberance of a young, militant socialist writer, through the more conventional sensibilities of a socialist aesthete, to the disenchantment of a social democrat dissatisfied with the structures of European modernity, and seeking an alternative frame of reference for understanding and managing the world.

The origins of Edgar's dramatic practice lay in a politically left-wing dramaturgical movement known as "agitprop theatre" that emerged in England in the late 1960s. The label stood for "Agitation and Propaganda," and applied to artists and groups who believed that all art is tendentious and ideologically loaded. Its adherents sought, through their art, not only to explicate the ideology of the dominant culture but also to propose strategies to contest and limit it. The movement boasted members such as the group known as "Blue Blouse," as well as the dramatists Erwin Piscator and Bertolt Brecht.

David Edgar's socialist esthetics, grounded in the traditions of agitprop, aimed to produce a counter-hegemonic culture both within the institutions of the establishment as well as on its fringes. Edgar did not belong to the avant-garde theatre movement but, rather, described his early politics as "a combination of the New Left and counter-culture."[4] Edgar's coming of age as a writer coincided with the Conservative Government's electoral success in 1970. His early plays include *A Truer Shade of Blue, Still Life: Man in Bed, Two Kinds of Angel, Acid,* and *Bloody Rosa.* By 1971, in collaboration with an agitprop group called The General Will, he had written *The National Interest,* which was an unsparing indictment of Conservative rule. As his relationship with the leftist theatre group deepened, he produced several other works including *The Rupert Show, State of Emergency, Rent, Or Caught in the Act,* and *The Dunkirk Spirit.*

These works responded to working-class disenchantment not only with the Tory government, but also with the Labour Party's drift toward a conservatism that seemed to make it unelectable. Unlike the preceding decade, the 1970s dawned in a spirit of gloom and cynicism. The socialist optimism that had spurred such dramatists as John Arden was in a state of decline. The left-wing writer David Hare lamented, "We have looked. We have seen. We have known. And we have not changed."[5] These adverse circumstances galvanized the resurgence of working-class consciousness and labor militancy during the four years of Conservative ascendancy from 1970 to 1974. As Edgar observed, "suddenly after thirty years the working class movement awoke with such speed and strode back onto the stage of history, like a broom sweeping people in its path . . ."[6]

Socialist theatre workers in England shared in the sense of urgency to resurrect the vision of a socialist revolution. As Edgar explained, he and others of his ilk responded to the heightened radicalism of the early 1970s "by rejecting the social realism of writers like Arnold Wesker that had dominated radical theatre for fifteen years." They joined artists like Brecht in proclaiming realism "inadequate" for a militant age. In addition, they felt that the rise of "mass populist culture," especially television, had sharpened the limitations of the realist strategy.[7] Agitprop emerged as the artistic approach of the hour.

True to the conventions of agitprop, Edgar's early plays were overtly didactic and politically topical.[8] They were performed in spaces appropriate to the economic and political identity of their audiences – streets, union conferences, church halls, pubs, and fringe venues. These plays interpreted the state of English society through the prism of Marxist economic theory, offering searing critiques of the "crisis of capitalism," and prescribing working-class strategies to resolve it.[9] Edgar insisted that psychologism, depth of character, and linearity of plot were irrelevant to the drama of socialist agitation – indeed, that they undermined the didactic function of agitprop plays. Using cartoon strip methods to present grotesque and contradictory imageries, the plays matched Marxist analyses of social reality with music hall and "stand-up" comedy performances. They aimed to package their political message in an entertaining garb. According to Edgar, the plays "worked best with what the jargon calls 'advanced workers' – at things like TASS weekend schools, shop stewards, Labour Party and IS socials." They made little impression on "apolitical workers."[10]

English agitprop drew encouragement from the spread of parallel genres in other parts of the world such as China, the former USSR, and East Germany. Artists such as *Blue Blouse*, Erwin Piscator, and Bertolt Brecht produced agitprop in countries where socialist states supported and promoted their endeavors. Agitprop practitioners in England sought to implant their esthetics upon the imagination of a social class (the working class) they hoped would help redefine English national culture. While the governments of socialist countries sought to use agitprop to assimilate their citizens into the state, English agitprop became an esthetic describing the marginalization of the working class that, it was hoped, would pave the way to socialism in England.

In the early 1970s, David Edgar mounted scathing challenges to Conservative Government policies through a series of agitprop works. *The National Interest* dramatized the Industrial Relations Act introduced by the Tories to emasculate the working class and their unions. *Rent . . .* explained the implications and contradictions of the Housing Finance Act designed ostensibly for the welfare of the less privileged. *State of Emergency* chronicled events culminating in the miners' and dockers' industrial disputes during the year 1972. *Death Story*, which was an adaptation of William Shakespeare's *Romeo and Juliet*, was a political allegory of England's colonial domination of Northern Ireland. *Tederella* adapted the fable of "Cinderella" to parody former Prime Minister Ted Heath's predicament with the European Common Market. *The Case of the Workers' Plane*, produced in 1973, explored the aerospace factory labor disputes.

By 1974, however, Edgar had parted company with The General Will over disputes that reflected the general fragmentation of the Left. One bone of contention between the playwright and the theatre group concerned the issue of performer/audience relationship. Edgar explained his version of the conflict thus:

> My feeling was that we should remain very slick and almost arrogant in our relationship with the audience. The group's feeling was that there should be much more room for a relationship with the audience in the sense of popular culture. Which I disagreed with because I was fearful that it will become vague and unspecific and imprecise.[11]

Moreover, with a gentrified Labour Party back in power between 1974 and 1979, Edgar felt that it was time to shift the focus of his practice from exclusively working-class and dissident middle-class audiences to a broader population representing a variety of political and social backgrounds. The discourse of socialist revolution in which agitprop was embedded, was in decline. The internecine bickering on the role of trade unions in parliamentary politics had weakened and compromised the effectiveness and reliability of the Labour Party as the home for radical politics. At the end of the decade, the election of a Conservative Government loomed imminently on the political horizon. It seemed necessary for any artist who, like Edgar, wished to enlarge the scope of his impact, to insinuate himself into the institutions of mainstream culture. Thus, the political and cultural dynamic from the late 1970s through the end of the 1980s, led Edgar in a new direction. His craftsmanship and political activism moved from the fringe esthetics of agitprop to the center of the political spectrum and into the dominant culture.

Returning to a context and audience he once excoriated, Edgar started working in state-subsidized establishment theatres and television in addition to fringe and community theatres. By the 1980s he had, in the words of John Bull, "declared War on All Fronts"[12] – for those were years dominated by England's popular and demagogic Prime Minister – the arch-Conservative Margaret Thatcher. The machismo of government never saw a better performer than Margaret Thatcher. Not only did she cultivate an overbearing patriarchal persona, she instituted an ideology equating conservative values with "common sense" and socialism with "loony thoughts." "Thatcherism" blossomed as an ideology based on competitive and solipsistic individualism, and an economy that boldly and arrogantly placed the interests of property ownership and wealth accumulation above social welfare and concern for the less privileged. Her government set out to limit the moral and material gains of working-class culture and modes of representation by a systematic process of economic strangulation. Thatcherism also redefined subjectivity for the popular masses by destroying trade unions and limiting their effectiveness with jingoistic nationalism. In her own words, the Prime Minister was determined to set up a government and dominant culture that:

> decisively broke with a debilitating consensus of a paternalistic Government and a dependent people; which rejected the notion that the State is all powerful and the citizen is merely its beneficiary; which shattered the illusion that Government could somehow substitute for individual performance.[13]

Thatcherism blossomed in a politico-cultural soil fertilized by a profound postcolonial identity crisis anchored in economic distress and large-scale immigration from England's former colonies. For centuries, England's

national self-assurance was shaped by its power to determine the carto-
graphic boundaries and cultural destinies of people within and outside its
little island. England's command over the vast resources and wealth of far
away Asia, Africa, the Caribbean, and the lower Pacific islands gave it an
exalted place in the career of European modernity. By the nineteenth
century, the riches of the British Empire far outshone the fabled bounty
of England's imperial forebears, Spain and Portugal. By the middle of
the twentieth century, however, English colonialism was in retreat.
Anticolonial nationalisms across the Afro-Asian world provided a global
impetus for counter-modernist cultural conflicts, which began to destabilize the English sense of national identity both in the context of empire
and within England. Decolonization was accompanied by the influx of
waves of immigrants from England's former colonies in the Caribbean,
Asia, and Africa to rebuild cities devastated by German bombs during the
Second World War as well as to meet the nation's dire need for menial
labor. England's immigrant population grew when the exclusionary fury
of African racial nationalism in Kenya and Uganda thrust large numbers
of Africans of Asian descent out of east Africa onto England's shores. By
the 1970s, debates over what constituted "Englishness" convulsed English
society. Economic hard times accentuated what came to be construed as
an essentially cultural debate over national identity, and added fuel to the
exclusionary fire of Conservative politics.

It was in this context that Thatcher effectively limited socialism's political
appeal as an effective mode of agency among the working class by fashioning a new nationalism that was imperialistic, culturally chauvinistic, and
racist. The political and cultural landscape forged by Thatcherism
confirmed Edgar's sense that progressive theatre must broaden its appeal
to include the "radically inclined middle class people."[14] By the early
1980s, he had jettisoned his past political activism in favor of a more
rhetorical estheticism. It became important to develop a multivocal
esthetics challenging the univocal nationalism shared by the dominant
culture and subordinated working class. Edgar expanded the range of his
concerns beyond the working class to include women's rights, and the
struggles against racism and homophobia, skillfully navigating a spectrum
of political and esthetic borders in an attempt to reach the broadest possible
audience. He moved from fringe to mainstream theatre, and television to
journalism, in a project to create what he called a "theatre of public life,"[15]
viewing the search for subjectivity by each constituency within that
"public" a potential source of a counter-hegemonic culture. For instance,
his 1978 play *The Jail Diary of Albie Sachs* dramatized the diary of a white
South African anti-apartheid campaigner. In a radical departure from the
flat characters of agitprop, the play highlighted the interiority of subjectivity in a context of intense political oppression.

It was, however, *Destiny*, written during the transitional period of Edgar's
theatrical practice in 1976, that most directly engaged the broad range of

issues – of race and nation, of class and citizenship, of colonialism and postcoloniality – that had begun to reshape the former agitprop artist's thinking. Deliberately mixing historical reality with fiction into a genre Edgar called "FacTion," the play presented a masterful illustration of the process by which nationality is invented and signified. As the historian Nicholas Dirks has observed:

> Claims about nationality necessitated notions of culture that marked groups off from one another in essential ways, uniting language, race, geography, and history in a single concept. Colonialism encouraged and facilitated new claims of this kind, re-creating Europe and its others through its histories of conquest and rule.[16]

David Edgar emerged as one of his nation's most trenchant commentators on England's imperial legacy and its postcolonial identity. The following section analyzes *Destiny* as a tract for the cultural conflicts of its time, as an exposé of the violence of chauvinistic nationalism.

Destiny

Destiny is set in the English Midlands in the 1970s. That this play about postcolonial beginnings dawns in darkness is highly symbolic. For darkness in this context is laden with multiple layers of meaning. On one level, it connotes a moment of renewal, both for the postcolonial nation and for its former colonizer. On another, darkness serves as a metaphor for the precarious foundation of that confident myth of imperialist ideology that asserted that the sun would never set over the British Empire.[17] Darkness also signifies a postcolonial moment akin to what Jacques Derrida calls "brisure"[18] – a simultaneous act of "join" and "break." In this case, the "join" forged Indians into a commonwealth of the formerly colonized loosely united by a shared, informal allegiance to England – what I call colonial nationalism. The "break" entailed a moment of anticolonial disidentification. Jawaharlal Nehru's call to his people to reawaken, and savor the moment when "the soul of a nation, long oppressed, finds utterance," with which Edgar opens *Destiny*, opens a space for enunciating the limits of colonial order and announcing a postcolonial desire. It signals the emergence of what Homi Bhabha terms "a third space,"[19] a moment of in-betweeness denunciating and fragmenting colonial order while projecting desires for postcolonial subjectivity.

Following Nehru's opening salvo to new beginnings, the lights fade onto the English Sergeant Turner and the Indian servant-soldier Khera as they pack up artifacts of the English colonial presence in India. They are joined by Major Rolfe and Colonel Chandler. The beginning of the end of the British Empire, which for Indians has opened up new vistas of freedom and opportunity, imbues the returning colonists with a sense of rootlessness. Will the England they call "home" live up to the expectations of their carefully preserved nostalgia? Or will it turn out to be an unrecognizable land, far, in fact, from the figments of their romantic imaginations? By opening the play in such a fluid setting in far away India, the playwright gives notice that all that is solid will crumble to dust, and all that is distant will unequivocally be brought closer to local struggles. In other words, Edgar schools his audience in the notion that the local is always global and vice versa.

In Act One Scene One Edgar makes colonial India the setting for what will turn out to be an English contest in England. Sergeant Turner, Major Rolfe, and Colonel Chandler all show a spectrum of emotions about the present state of the motherland they have long served, and appear to harbor different expectations about the reception they will be accorded upon their return home. The variety of their social backgrounds inserts them into different spaces in England's class hierarchy. The self-assured Chandler, born to wealth and educated at public schools, exudes confidence that he will be well rewarded for his loyal service to his nation. Far more insecure than Chandler about their hard-won middle-class status, Rolfe and Turner, by contrast, worry that their sacrifices will be undervalued and their gains eroded by the invasion of their pristine motherland by savage hordes of the colonized "Other." The parallel, yet different paths the three men traverse on their return to England will determine the nature and scope of the political and cultural conflicts in the play. The end of the scene is a particularly poignant lesson in English colonial history. As his imperial masters leave the stage, Khera, left alone to complete the packing of their colonial trophies, mockingly toasts a mural representing the colonial army's suppression of an anticolonial mutiny, declaring "Civis Britannicus Sum."

Why did Khera toast this mural? The mutiny represented in the mural is of great significance to any postcolonial inquirer. Jubilant cheers that serve as the backdrop for Khera's gesture of deference to the mural accentuate the painting's importance in announcing the imminent birth of a postcolonial nation. Displayed again in the next scene, this icon of anticolonial nationalism and colonial repression depicts the legendary Indian Sepoy mutiny of 1857 – a year that marked the centennial of English rule in India. On that memorable day, Indian troops belonging to the English colonial army enacted their insubordination to English rule in a rebellion that started in Meerut near Delhi and lasted a full year before it was brutally squashed by the English Army. The mutiny started when the circulation of a rumor that the English had introduced new bullets greased with fat derived from pigs and cows fueled the disaffection of Muslim and Hindu soldiers irate at the alleged desecration of their faith. An English dispatch published in the December 1857 edition of *The Atlantic Monthly* summed up the event thus:

The overt ground of the general mutiny was offence to caste feelings, given by the introduction into the army of certain cartridges said to have been prepared with hog's lard and cow's fat. The men must bite off the ends of these cartridges; so the Mahometans are defiled by the unclean animal, and the Hindoos by the contact of the dead cow. Of course the cartridges are not prepared as stated, and they form the mere handle for designing men to work with. They are, I believe, innocent of lard and fat; but that a general dread of being Christianized has by some means or other been created is without doubt.[20]

The rebellious troops moved to Delhi where they aligned themselves with the Mughal emperor, the titular head of a realm under the de facto suzerainty of the English. They attacked, maimed, and killed several English families, burnt down homes and colonial monuments. After a year-long struggle to crush the rebellion, the English brutally brought the revolt to an end on July 20, 1858. The mutiny of 1857 had a far-reaching impact on the organization of English India. The Parliament in London dismantled the authority of the East India Company which had hitherto exercised formal control, exiled the Mughal Emperor Bahadur Shah to Burma (now Myanmar), and imposed direct colonial rule by vesting overall governing authority in a newly appointed Vice-Roy. India became England's richest and largest possession from 1858 to 1947. The rebellion, however, exposed the fragility of colonial authority, while its repression became a symbol of England's military might. By raising a toast to the mural, Khera appears to acknowledge, indeed celebrate, anticolonial resistance by Sepoys like himself. Edgar's placement of such a significant gesture at the beginning of the play highlights the playwright's intent to demystify English nationalism.

The second scene shifts the locus of action to a Tory social gathering in England, which turns out to be a funeral for Colonel Chandler. The character makes a last dramatic entrance at his memorial service to offer a biographical sketch of himself before departing forever:

In '47. Came on home.
Colonel Chandler. Monochrome
Another England,
Rough and raw,
Not gentle, sentimental as before
Became a politician, not to master but to serve
To keep a careful finger on the grassroots Tory nerve;
Like any born to riches, not to plunder but to give:
Always a little liberal, a great Conservative.
But as his seat grows marginal, his powers less secure,
His responsive elder statements sound increasingly unsure;
Colonel Chandler, oyster eyed,
One fine summer morning, died.[21]

Chandler's death creates a vacancy in Parliament, which his cousin Peter Crosby is invited by Party members to fill. Unlike the Colonel, Crosby is a new kind of Conservative less obsessed with imperial nationalism than with global finance. Sleek, compassionate, and more tolerant than his forebears, Peter's persona is both repulsive and attractive to a propertied class clinging to mythologies of England's grander days. Peter accepts his anointment as Chandler's successor with enthusiasm and launches a political campaign to secure his dead relative's parliamentary seat.

Edgar uses the second scene to set up the ambiguous identity of the Conservative Party as it positions itself to narrate the destiny of the nation. The scene suggests that neither the Conservative nor Labour Party constitutes a coherent, consistent entity; rather, the identity of each is ridden with tensions and conflicts. Platt, the factory work manager, trade unionist, and local chairman of the Conservative Party, disagrees with Frank Kershaw, owner of Baron's Casing Factory that Platt manages, over workers' wages. Such differences become even more glaring when Kershaw meets the retired Major Rolfe and Sergeant Turner later on in the play.

The third scene of the first act shifts attention to the other political party involved in the conflict over narrating the nation. Edgar introduces the audience to Paul, Clifton, and Sandy at a meeting in a Labour club. Clifton, an aspiring Labour Party parliamentarian, is very dependent on Paul, a militant socialist with intricate knowledge of the Party's constituencies and internal politics. As in the previous scene, Edgar shows the presence of racial nationalism among Labour partisans. Paul informs Clifton and his wife Sandy that the Labour politician Mr Smalley whose parliamentary seat Clifton is seeking, has burnt his bridges with his largely Asian constituency by declaring, "Whatever one's sympathies – and I have many – with these unfortunate people, one must accept that the indigenous population will not for ever stay silent, faced with what appears to be the thin end of a very thick black wedge."[22]

In subsequent scenes the playwright underscores the readiness with which fascism sprouts roots not only within the dominant political party, but also among those marginalized by it, and even within its opposition. Scene Four exposes the dangerous logic of retired Major Rolfe's racial nationalism. Edgar showcases him thus:

> In '47. Came on home.
> Major Rolfe. A face of stone.
> Another England, seedy drab,
> Locked in the dreams of glories she once had.
> The Major looks at England and bemoans her tragic fate
> Condemns the mindless comforts of a flaccid, spongers state,
> Despairs of trendy idiocies repeated as rote,
> While the knot of old school tiredness is still tight
> Round England's throat.

Sees leaders fat with falsehood as they lick up every lie,
The people's blood grown sickly with their driving will to die.
Major Rolfe, sees the light,
Calls for a counter from the Right:
Major Rolfe, starboard seer,
Loses, for they will not hear.[23]

Major Rolfe has not come to terms with the imminence of the British Empire's end. Despite the minor issue of the loss of India, the empire is well and alive, its mandate to "civilize" intact: "it's not true that we've lost an Empire. Haven't found a role. We have a role."[24] Rolfe sees his own ascent from his working-class roots to upper middle-class respectability as the prize for his sacrifices to the national cause. As suspicious of the high-born as he is of groups he deems unfit for social mobility, the Major defines England's national identity in much the same terms, as does Enoch Powell. His experience in the colonial army has left Rolfe convinced that the boundaries of glorious Englishness are boldly delineated by the colonial "Other." Long years of policing and reorganizing the colonial order have helped him construct an exclusive idea of Englishness to which few outsiders can lay claim. The working classes and the poor whose dependency on the state he deplores, represent a potent threat to the purity of Englishness, as do the moderates within his own party who preach racial tolerance. As far as he is concerned "the flag they wave omits the red and blue."[25] The theatricality of his personality makes him memorable in the drama of nationalism.

Sergeant Turner's path to racial nationalism is paved with ambiguity born of disillusionment with the values of the contemporary Conservative Party. As someone who invests a great deal in the symbolic wealth of England – especially the glory of its imperial vision and achievements – the Sergeant is disenchanted with the modern Conservatives' crass materialism. The party to which he has long owed allegiance has mortgaged the country's future to selfish economic interests. The England defined by the traditional values of "thrift" and "prudence" which Turner had devoted his life to defending has all but passed. Edgar's sketch of Turner portrays him as a man out of sync with his time:

In '47. Came on home.
Sergeant Turner, to a Midland town.
Another England, brash and bold.
A new world, brave and bright and cold.
The Sergeant looks at England, and it's changed before his eyes;
Old virtues, thrift and prudence, are increasingly despised;
Old values are devalued as the currency inflates.
Old certainties are scoffed at by the new sophisticates:
And big capital and labor wield and ever bigger clout,

> And it's him that's in the middle and it's him that's losing out –
> Sergeant Turner, NCO:
> Where's he going? Doesn't know.[26]

Caught in limbo between "big capital" and militant labor, Turner eventually walks into the arms of the rabidly racist Nation Forward Party, although haltingly. His defection from the Conservative Party is triggered by the devastating news that Metropolitan Investments, owned by Frank Kershaw, is about to buy him out of the building housing his antique store. The carrier of these unhappy tidings is a Jewish character named Monty. This rubs Turner the wrong way. The messenger of his doom, after all, belongs to a "race" historically stigmatized as the "Other" – one whose decimation established the racial foundations of European modernity. Yet Monty's message is not one of his own making. Caught in a wave of anger and disappointment when he realizes that his betrayer is a man from his own party, Turner establishes a fringe party known as the Taddley Patriotic League, which, by the play's end, merges with the extremist Nation Forward Party (NFP).

The last scene of the act dramatizes the mentality of fascistic racial nationalism and its complicated relationship with empire by depicting the NFP's celebration of Hitler's birthday. The participants represent a motley crew – from working-class men to a rich older Canadian – who share a nostalgia for England's imperial glories and disdain for the alleged offscourings of its former empire, now in their midst to steal their jobs and adulterate their "culture." The Canadian Drumont recounts the anguish of an Enoch Powell constituent: "if I had the money to go, I wouldn't stay in this country . . . In this country in fifteen or twenty years time the black man will have the whip-hand over the white man."[27]

The paranoid imagination of racial nationalism has thus transformed England the great colonizer into the colonized, the lofty civilizer of savage lands into a land under siege by savages. The power of this imagination overwhelms distinctions of class among white men. As Edgar shows, Marxist theory notwithstanding, colonialism leaves its formidable imprint upon the nationalist consciousness of even those described by Ernest Renan as lacking "the social capital upon which one bases a national idea."[28] Conflating demands for protective wages and collective bargaining with imperialist tropes, the disenfranchised join the status quo in narrating an imagined nation premised upon racial purity and masculinity. The play's white male protagonists, no matter what their precise location on the political spectrum, proclaim their stake in participating in the racialized, masculinized discourse of nationalism, obscuring deep social cleavages among them in the process. As Benedict Anderson asserted, "Regardless of the actual inequality and exploitation that may prevail in each, the nation is always conceived as a deep horizontal comradeship."[29]

Into this racialized national narrative steps Khera at the end of the scene. Khera has immigrated to England as a formerly colonized subject who had rendered loyal service to his former masters. He makes no apologies, despite the fact that he understands that race and national origin disqualify him from narrating the English nation:

> Gurjeet Singh Khera. To a Midlands town.
> Another England, another nation,
> Not the England of imagination.
> The labor market forces have an international will,
> So the peasants of the Punjab people factory and mill,
> The sacred kess and kanga, kachka, kara and kirpan
> The Sikh rejects so he can be a proper Englishman;
> Keep faith in human virtue, while attempting to condone
> The mother country's horror at her children coming home.
> Gurjeet Singh Khera,
> Once a slave,
> Returns to haunt the Empire's grave.[30]

Sectarian unrest in the land of his birth – itself an invention, in part, of colonialism – has complicated the notion of a "home" for Khera. For him, the existential sites for being, belonging and becoming must be multiple, and he has come to England to assert such a pluralistic notion of identity. Khera's reference to his reception in England ("The mother country's horror at her children coming home") aptly captures the irony of imperialism's legacy. On the one hand, the paternalism inherent in the imperial mandate of the "white man's burden" facilitates Khera's English "homecoming," establishes his claim to England as one of her "children." On the other hand, he is an unwelcome stepchild, as it were, from whom the motherland recoils in horror. Khera's assertive presence and those of other postcolonial subjects contradict the univocal and singular narrative of English nationalism and provoke the vituperation of xenophobes like Enoch Powell. Edgar's crafty insertion of Khera's character at the end of the first act throws into sharp relief the dramatist's plea for an inclusive politics of humanism.

Edgar does not, however, romanticize Khera. Departing from agitprop traditions, Edgar problematizes the Indian character as much as he does the English protagonists of *Destiny*. Shunning his Sikh identity to become an Englishman, Khera is an ambiguous neo-colonial character. Khera seeks subjectivity through assimilation. Yet, his aspiration to assimilate also implicates him in the project to write a national narrative premised upon uniformity – of custom and culture, if not race. For "pukka" (a colonial coinage meaning "pure") English nationalists, he poses a particular problem. His postcolonial identity is one they prefer to forget. Yet he also represents the "Other" against which they define their identity and describe their history.

In the second act, the discourse of nationalism plays out on the floor of a factory – that familiar arena for conflict and consensus over race and class. The first scene pits Khera and another Indian immigrant Patel, against the manager Platt and a white worker Attwood. Khera and Patel protest the racialization of class by drawing attention to the low wages and lack of opportunity for promotions from which Asian workers suffer. Attwood responds with the familiar charge that Asians jeopardize the economic security of whites. Edgar develops the theme of intra-class racial conflict in the second scene by depicting the merger of two disgruntled splinter parties – Turner's Taddley Patriotic League and Nation Forward. Both groups seek to dissolve the schisms of class in a sea of white supremacy. As the Nation Forward spokesman Maxwell declares, "much more unites us than divides us. It's an old saying, but you can change your class and your creed. But you can't change the blood in your veins."[31] He goes on to promise that Nation Forward will restore England's brilliance by rooting out the darkness that stains the body politic: "I hope with all sincerity, that you will wish to join this party, join with us, and make our country great again."[32] Turner is persuaded to amalgamate his group with the racial nationalists with the hope that he will secure the combined party's nomination to run for Chandler's seat in Parliament. This moment of joining in racist fraternity is sealed by a new member Tony's rendition of Kipling's "The Beginning":

> It was not part of their blood
> It came to them very late
> With long arrears to make good
> When the English began to hate
>
> It was not preached to the crowd
> It was not taught by the state
> No man spoke it aloud
> When the English began to hate.[33]

Subsequent scenes trace Turner's growing popularity. Both mainstream parties – Labour and Conservative – envy the appeal of his populism, but are squeamish about his politics of racial essentialism. Meanwhile, schisms rack the ranks of Labour, as Khera and Patel denounce the racism of trade unions. Clifton, contesting Turner and Peter for Chandler's seat, walks a political tightrope between the concerns of the trade unions and the aspirations of their dissident immigrant members. Labour's predicament, as Edgar presents it, reflected the identity crisis the party experienced in the period when *Destiny* was written. In the late 1970s, the Conservative Party gained ground among Labour's traditional constituencies such as trade unions. Labour's ambivalence toward racialized class conflicts – as signified by Clifton's attitude toward the grievances of his working-class Asian allies – marked its willingness to move to the right in a strategic move to arrest its own marginalization.

An impending strike by lowly paid and largely Sikh workers at Baron Casings, acts of intimidation against immigrants followed by a race riot, and confusion among politically moderate members of the electorate combine to propel Edgar's plot to an uncertain climax. The riot provides the occasion for two white members of the working class to weigh the claims of racial nationalism against that of class solidarity. As these men, Tony and Paul, await police interrogation in the aftermath of the riot, they reveal the deep cleavage that the competing claims of race and class have wrought in the ideas of nationhood and citizenship:

PAUL: All history's the struggle of the classes.
TONY: No. All history's the struggle of the races.
PAUL: The workers of all races must unite.
TONY: The workers of all classes must unite.[34]

Meanwhile, Edgar highlights the anxieties among the mainstream parties generated by Nation Forward's racialized populism. The dramatist appears to be saying that the Conservative and Labour parties, by their opportunistic manipulation of racial divisions, have unleashed a monster that is now rapidly spinning out of their control. Peter Crosby, the Tory, is bewildered by the Nation Forward Party's lack of civility and its failure to pursue a decorous electoral process. As he confides in Platt:

CROSBY: (*to Platt*) And it was very strange, when talking to these people; thought, oh, no, these can't be with their grisly xenophobia, they can't or are they, our creation, Demons. Alter-ego. Somehow. (*Platt smiles*) And I remembered, being small, the coronation, and the climbing Mount Everest, a kind of homely patriotism, sort of harmless, slightly precious self-content. A dainty, water-color world, you know. (*Platt looks embarrassed.*) And then, their monstrous chauvinism. Dark, desire, for something . . . Kind of, something dark and nasty in the soul.[35]

Crosby pays an unexpected visit to Clifton and Sandy to urge that racial politics be taken out of the electoral process so as to keep the Nation Forward Party in check. Clifton then reminds Crosby that the Labour and Conservative Parties have created the problem in the first place and that both parties must take a more principled position on the subject:

Your deal, in '62. Then ours, a higher bid, the Kenyan Asians Bill, restricting entry purely on grounds of color. So, not to be outdone, the stakes go higher, back to you in '71, "Keep Race out of Politics, Keep Blacks out of England."

Thus, once again, Edgar implicates the mainstream political parties whose conflicting narrations of nationalism use race and class as markers of effective citizenship.

The racial moderation championed by Crosby and Clifton marks a moment of recognition and regret at the excesses of racial and imperial nationalism. Several scenes toward the end of the play tend in the same direction. A case in point is a scene at the end of the second act, when Edgar invokes audience sympathy for an unexpected casualty of nationalism. Major Rolfe, that icon of imperialism, reappears, this time to mourn the loss of a soldier-son, killed in Belfast where he had been dispatched to defend the claims of colonial nationalism. As he laments his child's death, Rolfe achieves a surprising state of political consciousness. Edgar uses this unusual character to map and reject the coloniality of English nationalism within and outside its borders. Contradicting his earlier assertion, Rolfe states that after all, "The sun has set. And we should remember. We should not look back, but should, instead, think only of the morning."[36] At the moment when the younger Rolfe laid down his life to sustain the nation's imperial narrative, his father said, enough. The time has come to draw the curtain on that narrative, and to launch new beginnings untainted by its legacy.

As Rolfe bids England's imperial destiny goodbye, so too, by the play's end, most of the remaining protagonists have come to realize the futility of rabid nationalism. The wedge issue of race has failed to buttress the electoral fortunes of the Nation Forward Party, and has undermined the integrity and electability of Labour. The Tory Party remains entrenched in power. The play ends like it began, with a voiceover. Lights fade out on Turner and Cleaver as their rhetoric wears out. And as darkness encroaches, a gentle voice rings out. It is Adolf Hitler at Nuremberg in 1933. In a brilliant stroke of irony, Edgar presents a fascist offering his advice on how to tame and resist fascism: "Only one thing could have stopped our Movement: if our adversaries had understood its principle, and had smashed, with the utmost brutality, the nucleus of our new Movement."[37] Like its beginning, the ending of the play promises the closing of old chapters and the dawn of new ones. Edgar admonishes partisans on the right as well as the left not to allow the fervor of nationalism to obscure the dangers of fascism. He invites them to close the chapter on the notion of a singular English identity that excludes more people than it admits, and to open a fresh one inscribed with the inclusive spirit of a multi-ethnic England.

Framed by a modified agitprop structure, *Destiny* tells a compelling story whose strength lies in its cast of tentative rather than emotive characters. As icons with deep discursive resonance, these characters act as ideograms seeking a common place where they can conjugate their identities. Edgar eschewed linearity of plot in favor of an emphasis on the play's political message. As he explained, "What I wanted the audience to do was actually view the play in terms of its theme, in terms of the social forces involved, not necessarily to be bothered with strict chronology."[38]

As a postcolonial subject, I read Edgar's text as interrogating mainstream and counter-cultural narratives of national identity at a time when England was trying to re-negotiate its place within a fragmenting European modernity. In the 1970s, the European Common Market and its cultural politics fractured uniform philosophies within and between political parties and labor unions in England. Great power rivalries among Europeans moved from colonial battlefields to the arena of global capitalism. England found itself caught between nostalgia for its imperial grandeur on the one hand, and a recession within its economy on the other. The result was a titanic struggle to redefine the national destiny, to draw and redraw the contours of nation and race. It is this moment of renewed cultural invention that Edgar captures in *Destiny*.

Since the age of European expansion in the sixteenth century, colonial encounters between the English and their Others had shaped England's sense of self. The racialized construction of the British Empire translated into an exclusionary definition of Englishness when, in the latter half of the twentieth century, masses of the formerly colonized immigrant Others flocked to England to complicate the meaning of nationalism. Mapping an archeology of colonial and anticolonial nationalism, Edgar's play portrays the racialization of class antagonism in times of social crisis. More than describing such an archeology, however, I believe that Edgar goes on to prise out fissures within which a socially democratic subjectivity is possible. The character of Khera, for instance, opens up the promise of such subjectivity. The indexical resonance of *Destiny* lies in its representation of the crisis of Euro-modernity by fragmenting solid discourses of national belonging. The play promises a more global means of restructuring the terms of becoming. If Edgar sees himself as a "Secretary of the times," recording the contradictions of nationalism, I see him as a theologian of nationalism, not merely documenting its overt manifestations as much as probing and explaining to the world its deepest meaning. For Edgar, socialism still furnishes the path to that meaning, a thesis for a theology he has so energetically textualized in his plays, television drama, films, journalistic articles, and essays. No other dramatist in recent times offers so much optimism for subjectivity among those "overpowered, but not tamed."

8 Caryl Churchill

Decolonizing the nation through gender and class

Come gather, sons of England, come gather in your pride,
Now meet the world united, now face it side by side;
Ye who the earth's wide corners, from veldt to priaries, roam.
From bush and jungle muster all who call old England "home".

Then gather round for England,
Rally round the flag,
From North and South and East and West
Come one and all for England![1]

This paean to imperial patriotism by the patriarch Clive sets the stage for a probing inquiry into the ephemerality and instability of colonial hegemony and its manifestations in bodies, spaces, and time in Caryl Churchill's *Cloud 9*. The empire emerges as a sexualized and racialized figment of a masculinist, heterosexist imperial imagination – a figment embodied in the cast of characters populating the family of a prototypical colonial master across two historical times and spaces – colonized Africa and postcolonial England. Churchill mines the history of imperialism not only to forge a critique of the Conservative culture and politics of Thatcherite England, but also to offer a language of anticolonial resistance anchored in a deliberate subversion of gender identities, roles, and expectations. The play's opening song, with its vision of the imperial "family" as a crypt of power and vehicle of civilization, introduces the audience to signifiers of objectification that expose the coloniality of discourses shaping the identities of gender, race, and sexuality. Illustrating Jean Genet's claim that there is "a parallel between colonial and sexual oppression,"[2] Caryl Churchill's *Cloud 9* simultaneously portrays a system of signification that describes the modernist landscape against which deviance and subjectivity can be imagined by the dominated, *and* establishes "identity" as a necessary site for asserting democratic citizenship. Empire and its microcosm, the patriarchal family, establish the framework within which various characters challenge their received identities of gender and sexuality as they proceed from the disfranchisement of informal citizenship

Plate 8.1 Cloud 9 directed by Awam Amkpa at Mount Holyoke College, South Hadley, US. Photograph by Lee Bouse.

to the empowering claims of non-formal citizenship within the polity of the household.

While John Arden and David Edgar use the paradigms of class and race in their dramatic commentaries on hegemony, Caryl Churchill conceptualizes the machinery of power and the modes of its subversion in terms of sex and sexuality. Although historians of imperialism and nationalism have offered sophisticated studies on the "feminization" of the "Other," few literary dramatists have treated the sexualized semiotics of dominance with the rhetorical brilliance and artistic gumption of Caryl Churchill. In this chapter, I argue that the style and substance of Churchill's elegant work of resistance turns sexuality into an intriguing prism for exploring the issues of colonial power and postcolonial desires.

The inter-modernist space from which Caryl Churchill sprang was that of England's counter-culture in the 1960s. As John Bull has written, the "bruised dreams" of that movement spawned a generation of British political dramatists committed to the cause of political and social transformation through drama: "From the outset, the predominant tone was of provocative confrontation, aimed as much at the values of the 'alternative'" society as of the establishment it opposed.[3] Churchill's works draw upon the semiotics of female subjugation and subjectivity not only to pose questions about the ideological role of women in the creation of a genuinely inclusive and democratic society, but also to question existing styles of representation. In the words of Sue Ellen Case and Jeanie Forte, Churchill depicts "a world of alternative identities and practices while demonstrating the link between dominant ideology and institutionalized gender roles and sexuality."[4]

I was first drawn to Churchill's dramaturgy in the early 1980s when a friend suggested we brave the wintry showers of a London December to see *Vinegar Tom*, produced by the playwright in collaboration with the feminist theatre company Monstrous Regiment. The witty boldness with which the show exposed femininity as a problematic medium through which dominant and subordinate cultures describe themselves, drove me immediately to the library of Bristol University to scour Churchill's other works, among them, *Blue Angel, Hotel, Skryker, Serious Money, A Mouthful of Birds, Fen, Top Girls, Light Shining in Buckinghamshire*, and *Owners*. Churchill's socialist-feminist gaze prompted me to look beyond class and race as the dominant theatre of struggles over hegemony to gender and sexuality as crucial and contested signifiers of England's imperial past and its postcolonial present.

Churchill began writing in 1958, mostly for radio in the early stages of her career. Years later, she made her mark as a noted practitioner of collaborative theatre, conceived and nurtured in workshops that brought together writers, actors, producers, and directors in an interactive endeavor to create and represent politically meaningful art. As Michelene Wandor has observed, the workshops sought to promote good working relationships among the members of theatre companies, as well as to supply the play-wright with a significant cache of raw materials for fashioning the play.[5] Such collaborative ventures turned actors into activists committed to cajoling audience identification with the discourses of subversion and inclusion embedded in the play. Churchill's personal history as a writer is closely tied to the fortunes of fringe and alternative theatre companies in the 1970s such as the workshop-oriented Joint Stock Theatre and Monstrous Regiments. Two of her most representative plays – *Cloud 9* and *Vinegar Tom* – resulted from these associations. The oppositional ideologies and styles of fringe companies situated them in contemporary England's inter-modernist landscape and helped fertilize the creative imagination of like-minded dramatists. Churchill acknowledged her debt to the dialogic mode of writing:

> If you're working by yourself, then you're not accountable to anyone but yourself while you are doing it. You don't get forced in quite the same way into seeing how your own inner feelings connect up with the larger things that happen to other people. If you're working with a group of people, one approach is going to have to be from what actually happened or what everyone knows about – something that exists outside oneself.[6]

The collaborative production of subversive drama occurred in the context of pungent ironies in post-1960s England. A volley of paradoxes surrounded the growing visibility and social mobility of women during Margaret Thatcher's years of ascent to political stardom. On the one hand, the passage of the Equal Pay Act in the 1970s signaled a victory for women's claims to justice in the workplace, while reproductive freedom became an established right recognized by public policy. Gillian Hanna, a member of the theatre group dedicated to producing alternative representations of feminist subjectivity known as Monstrous Regiment exulted, "To be a woman in 1975 and not to have felt the excitement of things starting to change, possibilities in the air, would have meant that you were only half alive."[7] It was, she recalled, an epoch where:

> The sense of being in the right place at the right time, in step with a great movement in history, part of history, making history ourselves. We were part of a huge wave of women and we were going to remake everything. It gradually dawned on us that we didn't have to go out and join any movement. We were already in it. We were the Movement.[8]

Yet, the 1970s also marked the burgeoning power of a counter-cultural backlash that threatened to rein in the mass political appeal of the women's movement – a backlash led, ironically enough by a beneficiary of the struggle for female emancipation. The rise of Margaret Thatcher symbolized not so much the realization of an inclusive feminist vision of the nation as much as the triumph of liberal individualism cloaked in the rhetoric of bourgeois feminism. As far as socialist-feminists like Churchill were concerned, the logic of liberal individualism was all too vulnerable to the politics of cultural conservatism. For instance, the conception of the fetus as an individual rationalized increasingly shrill denunciations of abortion rights by champions of traditional gender and sexual roles, while the reign of the "success ethic" fueled attacks against immigrants thought to lack the skills and temperament necessary for success in a free market society. Some "bourgeois feminists" urged a "post-feminist" world that celebrated the social mobility of a few women in patriarchal establishments. Artists and writers like Churchill who advocated structural change as the path to an inclusive and pluralistic postcolonial England, held that socialism promised a better means of achieving the goals of feminism, which after all, had little to do with a few white women ascending the rungs of a "capitalist ladder."[9]

Cloud 9

By 1979, when Churchill, in collaboration with Max Stafford-Clark and Joint Stock Theatre wrote *Cloud 9*, the "family" had become England's dominant semiotic field for struggles over the meanings of nation and race, gender, and sexuality. In the 1970s two mothers – Queen Elizabeth II (the Monarch) and Margaret Thatcher (the Prime Minister) – symbolically held their families together while narrating the nation as a familial place conferring the rewards of formal citizenship on deserving sons and daughters. Since women's imaginings and experiences make sense only in the context of a sexual politics as a whole, Churchill used "the family" as an ideogram for probing the gendered underpinnings of nationalism, citizenship, and subjectivity. As she told an interviewer:

> One of the things I wanted very much to do in *Cloud 9* . . . was to write a play about sexual politics that would not just be a woman's thing. I felt there were quite a few women's groups doing plays from that point of view. And gay groups . . . There was nothing that also involved straight men.[10]

The metaphor of the "family" helps Churchill contextualize the overlapping vignettes set in colonial Africa and post-imperial England that compose her play *Cloud 9* and launch signs of postcolonial desires for a radically alternative English society. Patriarchal and heterosexual, the paradigm of "family" undergirded the imperial mandate to dominate, "civilize," and acculturate, and was thus central to the ideology and rhetoric of what I have called "colonial nationalism." Its passion for cultural uniformity lived on in the static conservatism of English traditionalists in Churchill's own day. Thus, Churchill conceived of the dominant national culture of Thatcherite England as inherently colonial, sustaining its legitimacy through conventions of representations that made women and homosexuality visible, yet powerless as effective identities. In *Cloud 9*, the historical experience of imperialism frames and helps resolve the question whether the symbolic prominence of women in structures of national power signals the demise of patriarchy or whether such visible gains reinforce and legitimize heterosexist patriarchy.

Churchill approaches the issues raised above by setting the play in two inter-related moments in English history – the high holy days of empire at the turn of the twentieth century, and the renewed neo-imperialist nationalism of the Thatcher years. The same characters inhabit the two eras, which although separated by at least a couple of generations, are collapsed in the play into a short temporal continuum to signify their cultural continuities. If the creative manipulation of time serves as an effective strategy in underscoring the parallels between imperial and post-colonial England, subverting the representation of gendered, sexualized, and racialized identities supplies a means to destabilize the sexual underpinnings of colonial power across time and space. The play achieves this subversion of conventional modes of representation through cross-casting, cross-dressing, and doubling of roles. Churchill confessed in an interview with Jackie Kay in *New Statesman and Society*:

> I do enjoy the form of things. I enjoy finding the form that seems best to fit what I'm thinking about. I don't set out to find a bizarre way of writing. I certainly don't think that you have to force it. But, on the whole, I enjoy plays that are non-naturalistic and don't move in real time.[11]

The first act of *Cloud 9*, set in Victorian Africa, features a family apparently obsessed with a notion of Englishness that must be upheld to legitimize colonial domination. Their "home away from home" occupies an ecological landscape cultured by English bungalows, lavish verandahs, and a flagpole holding aloft the Union Jack. These material manifestations of colonial nationalism temper the natural menaces of noisome heat and humidity, of croaking frogs and flying insects kept at bay by netted windows, of unruly natives domesticated into colonial civilization. The battle between "nature" and culture forms an integral component of the imperial mission. The colonial administrator Clive, like Simon Pilkings in Wole Soyinka's *Death and the King's Horseman*, presides over an imagined patriarchal paradise that extends outwards from his own household, to a sea of colonized natives beyond the steps of his colonnaded bungalow. His authority begins at home, where he must maintain cultural order at all costs. Churchill suggests the synonymy of Clive's domestic dominance with his mastery over the empire he helps narrate, in the play's opening sequence in which the patriarch leads his family in singing "Come gather, sons of England . . .":

> This is my family. Though far from home
> We serve the Queen wherever we may roam
> I am a father to the natives here,
> And father to my family so dear.[12]

Clive proceeds to introduce the members of his family one by one, as he imagines each one of them. The characters play the roles prescribed by their received identities without question, even as the real-life sexual and racial identities of the actors playing the characters debunk the fixity of received identities. First, Clive's wife Betty, played by a man:

> I live for Clive. The whole aim of my life
> Is to be what he looks for in a wife
> I am a man's creation as you see
> And what men want is what I want to be.[13]

Next, we encounter the black servant Joshua, played by a white actor:

> My skin is black but oh my soul is white.
> I hate my tribe. My master is my light.
> I only live for him. As you can see,
> What white men want is what I want to be.[14]

On the one hand, these characters' rhetorical affirmation of deference to the same master unambiguously underscores the power relations governing the archeology of belonging in the colonial "family." The behavior of Betty and Joshua must conform to Clive's expectations in order for them to be recognized as citizens of his household and the colonial nation it represents. The aspirations and subjectivity of the colonial wife and the colonized servant are permissible only within the framework of Clive's absolute suzerainty. Within the overlapping familial realms they occupy – of household, colony, nation, and empire – they are formal citizens, but with minimal subjectivity. While Betty sees some opportunity for amassing cultural capital through racial affiliation, Joshua's path to empowerment lies in his masculine affiliation with Clive. In both cases, however, leverage stems from identification with the white patriarch, guardian of the imperial mandate.

Yet, the semiotic conundrum embodied in Churchill's resort to cross-casting in the opening sequence suggests the fragile, mutable foundations of absolute dominance, prompting the critic Elaine Aston to declare, "Churchill's theatre is not just a question of politics, but a politics of style."[15] For although the use of male actors to represent women has important precedents in Medieval and Renaissance theatres, the practice assumed a different resonance in the twentieth century when women played themselves in lead and supporting roles. Betty as a full-bearded big man in a Victorian dress or a white Joshua playing a subservient black man make quite a metaphorical leap in a context where naturalist and realistic performance conventions and readings of identities constitute the established norm of representation. Indeed, the opening act's stylistic refrain of cross-casting is carried forward by the character of Clive's son Edward, played by a woman. Edward's "effeminacy" proves a monumental challenge to Clive's campaign to make a "real" man out of his boy.

> EDWARD: What father wants I'd dearly like to be. I find it rather
> hard as you can see.[16]

Churchill's deliberate replay of cross-gender and cross-racial casting imposes a sexualized prism through which the referent identity is depicted. By using discordant bodies to represent supposedly immutable identities, the playwright destabilizes absolutist notions of "natural" identities. As Aston has pointed out, cross-dressing and cross-casting "allows the spectator the possibility of seeing beyond 'institutionalized' gender roles and sexuality by cross vestimentary signs of masculinity and femininity with the wrong body."[17] In my view, however, these surreal strategies go even further. They challenge the imperial project itself by deconstructing the gender notions embedded therein. *Cloud 9* draws attention to the colonizer's sexualized gaze on the colony and natives who inhabit it. For Clive, Africa is dark, mysterious, and waiting to be conquered as a woman might. He tells Betty: "I am pitching my whole mind and will and reason and spirit against it [Africa] to tame it, and I sometimes feel it will break over me and swallow me up."[18] The association of Africa with a feminine – or rather effeminate – sexual identity emerges again in the terms in which Clive expresses his desire for Mrs Saunders, the widowed, tantalizingly independent English-woman in the colony. He tells her, "Caroline, you smell amazing. You terrify me. You are dark like this continent. Mysterious. Treacherous."[19] Thus, most importantly for the purposes of my analysis, Churchill's resort to cross-casting defies the gendered assumptions of imperial mastery, namely the habitual dependence or servile effeminacy of the colonized native, opening up the possibility for change.

The tenuous foundations of patriarchal hegemony signified by racial and sexual cross-casting are further exposed by twists in the plot as the play proceeds. Scene after scene depicts the characters' departure from their prescribed roles in ways that shatter the illusion of the completeness of Clive's domination. Sexual transgressions and servile insubordination muddy the boundaries of family, race, and imperial relationships, disrupt-ing a colonial order rooted in the colonizer's familial assumption of well-defined, fixed, and separate social roles for all its members. For instance, Ellen the governess, ostensibly a good English girl charged with the responsibility of educating Clive's children in the niceties of English culture turns out to be a lesbian, whose sexual desire for Betty certainly contradicts, if not threatens, the patriarch's sexual and familial preroga-tives vis-à-vis his wife.

Further challenges to the imperial family's domestic bliss materialize with the visit of two characters who refuse to be reined in by the constraints of family: the sexually charged bisexual explorer Harry Bagley, and the carefree, attractive, and unattached Mrs Saunders. Declaring that "I would be insulted by any show of independence . . ." Clive proceeds to set up exploitative alliances with both these characters. From the outset, Clive and Harry, representing two male prototypes, enter into a barely concealed competition for the mastery of bodies and spaces. Clive's command over "family" in their social and political manifestations give him cultural capital with which he can trump the rootless Harry. Yet, Clive cannot help but envy the careless freedom of a man such as Harry, unshackled by wife, children, and the demands of colonial governance. While Clive seeks to institutionalize a patriarchal, "care-taking" male culture of dominance at home and in the colony, Harry embodies the adventurousness he would love to have. It is this very spirit of adventure that also stirs Betty's heart and libido, propelling her into an extramarital affair with Harry even as she continues to play the role of docile wife to Clive. Meanwhile, Clive too finds sexual solace and the pleasure of domination in the willing arms of Mrs Saunders against the background of a choir singing a "Christmas carol" off-stage.

Apart from revealing the fragile foundations of the heterosexual nuclear family upon which the colonial order ostensibly rested, the sexual adventures of the characters in *Cloud 9* also expose the excesses of male privilege epitomized by the rivalry between Harry and Clive. Harry is an unscrupulous philanderer whose predatory sexual impulses are themselves as masculinist as Clive's. Both young Edward and the hapless Joshua fall prey to his rapacious desires. Harry's sense of sexual domination is monumental – he imagines Betty with Harry on her lap as an exciting unit of bodies subject to his sexual domination. By the end of his visit, he leaves the impression that the boundaries of bodies and spaces for his sexual desires are endless, even as he leaves his multiple partners bereft of any sense of power. Thus, even when the objects of his attention desire him as much as he desires them, he appears no less than Clive, to signify the authoritarianism of patriarchy, however "liberal" in appearance.

Indeed, the competition for mastery between Harry and Clive, underscored in scene after scene by a variety of seemingly innocuous family games, culminates in a confession session in which each man brags about his sexual conquests. Disparaging women, Clive asserts:

> Friendship between men is a fine thing. It is the noblest form of relationship ... There is something dark about women, that threatens what is best in us. Between men that light burns brightly ... Women are irrational, demanding, inconsistent, treacherous, lustful, and they smell different from us ... Think of the comradeship of men, Harry, sharing adventures, sharing danger, risking their lives together.[20]

Clive's musings on male friendships stir Harry's omni-sexual impulses – he grabs Clive in a sexual embrace. Outraged by Harry's misunderstanding, Clive, as if declaring himself the winner in the patriarchal game, declares Harry's behavior immoral and "unmanly," quite unbecoming for a male member of the imperial race:

> I feel contaminated ... The most revolting perversion. Rome fell, Harry, and this sin can destroy an empire ... A disease more dangerous than diphtheria. Effeminacy is contagious. How I have been deceived. Your face does not look degenerate. Oh Harry, how did you sink to this?[21]

Harry seeks Clive's forgiveness and validation while accepting defeat in the game. Clive's response is to get Harry married with the hope that he will be "cured" of his homosexual proclivities. The task for leading Harry to heterosexual wedded bliss falls to the lesbian Ellen.

The first act ends in a verandah with the wedding of Ellen and Harry. Clive toasts the newly wedded couple in what appears like a self-congratulatory homage declaring himself the family and nation's "alpha-male." Yet, the patriarch's moment of triumph is cut short by a shot fired from an unexpected corner of the room. It represents the ultimate betrayal of the colonial nationalist faith by one of its seemingly most loyal adherents – the malleable Joshua.

Through the course of the play, Joshua's character evolves in unexpected ways. On the surface, he emerges as a subservient fellow thoroughly acculturated in the "civilizing" norms of the colonial nationalism, singing longingly of snow, as the governess Ellen has taught him:

> JOSHUA: In the deep midwinter
>   Frosty wind made moan,
>   Earth stood hard as iron,
>   Water like a stone.
>   Snow had fallen snow on snow
>   Snow on snow,
>   In the deep midwinter
>   Long long ago
>   What can I give him
>   Poor as I am?
>   If I were a Shepherd
>   I would bring a lamb.
>   If I were a wise man
>   I would do my part
>   What I can I give him,
>   Give my heart.[22]

Yet, by the end of Act One we learn that Joshua's submissiveness is performative, no more genuine than the antics of a black actor playing a minstrel. His behavioral conformity is meant to problematize the gaze with which his colonizers regard him on the one hand, and to mark the limits of his assimilation to their norms on the other hand. Joshua's musical reflections on snow reminded me of my own school boy rendition of the "Song of Colors" under the direction of the Catholic fathers of my primary school decades ago in Kano.[23] Joshua's fidelity appears at times to be complete. When a rebellion of the colonized breaks out in the course of the play, ruthlessly suppressed by Clive's colonial administration, Joshua reassures his English "family" that the rebellious natives "were not his people." The significance of the "black" servant's longing for snow, and his assertion of identity with the English causes lies in its suggestion of the limits of the inter-modernist space by which the colonized, ostensibly acculturated "native" is bounded. Because he will never be European, his affectation of Europeanness itself constitutes something of an act of resistance. Yet, at the end of the play, this subtle form of opposition on Joshua's part yields to a far more overt, radical, and violent act of resistance that belies the imperialists' complacent assumptions of "native" quiescence.

The stage directions indicate that Edward actually sees Joshua making preparations to kill Clive but does nothing to stop him. My reading suggests that Edward's stare, like Joshua's gunshot, represents the ultimate act of refusing domination even by men who apparently have a lot to gain from a culture of domination. In the end, neither Joshua nor Edward can live up to Clive's expectations of their roles. Their act of violence against Clive becomes their only means of performing dissent and subjectivity. However coherent Clive may have imagined the structure of his dominance to be, the power of his identity ultimately failed to induce complete subjection, thereby illustrating Chris Tiffin and Alan Lawson's assertion that "control is complete only up to the moment of its announcement; once enunciated it can never again be total, since the circulation of the knowledge loosens it."[24]

Churchill uses the highly inventive first act to establish two overlapping contexts of patriarchal domination – the household centered around a heterosexual family and its affiliates on the one hand, and a larger politico-cultural field of colonization in Africa on the other. The orderly sustenance of the one assures the stability of the other. By the end of the first act, both institutions – the heterosexual family and colonialism – were in disarray, brought down by the unruly actions of the apparently docile subordinate. Act Two explores the emancipatory implications of this disarray for the meaning of England's postcolonial identity.

Act Two occurs in a post-imperial, Cold War world separated from the colonial theatre of the first act by a hundred years or so. Yet, we meet the same characters from Clive's family, only twenty-five years older. I read this temporal dissonance between historical time and the characters' life spans as a clever strategy to reiterate the political and cultural continuities between imperial and contemporary England. In a reversal of Washington Irving's famous Rip Van Winkle scenario that sought to portray the rapidity of change in antebellum America, *Cloud 9* underscores the sameness of nationalist discourse across time. By the 1970s, in which the second act is set, England had lost her empire but retained significant symbols of its historic presence in the form of immigrant communities from its former colonies. Nor was nostalgia for imperial glory a thing entirely of the past. The Falklands re-energized the spirit of aggressive expansionism couched in the rhetoric of national pride and international respect. Thatcher's claim that "The lesson of the Falklands is that Britain has not changed,"[25] suggested that the imagined power of empire lay at the heart of the new nationalism of the 1970s. There existed other parallels with Victorian England. Despite the impressive advances of the feminist movement, many observers questioned whether women enjoyed real power. The paradox of early twentieth-century England in which the Queen gave women a symbolic presence in national discourse but exercised little effective power, seemed to replicate itself in the 1970s. For even as Queen Elizabeth II and Margaret Thatcher loomed large on the national stage, women's issues and concerns were often marginalized, especially if they did not conform to official expectations of gender and family. Indeed, Thatcher's welfare discourse demonized single mothers and upheld Victorian-era conceptions of heterosexual two-parent families as the norm. As in Clive's Africa, the traditional family became, once again, the bastion of order, the foundation of a stable polity within and imperial defenses without.

Against this new context of cultural conservatism and political reaction, Churchill proceeded to underscore the shifting nature of sexual identities and gender roles. If the first act of *Cloud 9* highlights the conflict between Clive's determination to impose social hierarchy and cultural uniformity on the one hand and subaltern desires for pluralism on the other, Act Two realizes the promise of relational identities as a strategy for the politics of coalition-building. Unconventional characters who move between identities offer the vision of non-formal citizenship as a vehicle for forging an inclusive, democratic society.

Act Two begins outdoors, in a London park. Clive's family has changed. In an act of ultimate resistance, Betty has left her husband who, we learn, survived Joshua's assault. The son Edward, lives an openly gay life, while the daughter Victoria, represented in the former act by an inanimate doll, has sprung to life as a bisexual wife. All characters are played by members of the sex they represent, with the exception of the precocious child Cathy, who is portrayed by a man. At the start of the act, two mothers, Victoria and Lin, sit by a pond in the park to discuss a range of issues – from their children's upbringing and education, to the machismo of popular culture as reflected in television programs. The class difference between working-class Lin and the middle-class Victoria produces some disagreement over social values especially as they relate to children. Lin, however, bridges whatever social distance may have prevailed between the two women by declaring her sexual attraction to Victoria. While Victoria is in a conventional marriage with Martin, Lin is the single mother of the macho Cathy. Lin chooses not to be encumbered by male companionship. Like Betty in Act One, Victoria is unfulfilled by marriage. Unlike her mother, however, she acts decisively to change her lot. She leaves Martin for Lin. Meanwhile, Betty arrives on the scene with her son Edward. She has finally found the courage to separate from the domineering Clive. She interrupts Edward's introduction to Lin by declaring, "I'm going to leave your father and I think I might need to get a job."[26] As she struggles to come to terms not only with her children's unconventional relationships but also with their parenting methods, Betty chooses to adapt to their ways rather than scold them into accepting traditional ideologies of the family as her mother Maud does in Act One.

While Scene One highlights Betty's new independence, Victoria's bisexuality, Edward's homosexuality and Lin's lesbianism, Scene Two explores the dynamics of the relationships defining their identities. Churchill uses Scene Two to distinguish the desire for difference from the politics of difference. While the former enunciates different and resistant identities, the latter highlights the politics of a heterogeneous socio-sexual landscape. Churchill uses the scene to stress the deep imprint of heterosexual power hierarchies on all kinds of relationships including the homosexual. We learn that Edward conceptualizes his role vis-à-vis his lover Gerry in much the same way that his grandmother Maud imagined Betty's mentality and conduct as a married woman in Act One. Edward values stability. While he seeks a sedentary role ("I like doing the cooking. I like being fucked. You do like me like this really."),[27] his partner Gerry persists in pursuing sexual freedom by sleeping with as many partners as possible without the encumbrances of "family." Gerry's solipsistic notion of pleasure is reminiscent of Clive's sexual encounters with Mrs Saunders in the first act. Gerry describes his orgasmic trysts with total strangers on trains and in parks and indeed stresses his preference for such anonymous meetings. Like Clive who could not care less about Mrs Saunders' sexual pleasure, Gerry is insensitive to Edward's fulfillment as long as he is at the epicenter of their coupling. Churchill seems to suggest that the political essence of heterosexual relations of domination and subordination can, and do, color gay couplings. Gerry enjoys Edward's constant companionship while disengaging himself from the responsibilities of a committed relationship.

The marriage of Victoria and Martin is no more a relationship between equals than Edward's partnership, despite Martin's assertion that he is a new man: "I'm not like whatever percentage of American men have become impotent as a direct result of women's liberation, which I am totally in favor of, more I sometimes think than you are yourself."[28] He wants his wife Victoria to have career choices and have a job anywhere in the country. He wants her to recognize his "generosity" toward her sexually: "my one goal is to give you rolling orgasms like I do other women." He denies dominating her even as he constantly disparages her dependence:

> I'm not putting any pressure on you, but I don't think you are being a whole person. God knows I do everything I can to make you stand on your own feet. Just be yourself. You don't seem to realize how insulting it is to me that you can't get yourself together.[29]

Martin's expression of liberalism is in fact an adept performance of a masculinist insecurity. Although he carefully cultivates a "politically correct" attitude ("I'm writing a novel about women from the women's point of view")[30] he punctuates his marital interactions with patriarchal threats, so that ultimately, his character seems little different from those of Clive and Gerry.

As Gerry and Edward, and Martin and Victoria reveal the unequal basis of their relationships, Lin and Victoria sort out a new partnership based on mutual respect, and unencumbered by their children or traditional notions of family. Edward gravitates to this new formula as the only context in which he can sustain a meaningful subjectivity. He reassures the women that he shares the hatred of patriarchy and even asserts, "I'm a lesbian."[31]

Scene Three shifts the focus of the narrative from the mundane realism of the characters' love lives to a fanciful flight into a supernatural realm where the inter-textual relationship between the imperial and Thatcherite settings of the play emerges with impressive clarity. Lin, Victoria, and Edward travel to the precinct of the dead. As they invoke the dead, they encounter Lin's brother who was killed in Northern Ireland, one of numerous soldiers who perished in one of England's last colonial wars. Martin interrupts the scene and is included in the drunken orgy that follows. The ghost of Lin's brother narrates the tale of his own fatal brush with militaristic nationalism. In this intermediate space that observes no boundaries between the material and the surreal, where identities shift and mutate, the characters metaphorically shake off their received and perceived identities for something less fixed, for a state of being embodied in the concept of "Cloud 9." It is Gerry, who upon joining the group, leads the others in singing the "Song of Cloud 9" – the celebration of a state of fragmentation where in the words of Marshall Berman "All That is Solid Melts Into Thin Air," unleashing, as Churchill seems to say, endless potential for emancipation:

> It will be fine when you reach Cloud 9 . . .
>
> Smoked some dope on the playground swings
> Higher and higher on true love's wings
> He said Be mine and you're on Cloud 9 . . .
>
> Twentyfive years on the same Cloud 9
> Who did she meet on her first blind date?
> The guys were no surprise but the lady was great
> They were women in love, they were on Cloud 9
>
> The wife's lover's children and my lover's wife,
> Cooking in my kitchen, confusing my life
> And it's upside down when you reach Cloud 9
>
> Upside down when you reach Cloud 9.[32]

Plate 8.2 Cloud 9 directed by Awam Amkpa at Mount Holyoke College, South
   Hadley, US. Photograph by Lee Bouse.

Cloud 9 is a dynamic theatre where transmutations are imagined, and
desires for democratic subjectivity lived and fantasized, posing a direct
threat to the hegemony of domineering discourses. Joshua's act of resistance against Clive made him the first to achieve the empowering shift
in identities embodied in the notion of "Cloud 9" at the end of Act
One. The last scene of Act Two on the other hand, suggests that the
remaining adult characters are moving in the same direction. Edward is
no longer dependent on Gerry's emotional charity, choosing instead to co-
habit with two bisexual women engaged in a lesbian relationship. He
co-parents their children and lives a more focused life. Martin is humbled
by Victoria's choice to live with Lin, away from his whining and dominance. Gerry feels alienated for the first time, recognizes the merits of an
equitable relationship, and longs for the return of Edward to his life. Betty
discovers herself sexually and socially. She realizes that she can achieve
sexual gratification without Clive: "I used to think Clive was the one who
liked sex. But then I found I missed it"[33] and goes on to describe her late
adult discovery of masturbation as a source of fighting back against Clive
and the patriarchal ethos that deemed her body an object of another's
sexual gratification. She is more assertive socially, attempting at one point
to pick up Gerry who she later discovers is her son's lover. She has also
come to terms with her children's unorthodox living arrangements and
even suggests buying a bigger house to accommodate the entire commune

including herself. In the end, the new Betty poignantly embraces and forgives the old Betty of Act One. Victoria on the other hand has become more confident in her new relationship and "family." Clive who reappears toward the close of the show, stubbornly refuses to change. He is greatly disillusioned by the goings-on of the new era:

> You are not that sort of woman, Betty. I can't believe you are. I can't feel the same about you as I did. And Africa is to be communist I suppose. I used to be proud to be British. There was a high ideal. I came out onto the verandah and looked at the stars.[34]

While the stars he saw in Act One firmly illuminated the ideal of empire, the stars at the end of Act Two are transient and their sparkling brilliance signifies a heterology that celebrates pluralism and defies domination.

I was fascinated by the subversive potential of *Cloud 9* when I first read it in 1985. Its embrace of unorthodox conventions of representation appeared to reject the very foundations of European modernism that emphasized the fixity of individual identity and legitimized nation states as the primary locus of citizenship and agency. Churchill's critique of the sexualized underpinnings of English nationalism and imperialism problematizes the nation state as an arbitrary construct. Ostensibly anchored in the stability of the patriarchal household, the colonizing nation proves as vulnerable to disorder as the heterosexual family it upholds. Churchill re-configures representational styles to illustrate the operation of an inter-modernist launching pad for the assertion of subaltern agency. She suggests that the nation state (in its imperial and internal colonial forms) is an inadequate framework for imagining citizenship and democracy, thus seeming to agree with Edward Said that:

> If the body of objects we study – the corpus formed by works of literature – belongs to, gains coherence from, and in a sense emanates out of the concept of nation, nationality, and even race, there is very little in contemporary critical discourse making these actualities possible as subjects of discussion.[35]

Instead, Churchill highlights the ideological conflict between the notions of "space" and "place." "Space" is a sphere of individuation and subjectivity while "place" tends to be hegemonic and in modernist terms imagined as "nations." Churchill seems to suggest that only when the pluralism and hybridity encapsulated in "spaces" impact upon "place" (usually constructed in homogenizing terms), will full and effective democratic citizenship be possible for all. As a metaphor, "Cloud 9," like Wole Soyinka's "The Fourth Stage," represents a "postcolonial desire" for fluid identities and non-formal citizens capable of forging coalitions to promote global democracy.

Such a project carries important implications for rewriting England's national identity in postcolonial terms – both epistemologically as well as experientially. It is true that the portion of "Cloud 9" that is set in contemporary England, is surprisingly lacking in ethnic characters representing the legacy of empire. The omission is especially curious given Churchill's position on the cultural politics of national identity definition in Thatcherite Britain. It may be that Joshua, having achieved emancipation in Act One, must, in Act Two, yield to those members of the imperial race who have yet to find "Cloud 9." Yet, notwithstanding the physical invisibility of non-white bodies in Act Two, the formula of "Cloud 9" itself, with its unending potential for coalition-building among diverse identities, offers the optimistic promise of cultural pluralism in postcolonial England.

9 Monstrosities, deviants, and darkies

Monstrous Regiment, Gay Sweatshop, and black theatre

> . . . it is from those who have suffered the sentence of history – subjugation, domination, diaspora, displacement – that we learn our most enduring lessons for living and thinking.[1]

Sentiments similar to Homi Bhabha's argument about the didactic role of history's most marginalized actors inspired my choice of England's Alternative Theatres as a field of graduate study. Not all my benefactors at the British Council, however, shared my perspective on the cultural practices of the dispossessed. Back in the days of my doctoral work in Bristol, at a reception organized by the Council for scholars from the Commonwealth, an eighty-year-old woman who had spent much of her adult life as a nurse and schoolteacher in colonial Africa asked me skeptically, "how useful do you think your study in England will be to your country?" Her question was perfectly understandable, for amid a roomful of fellows specializing in medicine and the physical sciences, I alone had elected to study something as seemingly impractical and esoteric as "Alternative and Fringe Theatres and the Cultural History of Post-World War II England." I explained that I was on a quest to investigate not only anticolonial resistance in Nigeria, but also its manifestations in the cultural works of radical theatre groups within an increasingly post-colonial England. My questioner was horrified. "Good God!" she exclaimed: "You mean Her Majesty's government pays you to study those monsters, deviants and Caribbean darkies who make England so inglorious?"

Yes, indeed. Those "monsters, deviants, and darkies" ensconced in radical English theatre companies as signifiers of postcolonial dissent held the key to an array of questions that had fired my imagination even before I left Nigeria. How, I wondered, did decolonization following the Second World War transform the official narrative of metropolitan nationalism, as also its *meaning* to its citizens and subjects at home? In what ways were contests over national identity or identities inscribed in the conventions of cultural representation? Did apparently counter-hegemonic discourses in post-imperial England parallel anticolonial forms of expression in countries like

Nigeria? For, as I have maintained throughout this text, my reading of history suggested that Edward Said was quite right to observe that "although the imperial divide in fact separates metropolis from peripheries, and although each cultural discourse unfolds according to different agendas, rhetoric, and images, they are in fact connected, if not always in perfect correspondence."[2] It is so because the ideological and cultural opposition to imperialism manifested at first in nationalist movements in the colonies, spills before long "into Europe and the United States, in the form of . . . dissent in the metropolis."[3]

My curiosity led me into the fascinating world of England's radical counter-culture, which challenged the stability of England's sense of national "self" by undermining its representative ideograms – from "family" to "citizenship." Companies with names like 7:84, Belt and Braces, Monstrous Regiment, Gay Sweatshop, Welfare State International, Joint Stock, Red Ladder, Black Theatre Co-op, Umoja, and Tara Arts boldly proclaimed the postcolonial character of contemporary England, and engaged the often raucous discourses of identity and belonging that such a reading of the nation implied. However diverse in their social origins and cultural backgrounds, they seemed to pursue new modes of representing communities created or re-formed by adjustments to European modernity prompted by national and global events. They all seemed to occupy varying states of exile from the official criteria of citizenship in what Said has called the "defiance of the classic canonical enclosures."[4] Their art, both within and outside traditional theatre institutions, embodied an unrelenting battle over cultural signs designed to alter traditionally circumscribed notions of culture, politics, and community, thereby complicating England's national culture. If the state sought to use ideograms such as the heterosexual, patriarchal nuclear family to "manufacture consent," as Noam Chomsky has put it, fringe and alternative theatres used their activities to "manufacture dissent" from the official norms of formal citizenship. Their drama served as a "desiring machine" by affording their often-marginalized audiences occasions and spaces to imagine themselves as democratic actors in the narrative of national belonging.

Notwithstanding their kinship to socialist movements, "fringe" and alternative theatres found the identity "class" by itself an insufficient signifier for describing the multifaceted nature of marginalization in post-war, post-imperial England. As the immigration of the formerly colonized, combined with the rising consciousness of women and homosexuals, strained the racialized and sexualized boundaries of "Englishness," counter-cultural dramatists embraced what Baz Kershaw describes as a "dilating spectrum of communities."[5] Their quest to build coalitions transcending fixed categories like "class" underscored the liberating potential of non-formal citizenship. Alternative theatres complicated, even fractured homogeneous constructions of national identity by turning the spotlight on what Stuart Hall calls "new ethnicities"[6] that staked claim to citizenship in the latter half of the twentieth century – ethnicities that acknowledged "the place of history, language and culture in the construction of subjectivity and identity."[7] Comprising affiliations of gender, sexuality, and race, these "new ethnicities" unleashed multivocal and multipositional movements for subjectivity all over the peripheries and centers of former empires. Transcending the nation state, they offered new frameworks for articulating ideas of political displacement and cultural alienation.

Although less studied than England's mainstream theatre, fringe groups have been rescued from the fringes of theatre scholarship by such able chroniclers as Catherine Itzin, Clive Barker, Peter Ansorge, Sandy Craig, Steve Gooch, Michelene Wandor, John Bull, Baz Kershaw, and a few others. In the present chapter, I seek to combine the insights of these scholars with my peculiar perspective as a postcolonial subject to argue that the very presence of radical theatre structured around the post-war "new ethnicities" of race, gender, and sexuality testifies to England's emergence as a postcolonial nation caught in lively contests over national identity similar to those that prevail in "Her Majesty's" former colonies. A particular configuration of these "new ethnicities" defined an official narrative of post-war Englishness that consigned certain groups of English society to the "Otherness" of colonial-style informal citizenship. It was to re-negotiate the terms of national belonging that "fringe" theatres representing the aspirations of alienated groups adopted counter-cultural themes and styles. They sought not only to "radically alter the whole structure of British Theatre," but also "to effect a fundamental modification in the cultural life of the nation."[8] They aimed to transform what I call "hegemonically coerced communities" into "grassroots voluntary communities." These voluntary communities saw themselves, as Edward Said described in another context as a "people compelled by the system to play subordinate or imprisoning roles" within which they emerged as "conscious antagonists, disrupting it, proposing claims, advancing arguments that dispute the totalitarian compulsions."[9]

I illustrate these themes through a discussion of the esthetic and discursive conventions of three fringe and alternative theatre phenomena in England in the 1970s. They include the feminist group, Monstrous Regiment; the gay company, Gay Sweatshop; and a Black British play by Tunde Ikoli. These dissenters challenged the gendered, racial, class underpinnings of official English national identity together with the cultural symbols which gave meaning to that identity, such as the family. The drama of these counter-culturists fashioned esthetics of desire that embodied demands for equity within which new identities could be symbolically and politically imagined.

The origins of alternative theatre in England may be traced to the bipolar re-orientation of twentieth-century European modernity into the competing systems of Soviet-style socialism on the one hand, and democratic capitalism associated most closely with a new superpower, the United

States, on the other. The Bolshevik revolution that spawned the Soviet Union in 1917 left a deep imprint upon England's own labor unions and its Communist and Socialist Parties. The Communist Party in particular provided an organizational network which supported theatre groups such as the Workers' Theatre Movement, Unity Theatre, and "Theatre of Action" run by Joan Littlewood and Ewan McColl. Although a socialist state did not materialize in England, the spirit of the socialist movement was bolstered in the 1930s and 1940s by what its activists saw as parallel events around the world – especially the wars of independence from imperialism in Africa and Asia. As the bloody ravages of the Second World War yielded to the tense anxieties of the Cold War between fresh constructions of "East" and "West," dissenters in each section adopted the ideology of the other to articulate their sense of displacement and rebellion. In Europe's colonies, for instance, nationalist movements critiqued colonialism as the logical extension of capitalism and found in Socialism and Marxism seemingly effective strategies of resistance. Nor did the currents of change leave the metropolitan center untouched. In postwar England, the Labour Party achieved power and nailed into place the structure of a welfare state committed to social justice. It accorded unprecedented political recognition to the working class by encouraging unionization and collective bargaining.

Yet, traditional notions of gender roles and expectations persisted. Moreover, the advent of masses of workers from England's former colonies to work in the transportation and nursing sectors racialized the official sense of "Englishness" more than ever before. The "new ethnicities" of "gender" and "race," fortified by the ideal of the heterosexual, nuclear family, became the most important signifiers of nationality in post-war England even as heightened opportunities for social mobility and cultural dissension expanded both the aspirations of marginalized groups, and the forums for their expression. Thus, the 1944 Education Act democratized education, paving the way for the ascension of segments of the working class, while the theatres sustained by state patronage offered outlets for the articulation, indeed professionalization of dissent through art. Groups subjected to "internal colonization" by their relegation to the margins of national identity, forged alliances with each other as they struggled for citizenship and agency. Like their counterparts in the emerging republics of the "Third World" who found that the end of European imperialism did not guarantee either democracy or social justice, England's "neo-colonized" groups found that the welfare state did not necessarily fulfill promises of equity or cultural pluralism for all its citizens. As in the former colonies of the British Empire, alienation and conflicting notions of "home" shaped postcolonial contests over identity. These struggles sought, through the path of nonformal citizenship anchored in coalition building, to achieve the goal of formal citizenship within a broadened, more inclusive paradigm of national identity. Counter-cultural coalitions united socialist oriented antinuclear movements with groups committed to cultural pluralism. These coalitions launched their campaigns from the inter-modernist spaces they occupied on the margins of mainstream culture.

Such coalitions, by transcending fixed identities like those of "class," illustrated the emancipatory possibilities of non-formal citizenship. The social and cultural affiliations of their members varied. Middle-class radicals acted in concert with working-class and immigrant organizations to produce hybrid communities and political attitudes that challenged both the rhetoric of national belonging, as well as its institutions of representation. The Royal Court Theatre of London, the Theatre Royal Stratford East and other mainstream regional venues newly refurbished after the war to reinstate cultural order in devastated cities, had no choice but to engage the new post-war social classes and their language of alienation. Sandy Craig in his edited volume, *Dreams and Deconstructions*, has observed that counter-culture registered its first major victory with the formal establishment of subsidized theatres in England, particularly the Royal Court Theatre and the English Stage Company in 1956. These venues presented the works of writers, artists, and directors such as John Osborne, John Arden, Harold Pinter, Snoo Wilson, and Joan Littlewood, that addressed the existential and political questions of their day. The plays of John Osborne reflected the angst of the new middle class, and adopted the subversive stylistic conventions of the "angry" dramatists in mainstream forums like the Royal Court and National Theatre. At the same time, more grassroots-oriented community activists articulated dissent in non-traditional arenas. Such dramatists were less committed to the esthetic perfection or stylistic purity of their art than to its social relevance. They adopted highly experimental forms that reflected the levels of "deviance" with which they identified. These "fringe" or "underground" groups adapted European avant-garde, counter-cultural, and left-wing theatre conventions to the particular purposes and terms of their engagement with the dominant culture. According to theatre historian Peter Ansorge, this "fringe" movement attracted artists working in subsidized mainstream theatres to the more informal, socially activist drama of community halls, churches, schools, pubs, cellars, and, of course, the streets.

The trans-Atlantic climate of protest in the 1960s shaped by large-scale decolonization in Africa, the Vietnam War, the American civil rights and feminist movements, and England's military occupation of Northern Ireland, propelled the activism of "fringe" theatre to a crescendo. It was in this era that England abolished the archaic government institution for censorship (Lord Chamberlain's office), and instituted the Arts Council to help develop the arts across the nation, including those on its "fringes." A festival in Edinburgh, Scotland, became the largest venue for exhibiting the thematic and stylistic exuberance of the "fringe." The growing political relevance and state support of "fringe" theatre helped transform the genre into something more than simply a vehicle of protest. What emerged in the 1970s especially, was a new "alternative theatre" that offered a well-developed vision of alternatives to the racially and sexually limiting versions of national identity.

Such alternative visions were timely indeed. For, by the end of the 1970s, progressive politics were in retreat, at least in the halls of power. In the course of the 1970s, the Labour Party fell prey to a fall out with trade unions, lapses in leadership, economic hard times, and the vicissitudes of a fickle fortune. James Callaghan's unsuccessful tenure, his resignation and Harold Wilson's cosmetic attempts at reinstating Labour's integrity, and Edward Heath's defeat by the more conservative Margaret Thatcher – all exacerbated existing cleavages over ideology, class, and culture. In this environment, alternative theatre groups produced a dramatic tradition that went beyond reconfigurations of theme, narrative structure, and language by adopting collectivist production methods. Even writers and directors accustomed to solitary and individualistic styles had to adapt to the more democratic and populist creative process embraced by the Alternative Theatre Movement. Managing such organizations was similarly collectivist by tradition. In addition, these companies toured England in an attempt to promote interactions among various performance styles and practitioners. Festivals such as those in Edinburgh and London resulted. One such festival organized by the American Ed Berman's "Inter-Action Ambience Lunch Hour Theatre Club" in London launched among others, the companies Monstrous Regiment, Gay Sweatshop and the Black Theatre Co-op. As the companies and venues became more culturally diverse, so did their audiences, driven by the quest for subjectivity in an increasingly conservative political climate. The Arts Council of Great Britain also increased its support for the companies and, ironically, made the rapid and systematic professionalization of the theatre of dissent possible.

There was much to dissent from in Thatcher's England. Having discovered the political dividends that stemmed from a nationalist language of imperial glory, Thatcher was about to lead her country in a nostalgic expedition to the far away Falklands. Meanwhile, England re-drew its boundaries to consolidate Northern Ireland as its adjoining territory while developing a more emotive rhetoric that paralyzed moves to snatch Scotland and Wales from the United Kingdom. The appeal of Thatcher's language of nationalism blended with a brand of ethnocentric populism designed to resonate with the white working classes, gave the Prime Minister an electoral majority over and over again, while opening up schisms within traditional Labour constituencies. "Skinheads," the National Front, and other grassroots racist organizations (as David Edgar portrays in his *Destiny*) emerged to limit the political coherence of the counter-hegemonic movement of previous years. Thatcher's government succeeded in breaking into the labor movement, made membership in trade unions optional even as it supported dissenting groups. "Thatcherism" came to mean a more vibrant nationalism that undermined the project of alternative theatres. By the 1980s the Arts Council that had aided the groups to achieve professional standards, had become the target of conservatives who rejected state support for allegedly subversive cultures. The collectivist management traditions of the companies came under scrutiny and were found wanting. The Arts Council began to impose strict managerial criteria mandating the operation of the organizations by boards of managers headed by an executive.

Thus, when I arrived in England in the 1980s, alternative theatre was in a state of crisis, forced back into the most limiting of inter-modernist spaces by the ravages of Thatcherism. While some companies, starved of support, disappeared, others, in the words of Clive Barker, "became gradually absorbed into the Establishment by subsidy." Under the circumstances, alternative dramatists engaged in a dialectic of accommodation and resistance that emphasized subversion from within. As Barker has written:

> What characterizes this period is a remarkable display of skill and ingenuity as playwrights and companies tried to subvert the system and exploit its advantages to create theatre which had political potency and to breakthrough to non theatre-going audiences.[10]

I was fortunate enough to witness some of these strategies in person. For, as I probed the world of England's alternative theatres, I uncovered an extraordinarily friendly and gracious network of activists who generously permitted me to tag along to rehearsals and performances in smoky pubs, community halls, abandoned churches, and school gymnasiums. My postcolonial understanding of these dramatists' treatments of clashes over power and culture in England was shaped in no small measure by these encounters. What follows are my musings on the continuities of postcolonial clashes over the boundaries of national belonging across the metropolis and its former colonies, based on dramatic works representing feminist, gay, and black perspectives.

Monstrous Regiment

A chance meeting at a 1970s' abortion rights rally in Hyde Park became the occasion for a fruitful creative collaboration between the activist writer Caryl Churchill, and a rambunctious feminist theatre company, parodically titled "Monstrous Regiment" (MR). The company had recently germinated in the radical ground laid by the "Almost Free" program of North London's Inter-Action Theatre (IAT), designed to give voice to feminist, gay, black, and other minority perspectives in the nation's capital. In 1973 – a moment of ferment in the women's movement – the Inter-Action

Theatre's advertisement of a short festival of plays written, directed, and stage managed by women, drew an enthusiastic response. It brought together professional and amateur theatre artists in a sympathetic forum to reflect on the shape and political meaning of a feminist esthetics, thereby providing organizational structure and ideological coherence to the existing efforts of women's theatre companies such as Women's Street Theatre Group and Women's Theatre Group, as well as feminist interventions within established political theatre companies such as Red Ladder.

Exchanges between some women in professional and amateur theatre circuits brought in touch by the successful IAT festival culminated in the inauguration of a theatre company later known as "Monstrous Regiment," in a basement flat in Gospel Oak, London on a cold rainy day in August 1975. From the outset, the company was imbued with a sense of social mission. According to one of its founding members, Gillian Hanna:

> We set out at the very beginning to make theatre and over the weeks and months of discussions we discovered that we were involved in something bigger than that: we wanted to change the world ... All around us, women in every area of the world we knew were doing the same thing.[11]

The name "Monstrous Regiment" was inspired by an anti-feminist diatribe authored by the Scottish Presbyterian polemicist John Knox. In an article apocalyptically titled "The First Blast of the Trumpet Against the Monstrous Regiment of Women," Knox raised the un-Godly specter of women launching an invasion against male institutions of rulership. The women's defiant appropriation of Knox's label of denunciation signaled the reformist tenor of their creative enterprise. They embraced a political and cultural mandate to critique the inequities of *internal colonization* within a feminist framework. Moreover, they saw their theatre practice as posing a challenge to social relations not only within hegemonic discourses but also within counter-hegemonic discourses like socialism and the women's movement. In particular, they strained to distinguish themselves from the adherents of what they described as "bourgeois feminism" by championing a socialist feminism that wove the strands of class and race, and gender and sexuality into a holistic vision of subjectivity.

With a majority of its original membership drawn from the Women's Movement, the International Socialists, the Communist Party, and the Labour Party, the "Monstrous Regiment" proclaimed a wide-ranging cultural agenda with an overtly political purpose:

> To produce great shows.
> To discover and encourage women writers.
> To explore a theory of feminist culture. "What is a feminist play?"

To resurrect women's "hidden history."
To give women opportunities for work especially in technical
    areas which had always been male preserves.
To put real women on the stage. No more stereotypes.
To be a consciousness-raising group.
To attempt a theory and practice of collectivity.
To find a new audience.
To explore the relationship between music and theatre.[12]

By December of the same year the company had commissioned its first play titled *Scum: Death, Destruction and Dirty Washing* written by Claire Luckham and Chris Bond, and performed all over England. The company's endeavor to use theatre to create an anti-hegemonic space for the assertion of feminist identities received an impetus from its members' fateful encounter with the writer Caryl Churchill at a London rally for reproductive freedom. There, the women of MR were able to interest and enlist Churchill in their current project – a play purporting to use the language of witchcraft to inveigh against the subjugation of women. The company devised a communitarian approach to all phases of the play's production – from collective research to workshops where lively exchanges of ideas facilitated the playwright's writing process. The result was a provocative inquiry into the structural disempowerment of female identity titled *Vinegar Tom*. This play – the second dramatic production for the company – rendered its political message in a mode of intense esthetic experimentation.

Vinegar Tom uses the seventeenth-century hysteria over witchcraft as a metaphor for twentieth-century contests over the politics of difference by collapsing time into space. Twentieth-century characters decked out in contemporary costumes enact seventeenth-century events to the tune of twentieth-century music in a cabaret narrative style. The discourse of witchcraft becomes a way of exposing and critiquing the conscription of women's identities into the sexualized project of the modern nation state. Such identities must conform to their prescribed social roles determined by biology and defined by dependency, or be cast out of the body politic. The logic of exclusion for non-conformism leads to the physical elimination of the rebel through hanging as a punishment for alleged acts of witchery or "whoring." Constructions of marriage, family, and work uphold a hierarchical and organic society not unlike the empire, by limiting women's senses of belonging and becoming to the inter-modernist fringes of heterosexual male power. In such a society, women are by definition colonized subjects, their sexuality confining the boundaries of their informal citizenship to male-contingent identities like "mother," "lover," and "daughter."

The logic of woman's received role as wife in the patriarchal empire-like nation state of contemporary England emerges in a song by the character Margery, who is married to the landowner Jack:

If everybody worked as hard as me
If our children's shirts are white
If their language is polite
If nobody stays up late at night
Oh, happy family
Oh, the country's what it is because
The family is what it is because
The wife is what she is to her man
Oh I do all I can
Yes, I do all I can
I try to do what's right
So I'll never be alone and afraid in the night
And nobody comes knocking at my door in the night
The horrors that are done will not be done to me.[13]

Like subjects in England's former colonies, Margery can only speak within the confines of a structure which she inhabits intimately, and buttresses by her role. She must speak in the very language of patriarchy that dominates her. I read *Vinegar Tom*, then, as suggesting, however implicitly, that women's bodies have historically constituted the "first colony" within which discourses of domination were perfected and enacted. Interpreted in this light, the play's feminist message becomes a stirring counter-hegemonic strategy, not only for mounting anticolonial resistance, but also for paving the way to postcolonial regeneration.

Other characters illustrate the limits of dissent, enforced by the informal sanctions of society, as well as by the formal institutions of "justice." They include Alice and Betty, both young and unmarried. Alice, the daughter of a middle-aged widow named Joan seeks male validation by wooing a potential mate. Yet, she is already stigmatized by her status as an un-married mother – a mark of sexual waywardness that violates acceptable norms of the "family." Betty, too, is in her own way a social and moral misfit. For she rejects marriage in defiance of the wishes of her family, provoking them to seek a medical diagnosis of her intransigence. Unsurprisingly, the doctor renders a physiological interpretation of Betty's act of rebellion:

> Hysteria is a woman's weakness . . . Excessive blood causes an imbal-ance in the humors. The noxious gases that form inwardly every month rise to the brain and cause behavior quite contrary to the patient's true feelings. After bleeding you must be purged.[14]

The doctor prescribes as a remedy, the procedure of leeching, to which the young woman is duly subjected. The only female character of inde-pendent means is Ellen, who as a discrete herbalist, specializes in the treatment of women's medical afflictions. Her survival depends on how well she is able to negotiate the minefields of morality laid by the church-led society she inhabits.

The fragility of these women's existence is bared by their confrontations with Margery and Jack, who see them as posing threats to their harvests and fortunes. Joan is accustomed to begging these landowners for yeast or flour, and cursing them when rebuffed. Her identity as a single woman who owns and shares a bed with her tomcat marks her out for potential persecution. Her daughter Alice, notorious for her alleged sexual promis-cuity, is likewise, an ideal candidate for ostracism. Thus, when Jack and Margery persuade the community to invite Kramer and Sprenger, professors of Theology, to investigate their suspicions of witchcraft in their midst, it is only a matter of time before Alice, Joan, and Alice's friend Susan – all unmarried women belonging to the "underclass" – are condemned to hang for their departures from the norms of their society. For their unconventional behavior ultimately violates nothing less than the integrity of the "country" that Margery celebrates in song. Betty, thanks presumably to the privilege of her class and the security of a normative family, is spared the punishment of physical extinction.

With the help of twenty-one scenes and seven songs, this one-act play underscores the continuity of women's institutionalized subordination across space. The work's rejection of the patriarchal morality anchoring the nation state embodies a plea for reconfiguring nationalism to accom-modate women as autonomous *subjects*, with identities not wholly contingent on their relationships with men or their places within the struc-ture of the heterosexual family as daughters, wives, and mothers.

I see in *Vinegar Tom*'s semiotic vocabulary of feminist dissent, a broader discourse of *difference* shaped by the new postcolonial context of English society in the 1970s. Witchcraft, given its historic association with the proscription of all kinds of peculiarities – of difference, in other words, is a particularly apt metaphor for talking about conformity and cultural pluralism as they relate to official narratives of nationhood. In the play, allegations of witchcraft become a rationale for punishing all kinds of idio-syncracies, all manner of departures from the expectations of received identities, and all *forms* of protest:

> If you float you're a witch
> If you scream you're a witch
> If you sink then you are dead anyway
> If you cure you are a witch
> Or impure you are a witch
> Whatever you do you must pay
> Fingers are pointed, a knock at the door
> You may be a mother, a child or a whore
> If you complain you are a witch.[15]

For subordinate groups, defined by race, class, and sexuality, as much as by gender and marital status, their very survival – even as informal citizens – rests on their obedience to authority, to their *place* in the imagined nation. The victims of execution in *Vinegar Tom* were after all multipositional, their crime of committing unconventional behavior exacerbated by their affiliations of class as much as by their gender. The play's feminist message, must then be understood and seen as part of the larger counter-hegemonic movement critical of a unitary national identity limited by class and ethnicity as well as by gender. Decolonization overseas, and non-European immigration to England in the latter half of the twentieth century did, after all, re-frame the context of feminist activism, and set in motion transnational exchanges of semiotic strategies for achieving independence – whether defined as personal, political, or national, as well as for promoting equity and cultural pluralism. Thus, companies like "Monstrous Regiment" shared with like-minded activists against both European imperialism and Developing World neo-colonialism, an interest in using the body as a site for enunciating subjectivity, exploring the nation state as a problematic place of belonging, and theatre as a tool for politicizing marginalized communities. For the audiences who watched *Vinegar Tom* in community centers, schools, and traditional theatre venues, the play issued a call for action against the neo-colonialism of social oppression by stressing that its victims had little to lose – presumably their very identities as subordinates marked them out for opprobrium no matter how hard they hard they tried to "fit in":

So don't drop a stitch
My poor little bitch
If you are making a spell
Do it well
Deny it you are bad
Admit it you are mad
Say nothing at all
They'll damn you to hell.[16]

Monstrous Regiment followed up the success of *Vinegar Tom* with another collaborative effort known as *Kiss and Kill*. There followed *Floorshow*, jointly written by Michelene Wandor, Caryl Churchill, Bryony Lavery, and David Bradford, and David Edgar's *Teendreams*. By the early 1980s, the company had succeeded in performing a total of nineteen plays exploring a variety of styles, venues, and audiences. The second term of Margaret Thatcher's premiership, however, did not augur well for the group. The Arts Council became more ideological in its funding strategies. Initial demands for a more corporate managerial structure to ensure what the Arts Council considered "judicious use" of its funds, undermined MR's spirit of collective ownership. It began a new managerial mode of appointing full-time administrators charged with running the company as a professional business rather than a political and ideological outfit. The group eventually broke its own ideological commitment to working exclusively in the fringe and alternative venues in 1984 when it produced *Origin of the Species* written by Bryony Lavery at the Birmingham Repertory Theatre. Such a move was a necessary reaction to cuts in its funding. Signaling the beginning of a new battle for survival, it led the company to produce *Waving* in 1988 at the Sheffield Crucible Theatre and *My Sister in This House* at the Leicester Haymarket Theatre. "Monstrous Regiment" had crossed over to the very mainstream theatre venues they had once avoided.

The gravest ideological threat to the social commitment of MR, was leveled not by its funding exigencies, however, but rather by a phenomenon known as "post-feminism." Encouraged by the small victories of women in the corporate world and mainstream politics, certain middle-class women (whom Churchill called bourgeois feminists), decried feminism as out of step with the times. As Gillian Hanna explained:

> While red-braced Porsche-driving yuppies were let loose to roam the floors of the commodities market, and successful career women were falling over themselves to deny they even knew what that nasty word "feminism" meant, what place was there for these old lady dinosaurs who would keep banging on about sisterhood and solidarity? What place was there for the word "sisterhood" itself when the cult of unrestrained individualism told us that any woman could be Prime Minister if she had the guts and worked hard enough?[17]

The company distinguished itself from the prophets of "bourgeois feminism" by continuing to uphold its brand of socialist feminism even as it shifted its productions to mainstream venues. Unfortunately, the early 1990s brought an end to the group's financial support. Yet, it remained firmly committed to its mission for as Hanna observed:

> the women's theatre companies have to keep fighting for their right to exist. Fifteen years ago, we were looking forward to the day when we could pack up and go home knowing that women's experience, women's vision, women's culture had become an acknowledged part of culture in general. Unfortunately we can't pack those cases yet.[18]

Gay Sweatshop

The house lights fade out and stage lights fade in to illuminate a Victorian piano on one side of the set and a radio perched on a small table nearby. It is 1944. The end of the Second World War is near, although the world's people may not yet know it. As the lights pick out the bodies on stage, the strains of a song titled "The Body Electric" fill the theatre. A company of men render the song to the accompaniment of a piano with a passion that suggests that they are deeply invested in the history of the song or perhaps, in the identity of the person who wrote it. The song peters out as the stage lights dim and a spotlight bathes the radio in a glow of brilliance. A voice rings out over the radio just as the speaker steps into a pool of light. It belongs to E.M. Forster, one of England's most celebrated chroniclers of empire, and author of *A Passage to India*. As the narrator, the character of Forster introduces his audience to the protagonist of the play:

> One hundred years ago on August 29th 1844, Edward Carpenter was born, and I want to talk about him. Do you know the name Edward Carpenter? It is being forgotten, partly because he was a pioneer, and his work has passed into the common stock. He was a good man, certainly an unusual one.[19]

The play is Noel Greig's *The Dear Love of Comrades*. It premiered in London in 1979 under the auspices of the alternative theatre group known as "Gay Sweatshop." It tells the story of Edward Carpenter, a prominent architect of England's socialist politics whose homosexuality excluded him from genuine formal citizenship in the very welfare state he helped craft. Carpenter was an artist as well, an activist artist whose songs and poetry championed the cause of the downtrodden of various descriptions. His character in the play observes:

> *The Times* was quite enchanted
> By his bold and witty fervor
> And made clear that it hoped
> His writing would go further
> His desire for social justice
> Was a theme to be admired
> And a subject to which many
> Striving writers had aspired.[20]

Both the play's narrator E.M. Forster, and its protagonist, Carpenter, embody the connections between anticolonialism overseas and metropolitan struggles for subaltern subjectivity at home, making them appropriate dramatic subjects for artists concerned with the postcolonial England's culture wars in the 1970s. Greig's Carpenter has lived in India and sympathizes with its independence movement, finding in Mahatma Gandhi's philosophy of non-violent resistance an especially compelling strategy for achieving democratic inclusiveness. His Indian experience shapes his opposition to English colonialism in Ireland. Yet, in the demise of imperialism, he finds hope for a new, more just, more equitable beginning in England:

England arise, the long, long night is over,
Faint in the East, behold the dawn appear;
Out of your evil dream of toil and sorrow
Arise, oh England, for the day is here.[21]

This song, at once a dirge and a celebration, goes on to become a hit in pubs and Labour Party conventions.

As in the case of E.M. Forster, Carpenter's broad, transnational vision of social justice is inextricably woven with his sexuality. He presents a perfect example of the possibilities of non-formal citizenship – the sort of coalition-building that transcends the insularity of rigid, uni-positional group identities. His sexuality becomes the medium for challenging the boundaries of race, class, and nationality. Like Forster, he loves Indian men, Bengalis in particular. He also consorts with working-class Englishmen lacking in the frills of elite culture such as the Cambridge education that Carpenter himself possesses. Moreover, such associations are founded on terms refreshingly free of the unequal power dynamics of contemporary heterosexual relationships. His sexual desires and pleasures, then, are encoded with the politics of democratic inclusiveness and cultural pluralism that inform his work as a Labour Party leader and his art as poet and song writer.

Carpenter's sexual politics serve to undermine not only hierarchies of class, race, and nationality, but those of gender as well, by redefining the social meaning of "masculinity":

> What was considered "unmanly" in polite society, was allowed by people who, I had been brought up to believe, were a lower race. Brutes and animals with no human feeling. And yet, I found love. Not an abstract notion, or an old man in the sky, but an active force. The island wasn't necessary. I knew I had to throw my lot in with them, because if a new order and vision of the world was possible, it could only start here.[22]

As the above passage suggests, Greig's Carpenter juxtaposes "polite society's" construction of manliness with its representation of humanity itself, suggesting the readiness with which such constructions lend themselves to dehumanizing *difference*. His use of the term "a lower race" deliberately obfuscates boundaries between different groups who deviate from the norm, suggesting the importance of subaltern solidarity across lines of class, sexuality, ethnicity, and nationality in the postcolonial campaign for social justice. Carpenter's character inverts the social meaning of these "deviant" identities: their value stems not from their conformity to acceptable norms of class, color, culture, or sexuality, but rather from their capacity to give and take love. It is such a reading of value, wrested from its material foundations in formal institutions of power and the heterosexual family, that makes possible an alternative vision of the universe. Carpenter "throws [his] lot" with those castigated by dominant society as "brutes" in order to realize his and, no doubt, Greig's vision of postcolonial harmony.

Given the expansive range of his concerns, it is not surprising that Carpenter should also champion women's rights with the same forthrightness with which he acknowledges his own homosexuality (and which liberates E.M. Forster from the closet). In so doing, he challenges the racialized, sexualized, gendered, and familial underpinnings of English national identity both in his own time, as well as in Greig's vastly more complex, more pluralistic, more *visibly* postcolonial world. The timeliness of his message stems in part from the overt link that he establishes between imperialistic constructions of the white man's burden vis-à-vis the "unmanly" colonized overseas on the one hand, and "polite society's" attitude toward all manner of "unmanly" deviants at home, not to mention women. That homosexual, female, and working-class identities should remain as signifiers of exclusion from the privileges of national belonging, implies the reach of domestic colonization.

The *Dear Love of Comrades* represented one of Gay Sweatshop's most interesting and broadly conceived engagements with the issue of all forms of discrimination including homophobia in 1970s' England. This new theatre company, like Monstrous Regiment, grew out of a 1974 festival organized by Ed Berman's Inter-Action "Almost Free" group in London. Designed to promote outreach work among gays, the festival featured four plays that drew enthusiastic audiences. They included *Thinking Straight* by Laurence Collinson; *Passing By* by Martin Sherman; *Limitations* by John Baker, and *Ships* by Alan Wakeman. At the outset, most of these and other works crafted against the backdrop of the gay rights movement on both sides of the Atlantic focused more narrowly on contesting homophobia than Greig's play would. England's Gay Liberation Front and New York's Stonewall, as well as the government-instituted Commission for Homosexual Equality provided the political context for their enterprise which was both esthetic and political in mission.

Gay Sweatshop, formed a full year after the Inter-Action festival as the nation's first gay theatre company, threw itself into the work of making gay identities visible as something more than "near-male," "near-female," "effeminate male," or "masculine-female" objects of derision – representations that reinforced heterosexual patriarchal dominance. According to Philip Osmet, the company was:

> set up in response not only to the way homosexuality was portrayed on stage but also to the way in which gay people working in theatre were often put in the position of colluding with those portrayals. Since its inception the company has worked to dispel the myth that theatre provides a haven for gay people.[23]

The success of the group's maiden enterprise – *Mister X* in both England and Ireland won it its first grant from the Arts Council of Great Britain. *Mister X* was as much an exercise in consciousness-raising as a critique of the sexualized limits of national belonging. According to Gay Sweatshop founding member Drew Griffiths, the play:

> was about all the ways gay people put themselves down, put obstacles in the path of their own liberation, believing all the lies that society tells about homosexuals. It was about getting rid of self oppression so that you can start fighting society's oppression.[24]

Along with another play titled *Any Woman Can* by Jill Posner – previously rejected at the Inter-Action Theatre festival – *Mister X* helped launch a festival of gay plays at London's ICA venue. The success of *Any Woman Can* also brought lesbians into Gay Sweatshop. The company not only developed its own audiences within the fringe touring circuit and community venues, but also fashioned educational programs targeting younger people in schools and youth organizations.

One of Gay Sweatshop's immediate challenges was to find authors willing to write about gay subjects, prompting questions over whether the company should commission non-gay writers to write for them. The socialist playwright Edward Bond's contribution of a play entitled *Stone* became the occasion for debating the merits of the issue in some depth. Though largely successful, the play evoked criticism for conflating the cause of gay rights with the larger goal of socialist transformation, thus ignoring the homophobia that prevailed in the organized left. Another controversy over identity stemmed from the question whether lesbians belonged in the company, and therefore involved the larger issue of the Gay Sweatshop's relationship with the women's rights movement. Although lesbians eventually separated from the company under the auspices of a common administrator, they promoted parallel goals through plays like Michelene Wandor's *Care and Control*, which publicized the institutionalized persecution of gay mothers.

Greig's work, *The Dear Love of Comrades*, commissioned and performed by Gay Sweatshop at the end of the decade addressed some of these issues of identity and focus. Although written by a gay man, the play was, as I have argued, broadly conceived to meet the challenge of a postcolonial England by advocating an equitable, pluralistic, democratic order inclusive of *all* groups left out of the narrative of "Englishness." Speaking through Carpenter, Greig used the prism of gay rights to talk about all kinds of markers of disenfranchisement – whether those stemming from class, color, or gender, besides sexuality. This expansive vision of democratic identity ensured Gay Sweatshop an enduring legacy not only in the movement for equal rights for gays, but in the culture of *all* resistance even when, by the late 1980s, its sources of funding, especially from the Arts Council, had dried up.

Black British theatre

It is early in the morning. A solitary white woman sits desolately in a damp and dark flat in East London. Wrapped in sweaters, she sits uncomfortably on a worn settee. Her curtains are pulled to avoid light as well as to keep her creditors at bay. She stares at a framed photograph as she smokes. A telephone rings and several knocks on the door follow. As she gets up and walks toward the door swearing beneath her breath, we notice a slight limp. Rose is a lonely and mostly sad woman. Her appearance and demeanor suggest an air of pessimism, a despondent lack of hope. An avid drinker and smoker, Rose's only source of excitement lies in the promise of winning money in a game of bingo with which she is obsessed. When Rose eventually opens the door, a bi-racial man walks in with an air of familiarity and fondly calls her "Mum." Such is the static, somber setting for Tunde Ikoli's play, *Scrape Off the Black*.

First performed at London's Riverside Theatre in 1981, the play portrays the lives of an Englishwoman Rose and her two hybrid sons Trevor and Andy Ikoyi. Rose's story is one of migration, displacement, and exile, not unlike the experiences of immigrants from England's former colonies who crossed several seas in pursuit of a better life. Rose has not had to travel quite that far. Many years before, she left a simple bucolic life with middle-class parents in Cornwall to explore life in cosmopolitan London. There she met and married an African immigrant from Nigeria. Two children later, Rose's husband runs afoul of the law and is sent to prison, a situation that not only subjects Rose to penury but also exposes her to racial prejudice as she had to raise two "black" children on her own. She is forced to send her sons into foster care. Twelve years later, she lives alone, divorced, bitter, still poor, and lumbered by the history of her association with an African immigrant through her children. Her older child Trevor is married to a black woman and identifies himself as black while the younger Andy has been in and out of prison. Indeed, the play is set on a day when he is released from prison. The unemployed Trevor arrives at his mother's doorstep when the play opens, partly in order to greet a younger brother he has helped raise. The banter between mother and son reveal the complex intersections between class and blackness that shape the depths of their poverty. As mother and son talk about their poverty, smoking cigarettes, tea and toasts, they are joined by Rose's friend Mary. Mary is a migrant like Rose, originally from Scotland. She crawled out of poverty by prostituting herself, before a drinking habit and her addiction to hallucinogenic pills sent her spiraling back into destitution.

The title of Tunde Ikoli's dark drama is derived from a conversation between Rose and Trevor in which she insists she would eat a brown toast even if it were burnt by simply scraping off the black. Ikoli, himself the bi-racial child of a Nigerian immigrant father and an English mother, has coyly refused to comment on his play's title. Notwithstanding the author's reticence, the provocative nature of the title invites reflection on the meanings it might encode. On one level, it suggests that blackness as a signifier is not immutable but, rather, subject to subversion. While Trevor calls himself "black," Andy insists that they are "brown." In the end, however, what matters is not whether they are "black" or "brown" but, rather, that they are not "white." Excluded from the privileges of whiteness which constitutes the prime signifier of "Englishness," and condemned by their class status, the brothers are confined to the ethnicized liminal margins of informal citizenship in the land of their birth. By the end of the play each character achieves a cathartic understanding of his or her predicament only to return to the static misery of underclass existence. For, as Paul Gilroy has suggested in *There Ain't No Black in the Union Jack*, "Black English" is a contradiction in terms. There is no question that Englishness dictated the discourse of colonial nationalism into which the English as imperial masters sought to acculturate their Afro-Asian colonized subjects, thus creating a hybrid inter-modernist landscape that limited the extent of belonging to the master "race" even as it launched anticolonial resistance. In the metropolis, however, racial purity turned English identity into a more or less closed caste. Gilroy has suggested that the semantics of "Black British," on the other hand, make concessions to a more hybrid identity by accommodating the history of empire. "Black British" is simultaneously an identity of resistance, for it shapes the grounds for asserting agency and citizenship by those who are touched by Englishness but are deprived of the right to claim it. Thus, no term signifies England's postcolonial character better than "Black British."

The postcolonial implications of the term stem in part from the variety of peoples it encompasses – becoming in effect a description of the microcosm of empire which now resides in its metropolitan center. Yet, its homogeneous construction of that very cultural diversity through the application of a unitary label, smacks of the totalizing effect of "race" on colonial discourse. The bi-polar construction of the world into colonizer and colonized, "white" and "black" appears to endure in the representation of all non-European Englishmen and women as "Black British" be they Indian, Pakistani, Bangladeshi, Nigerian, Ghanaian, South African, Jamaican, or Hong Kong Chinese. As a signifier, then, "Black British" simultaneously denotes exclusion and connotes immigrants from England's vast former empire. The occasional label "ethnic minorities," further undermined the subjectivity of the homogenized Black British, for as Kobena Mercer has argued it made the "black subject" a "minor, an abject childlike figure . . . necessary for the legitimation of paternalistic ideologies of assimilation and integration that underpinned the strategy of multiculturalism."[25] Yet, the term "ethnic minorities" also implied a coalitional politics between former colonial subjects aimed at creating a multicultural society.

Thus, by the time Ikoli's play was performed in 1981, blackness had become a more complex and fractious inter-modernist signifier. It was simultaneously used to refuse assimilation while providing the people whom it defined a platform for opposing the racialized coloniality of English national culture. It linked anticolonial nationalism with a desiring process that imagined an inclusive, equitable postcolonial England. It also implied memories of the violence of Empire would help eradicate the violence of contemporary racism. People of non-African ancestry however, took exception to the nomenclature or, rather, the stigma (as they saw it) of blackness. An intra-modernist crisis reared its head in various communities as Asians, West Indians, and Africans sought to define themselves on their own terms, in ways that took account of the uniqueness of their respective cultural heritages. While non-formal citizenship became an option for those willing to embrace a common agenda for democratic change, others clung to ethno-cultural particularisms with passion. Before long, "blackness" became a floating signifier tossed around within inter-modernist and intra-modernist landscapes. Cultural practices such as theatre and popular music became common arenas for playing out these semiotic contests.

For people of African ancestry, "blackness" promised an avenue to affirm cultural identity and group solidarity and to prescribe an agenda for progressive reform. To them, plays like *Scrape Off the Black* served as poignant reminders of the burden of history – of centuries-old slavery and colonization, and of the legacy of racism. Trevor and Andy in Ikoli's play illustrate the jeopardy of that legacy: effective exclusion from economic opportunity and social mobility, overrepresentation in the nation's prison system. The egalitarian promise of decolonization in Africa, and civil rights and pan-African movements in the United States and the Caribbean, remained largely unrealized.

In this context, Ikoli built on the pioneering works of Mustapha Matura, Norman Beatty, Yvonne Brewster, Alby James, and Bernadine Evaristo. There was, however, no definitive sense of black British theatre until companies such as Temba, Umoja, Black Theatre Co-op, Black Mime Troupe, and venues such as Talawa Arts emerged across cities with large black communities like London, Birmingham, Bristol, Liverpool, and Manchester. This dramatic tradition received an impetus from calls for black representations as a necessary component of anticolonial and human rights struggles in Africa, the United States, and the Caribbean. The companies that resulted received some funding from the Arts Council of Great Britain as well as from the more liberal regional sponsors like the Greater London Council. Companies such as Temba and Black Theatre Co-op toured the country performing plays dramatizing the experiences of black Britishness, thus complementing the portrayal of some of these themes in other forms of popular media such as music and television.

A pervasive sense of history and structural context distinguished black British drama from other forms of alternative theatre. As Kobena Mercer has argued, black themes and modes of representation centered not exclusively on "individualizing and psychologizing theories of subjectivity" but, rather, acknowledged "the contingent social and historical conditions in which new forms of collectivity and community are also brought into being as agents and subjects in the public sphere."[26] Over time, black British theatre emerged as a subject of serious scholarly inquiry, aided by the appearance of such works as Yvonne Brewster's edited three-volume collection of plays entitled *Black Plays*. I taught one of the first of such courses at King Alfred's College in Winchester in the late 1990s.

Fifteen years after that British Council reception in Bristol, I look back on my learning experiences in the worlds of England's alternative theatre with not simply gratitude, but with a certain degree of satisfaction as well. Those dramatists and artists who used their craft to fashion a language for describing and resisting the coloniality of a unitary English nationalism proved more successful than not in complicating the meaning of Englishness. Even as Margaret Thatcher's Tory Party sought to return England to an exclusionary brand of politics harking back to the days of a racialized empire, the last quarter of the twentieth century witnessed the evolution of a remarkably diverse popular culture truly reflective of the postcolonial nation England has become. The activities of dramatists such as those in Monstrous Regiment, Gay Sweatshop, and the black British companies, have opened up democratic spaces for contesting various forms of marginalization. As long as these folks persist in using their art to manufacture and sustain dissent, the future of postcolonial desires seems secure. For it is these victims of what Homi Bhabha calls "the sentence of history" – of subjugation and displacement – who offer the most compelling demonstrations of agency in the face of adversity.[27]

Conclusion

> The job facing the cultural intellectual is therefore not to accept the politics of identity as given, but to show how all representations are constructed for what purpose, by whom, and with what components.[1]

Edward Said's prescription of the cultural scholar's task has guided my efforts to interpret diverse theatrical traditions throughout this work. The march of recent international events has, however, shown Nigeria, England, as well as the world at large to be so dynamic, disconcerting, and unpredictable, that I am wary of offering a reading of contemporary conditions as they relate to the politics of representation. A few weeks after two airplanes were crashed into the World Trade Center in New York City where I now live, I found myself more disconnected from the world of my childhood than ever before, for the telephone, my single most important mode of communication with my octogenarian parents, suddenly ceased to function. When we finally made contact through the medium of a Nigerian friend's cell phone, I learned that the battles in the American theatre had spilled across the ocean into older battles in the Islamic city of Kano, where my parents still live. Old and much too committed to Kano to relocate, my Christian parents had taken refuge in a military barracks when militant religious fundamentalists – both Muslim and Christian – took to the streets of Sabon Gari in their neighborhood in order to settle old scores resuscitated by new issues arising in the world. I was told that Muslim youths wielded placards bearing photographs of Osama Bin Laden while their Christian opponents waved makeshift flags of the United States. My father, always a great storyteller with an eye for drama, offered a graphic portrayal of the terrifying real-life circus that unfolded on Kano's streets, including the one where he had lived for over sixty years. One faction, he recounted, chanted "Osama, Osama," eliciting from the other, the war cry: "USA, USA."

A year and a half later, two news items from Nigeria caught my eye. The country's Minister for Justice and its chief law officer had been assassinated in a burst of neo-colonial lawlessness. The other concerned a young woman condemned by a Sharia court in northern Nigeria to die by stoning for allegedly committing adultery. It appeared that representative democracy and electoral reform had not fulfilled the promise of either emancipation or equity after all. An overwhelming majority of Nigerians remain excluded from their share of the nation's vast resources even as the institution of a federal system of governance designed to promote regional autonomy blew the lid off old antagonisms and fueled new ones. The inter-modernist conflicts of the colonial era had yielded to a state of perpetual intra-modernist crises. The resurgence of regional rivalries and perennial economic want translated into destructive forces of ethnic and religious nationalism that pitted Muslims against Christians, the Sharia against civil law, and the North against the South. And now, a re-oriented Western modernity centered in the United States, arrayed against what supporters saw as the primitive authoritarianism and irrational impulses of militant Islam, and detractors decried as a modern-day crusade powered by imperialistic designs, gave fresh meaning to Nigeria's historic civil wars.

As Nigerians hack each other limb from limb in city after city, I look back at the themes of postcolonial liberation promised in the dramas of Wole Soyinka, Femi Osofisan, and Tess Onwueme and come to the conclusion that those impulses of freedom are locked in what my former teacher Biodun Jeyifo aptly calls a state of "arrested decolonization."[2] For those Nigerians who, like me, dreamed of a future founded on democratic non-formal citizenship, the present situation leaves little scope for optimism. The country I introduced earlier in this book as a site of overlapping modernities that afforded its dispossessed, invaluable cultural resources for developing multivocal and pluralistic identities, offers today a spectacle of bloody carnage cloaked in a new global rhetoric of religious purity and moral absolutism exacerbated by the persistence of a neo-colonial, oil export-oriented economy with little to offer its citizens. For now at least, postcolonial desires for a prosperous, inclusive, democratic society remain singularly unfulfilled.

On one level, England looks as though it offers more hope for "redemption" than Nigeria does. There is no question that the intense hybridization of contemporary English popular culture offers an unprecedented pluralistic window to English society. Yasmin Alibhai-Brown recently reported in the *New York Times* that "Bend it Like Beckham," a lighthearted romantic comedy about culture clashes in immigrant England, became "the first Britflick by a nonwhite Briton to be No. 1 on the film charts here."[3] The black British writer Zadie Smith's exuberant portrayal of the chaos and color of multiculturalism in her novel *White Teeth* inspired a television adaptation by Channel 4. In the realm of theatre, Andrew Lloyd Webber has collaborated with the Indian composer A.R. Rahman to produce a West End musical set in Bombay but embodying a blend of Western musical traditions with the esthetic styles of Bollywood. It would appear that yesterday's counter-culture has moved into the mainstream, facilitated by – among other factors – a Prime Minister's office hospitable to a hybrid definition of postcolonial national identity.

Ironically enough, the "melting pot" of English popular culture, by its very nature a product of miscegenation, sometimes obscures the deep sense of alienation that significant elements of the English citizenry feel. Nor does it always reveal the depths of class, racial, and ethnic antagonisms of the kind that recently erupted into bloody riots in working-class towns like Oldham and Leeds. Economic crises like the disappearance of factory jobs in industrial towns fuel disaffection among second-generation immigrants willing to assert their claims to formal citizenship more aggressively than their parents did. The advent of populist white supremacist movements intent on circumscribing the definition of national belonging by race has set the stage for fractious intra-modernist contests for agency among those on the margins of English society. Thus, the limiting boundaries of "Englishness" have by no means evaporated into a hybrid cloud of inclusiveness. Rather, they remain a matter of severe contest. While modern incarnations of "skinheads" seek to racialize such boundaries, some second-generation immigrants reject the notion of integration to any sense of "English" identity altogether.

In this context, the movement – some would say co-optation – of fringe cultures by the mainstream may have served to drain some of them of the political meaning and mission that originally animated their art. The decolonizing attitude of oppositional culture has sometimes mutated into ethnic celebrations of simple pleasures. Gurinder Chadha, the Indian-British director of *Bend it Like Beckham* explained that her film was popular not only because it reflected and celebrated the "mixed race nation" into which England had evolved, but also because it did not emphasize racism: "I have had white pensioners saying 'Well done, love' – saying I have shown the world they see around them, without the focus always on racism."[4] Like Chadha's film, Webber's musical deals with romance rather than with the gritty issues of immigrant or working-class alienation and race riots. While dramatic affirmations of inter-cultural mixing are necessary and good, I fear that art drained of political purpose may well leave large segments of marginalized populations voiceless and invisible, thereby ultimately arresting the progress of decolonization in the metropolis as in its former colony.

Yet, the need for a politically conscious art that transcends times and spaces remains as dire as ever. As I was bringing this book to a close, I walked past the United Nations building in midtown Manhattan one spring afternoon. That edifice, symbolizing a war-weary world's quest to forge an international forum of non-formal citizenship for settling all sorts of human crises, is of course, itself in crisis. It is no small irony that the nation in which the United Nations is headquartered – a nation once thought of as a marginal enclave of European dissidents – has, it would appear, itself become the final frontier for re-inventing the dynamics of European modernity. America's Iraqi war appears to resurrect the nationalistic adventures of imperial war in defiance of multilateralism at the very moment that the old masters of imperialism, the Europeans, seem intent upon breaking down the barriers of national boundaries and identities. Edward Said captured the transcendent nature of imperialism and its antagonists thus:

> So vast and yet so detailed is imperialism as an experience with crucial dimensions, that we must speak of overlapping territories, intertwined histories common to men and women, whites and non-whites, dwellers in the metropolis and on the peripheries, past as well as present and future; these territories and histories can only be seen from the perspective of the whole secular human history.[5]

The international scope of opposition to the Iraqi war – embracing diverse constituencies both within and without the United States – highlights not only a dramatic tension between the state and a substantial proportion of the people who define it, but also the viability of non-formal global coalitions. In this context, theatre can use its textuality to fragment fundamentalist concepts of nation, identity, and community, thus disabling the forces of cultural chauvinism, and facilitating the creation of universalist coalitions of fluid, non-formal identities, united in their quest for subjectivity and social justice, freedom and cultural pluralism, in other words, their quest for *postcoloniality*. For as I have argued throughout this book, colonialism, anticolonialism, neo-colonialism, and postcolonialism represent significant moments of exchange, of overlaps between and within the modernities that link communities and people together.

I conceptualize "postcolonial" as a vision and resource of hope in the face of domination, and hold that those cultural practices that textualize such hope have touched and altered the cultures of environments in which they operate. The "hope" implied in my notion of "postcolonial desires" is both an act of refusal and an affirmation. It refuses to adopt fatalism and hopelessness in the face of corruptions of humanity by mechanisms of nation states and the modernities they thematize and sustain. What "hope" affirms on the other hand, is the impulse to find modes of articulating subjectivity and democratic citizenship regardless of the barricades cultural and political crises place in our way. Such affirmation is existentially imperative for producers of culture who must confront and use it to imagine and practice perpetual decolonization of our minds, places, and histories. As Paulo Freire has observed:

> Without a minimum of hope, we cannot so much as start the struggle. But without the struggle, hope as an ontological need, dissipates, loses its bearings, and turns into hopelessness. And hopelessness can become tragic despair. Hence the need for a kind of education in hope.[6]

The challenge for theatre in the twenty-first century consists in articulating a postcolonial politics of representation of the global crises that confront us, of translating an emerging internationalist civic consciousness into constructive discourses of decolonization and democratic citizenship.

Notes

Introduction: from colonial modernity to postcolonial desires

1 Smith, B.S. *Recollections of British Administration in the Cameroon and Northern Nigeria 1921–1957 "But Always As Friends,"* Durham: Duke University Press, 1969. Tafawa Balewa – an opponent of independence whom the British ensured would be the first Prime Minister in an independent Nigeria, apparently gave the tribute from which the sub-title to this colonial administrator's book is derived. The tribute reads: "We are grateful to the British officers whom we have known, first as masters and then as leaders, and finally, as partners but always as friends." He and his wife Margaret Perham Smith lived at my childhood home at Dawaki Road in Nassarawa, Kano.

2 Volosinov, V.N. *Marxism and the Philosophy of Language*, New York: Seminar Press, 1973, p. 23.

3 See Diakhate, O. and Eyoh, H. "Of Inner Roots and External Adjuncts" in Rubin, D., Diakhate, O., and Eyoh, H. (eds) *World Encyclopedia of Contemporary Theatre: Africa*, Volume 3, London: Routledge, 2001.

4 Tiffin, C. and Lawson, A. (eds) *De-scribing Empire: Post-colonialism and Textuality*, London: Routledge, 1994, p. 3.

5 Ibid.

6 Bhabha, H. "Signs Taken for Wonders: Questions of Ambivalence and Authority under a Tree Outside Delhi, May 1817" *Critical Inquiry*, 12 (1), 1985, p. 154.

7 Bhabha, H. *The Location of Culture*, London: Routledge, 1994, p. 25.

8 Appiah, A. *In My Father's House*, Oxford: Oxford University Press, 1992, p. 28.

9 Nkrumah, K. *Neo-colonialism: The Last Stage of Imperialism*, London: Thomas Nelson and Sons, 1965, p. xi.

10 Young, R. *Colonial Desire*, London: Routledge, 1995, pp. 159–182.

11 Kiberd, D. *Inventing Ireland*, Cambridge: Harvard University Press, 1996, p. 6.

12 See my essay "Colonial Anxieties and Postcolonial Desires" in Goodman, L. and DeGuy, J. (eds) *The Routledge Reader in Politics and Performance*, London: Routledge, 2000.

13 Deleuze, G. and Guattari, F. *Anti-Oedipus: Capitalism and Schizophrenia*, Volume 1, 1972, (trans. Hurley, R., Seem, M., and Lane, H.), New York: Viking Books.

14 Young, R. *White Mythologies: Writing History and the West*, London: Routledge, 1990, p. 174.

1 Wole Soyinka: theatre, mythology, and political activism

1 Soyinka, W. *Death and the King's Horseman* in Worthen, W. (ed.) *The HBJ Anthology of Drama*, New York: Harcourt Brace Publishers, 1993 (my italics for emphasis).
2 Like Augusto Boal in his *Theater of the Oppressed*, I interpret Aristotle's schema on "Tragedy" as a call to ideological adherence to the dominant culture, in his case a romantic backward glance to the Golden Age of Athens. The cathartic essence of Tragedy through the purgation of emotions of "pity" and "fear" is a poignant moment of soliciting audience identification with the play and ritual's ideology.
3 Dirks, N. (ed.) *Colonialism and Culture*, Ann Arbor: University of Michigan Press, 1992, p. 10.
4 Soyinka, W. *Myth, Literature and the African World*, Cambridge: Cambridge University Press, 1976, pp. x–xi.
5 Ibid., p. ix.
6 Soyinka, W. *Idanre and Other Poems*, New York: Hill and Wang Publishers, 1968, p. 83.
7 Fanon, F. cited in Bhabha, H. "Remembering Fanon: Self, Psyche and the Colonial Condition" in Williams, L. and Williams, P. (eds) *Colonial Discourse and Postcolonial Theory*, Hemel Hempstead: Harvester Wheatsheaf, 1993, p. 113.
8 Soyinka, W. *Myth, Literature and the African World*, p. 146.
9 This means those who have to commit customary suicide after the king's death. They are usually buried with the king.
10 There are conflicting dates for the actual incident – 1944, 1946, and 1947 are often cited. I find James Gibbs's date 1944 more reliable only because of his astute sleuthness on matters of historical detail. This can be found in his *Wole Soyinka*, Basingstoke: Macmillan, 1989.
11 Soyinka, W. *Death and the King's Horseman* in Worthen, W. (ed.) *The HBJ Anthology of Drama*, New York: Harcourt Brace Publishers, 1993, p. 822.
12 Ibid.
13 Ibid.
14 Ibid., p. 822.
15 See Olaniyan, T. *Scars of Conquest, Masks of Resistance*, Oxford: Oxford University Press, 1995.
16 Soyinka, W. *Death and the King's Horseman*, p. 826.
17 Ibid., p. 833.
18 Dirks, N. *Colonialism and Culture*, Ann Arbor: University of Michigan Press, 1996, p. 8.
19 Soyinka, W. *Death and the King's Horseman*, p. 834.
20 Ibid., p. 838.
21 Callaway, H. *Gender, Culture and Empire: European Women in Colonial Nigeria*, Urbana-Champaign: University of Illinois Press, 1987, p. 57.
22 Bradley, K. *Once a District Officer*, London: Macmillan, 1966, p. 15.
23 Perham, M. *Lugard: The Years of Authority 1898–1945*, London: Collins Publishers, 1960, p. 52.
24 Soyinka, W. *Death and the King's Horseman*, p. 840.
25 Ibid., p. 839.
26 Ibid., p. 839.
27 Fanon, F. *Black Skin, White Masks*, New York: Grove Press, 1967, pp. 110–112.
28 Ibid., p. 218.
29 Olaniyan, T. *Scars of Conquest, Masks of Resistance*, p. 58.
30 See Stoler, A. "Carnal Knowledge and Imperial Power" in *Race and the Education of Desire: Foucault's History of Sexuality and the Colonial Order of Things*, Durham: Duke University Press, 1995.

31 Callaway, H. *Gender, Culture and Empire: European Women in Colonial Nigeria*, pp. 4–5.
32 Bradley, E. *Dearest Priscilla: Letters to the Wife of a Colonial Civil Servant*, London: Max Parrish Publishers, 1950, pp. 119–120.
33 Volosinov, V. *Marxism and the Philosophy of Language*.
34 Ibid., p. 23.
35 Hall, S. "On Postmodernism and Articulation" in Morley, D. and Chen, K. (eds) *Stuart Hall: Critical Dialogues in Cultural Studies*, London: Routledge, 1996, p. 141.
36 Bhabha, H. *The Location of Culture*, p. 25.
37 See Soyinka, W. Preface to *The Bacchae of Euripides*, London: Methuen, 1975.
38 Jeyifo, B. "Introduction" in Soyinka, W. *Art, Dialogue and Outrage*, Ibadan: New Horn Press, 1986, p. xx.
39 Soyinka, W. *Myth, Literature and the African World*, appendix.
40 Ibid., pp. 147–148.
41 Ibid., pp. 38–39.
42 Ibid., p. 179.
43 See Chinweizu, Jemie, O., and Madubuike, I. *Towards the Decolonization of African Literature*, Enugu: Fourth Dimension Publishing, 1980.
44 Hall, S. "On Postmodernism and Articulation" in Morely, D. and Chen, K. (eds) *Stuart Hall: Critical Dialogues in Cultural Studies*, London: Routledge, 1996, p. 145.

2　Femi Osofisan: theatre, nation, and the revolutionary ideal

1 Osofisan, F. "'The Revolution as Muse': Drama as Surreptitious Insurrection in a Postcolonial, Military State" in Boone, R. and Plastow, J. (eds) *Theatre Matters: Performance and Culture on the World Stage*, Cambridge: Cambridge University Press, 1998, p. 11.
2 Fanon, F. *The Wretched of the Earth*, New York: Grove Press, 1963, p. 250.
3 Osofisan, F. "'The Revolution as Muse': Drama as Surreptitious Insurrection in a Postcolonial, Military State," p. 15.
4 Ibid.
5 Osofisan, F. "Do the Humanities Humanise?: A Dramatist's Encounter with Anarchy and the Nigerian Intellectual Culture." Faculty of Arts Lecture, Ibadan: University of Ibadan, January 9, 1981, p. 5.
6 Osofisan, F. "The Alternative Tradition: A Survey of Nigerian Literature After the War" in Gerard, A. (ed.) *European Language Writing in Sub-Saharan Africa*, Volume 2, Budapest: Akademiai Kiado, 1986, p. 783.
7 Osofisan, F. "Beyond Translation," Ile-Ife: Ife Monograph Series, No. 1, 1985, p. 185.
8 Richards, S. *Ancient Songs Set Ablaze: The Theatre of Femi Osofisan*, Washington: Howard University Press, 1996.
9 Osofisan, F. *Once Upon Four Robbers*, Ibadan: Heinemann Educational Books, 1991, p. 98.
10 Osofisan, F. "'The Revolution as Muse': Drama as Surreptitious Insurrection in a Postcolonial, Military State," p. 21.
11 Ibid., p. 30.
12 Osofisan, F. *Once Upon Four Robbers*, p. 84.
13 Ibid., pp. 39–40.
14 Osofisan, F. "'The Revolution as Muse': Drama as Surreptitious Insurrection in a Postcolonial, Military State," p. 11.
15 Ogungbade, A. "Vision and the Artist: The Dramaturgy of Femi Osofisan," unpublished MA thesis, Ibadan: University of Ibadan, 1983, p. 33.

16 Osofisan, F. "'The Revolution as Muse': Drama as Surreptitious Insurrection in a Postcolonial, Military State," p. 18.

17 Osofisan, F. *Once Upon Four Robbers*, p. 53.

18 Gordon, L. *Fanon and the Crisis of European Man: An Essay on Philosophy and the Human Sciences*, New York: Routledge, 1995, p. 50.

19 Spivak, G. "The Making of Americans, the Teaching of English, the Future of Colonial Studies" *New Literary History*, 21 (4), 1990, p. 28.

20 Osofisan, F. *Once Upon Four Robbers*, p. 51.

21 Ibid., p. 81.

22 Osofisan, F. "Warriors of a Failed Utopia?: West African Writers Since the 1970s II," Lagos: *Post Express Newspaper*, November 8, 1997.

23 Ibid.

24 Ibid.

25 Garuba, H. "*The Album of the Midnight Blackout* and the Aesthetics of Levity," Lagos: *Post Express Newspaper*, July 26, 1997.

3 Tess Onwueme: theatre, gender, and power

1 Onwueme, T. *Three Plays: The Broken Calabash, Parables for a Season and the Reign of Wazobia*, Detroit: Wayne State University Press, 1993, p. 166.

2 Ibid., p. 148.

3 Jeyifo, B. "Wole Soyinka and the Tropes of Disalienation" in Soyinka, W. *Art, Dialogue and Outrage*, pp. vix–xxx.

4 Radakrishnan, R. "Nationalism, Gender and the Narrative of Identity" p. 78 in Parker, A., Russo, M., Summer, D., and Yaeger, P. (eds) *Nationalisms and Sexualities*, New York: Routledge, 1992, pp. 77–95.

5 Onwueme, T.O. "Buried in the Rubble: The Missing Face in African Literature" keynote address at the 28th Annual African Literature Association (ALA) Convention, San Diego, California, April 5, 2002.

6 *The Reign of Wazobia* in Onwueme, T.O. *Three Plays*, p. 126.

7 Ibid., p. 127.

8 By this I mean the patriarchal gaze through which women's bodies are only imagined and seen as lovers, daughters, and mothers thereby denying women agency by barricading femininity within these frames. As expected colonial nationalism focused on masculinity as the identity that must be colonially castrated, refined, and dominated while assuming women's ontological marginality as identities they expect colonized men to "control."

9 Onwueme, T. *The Reign of Wazobia*, p. 131.

10 Ibid., p. 135.

11 Ibid., pp. 142–143.

12 Ashcroft, B. "EXCESS: Post-colonialism and the Verandahs of Meaning" in Tiffin, C. and Lawson, A. *De-scribing Empire: Post-colonialism and Textuality*, London: Routledge, 1994, p. 38.

13 Onwueme, T. *The Reign of Wazobia*, p. 146.

14 Ibid., pp. 155.

15 Ibid., p. 157.

16 Ibid.

17 Ibid., p. 175.

18 Loomba, A. *Colonialism/Postcolonialism*, London: Routledge, 1998, p. 222.

19 Ebogu, A. "Feminism and the Mediation of the Mythic in Three Plays by Tess Onwueme" *The Literary Griot*, 3 (1), Spring 1991, pp. 97–111.

20 Onwueme, T. *The Reign of Wazobia*, p. 128.

21 Ibid., p. 140.

22 Ibid., p. 169.
23 There are contending narratives on indigenous political and cultural institutions among the Igbos. Neither Onwueme nor any other playwright focuses on the authenticity of such historical accuracies. Rather, they use history as dramaturgic resource. The argument suggesting the inauthenticity of monarchies among the Igbos is proposed by Onwuejeogwu, M. *Evolutionary Trends in the History of the Igbo Civilization in the Culture Theatre of Igboland in Southern Nigeria*, Owerri: Ministry of Culture, Youths and Sports, 1987, p. 34.
24 I directed a film version of the play titled *Wazobia!* in 2002. It was produced by Tess Onwueme.

4 The Yoruba Traveling Theatres: popular theatre and desires for postcolonial subjectivity

1 Jeyifo, B. *The Yoruba Popular Traveling Theatre of Nigeria*, Lagos: Nigeria magazine, 1984, p. 1.
2 Mabogunje, A. "The Land and Peoples of West Africa" in Ajayi, J.F.A. and Crowder, M. *History of West Africa*, London: Longman Publishers, 1971.
3 Jeyifo, B. *The Yoruba Traveling Theatre of Nigeria*, p. 16.
4 Ibid., p. 9.
5 In 1968 the Institute of African Studies at the University of Ife (now Obafemi Awolowo University) set up a novel idea of creating a forum for interacting performers from such non-literary traditions as Yoruba Traveling Theatre and university-trained performers. In an effort to also attract a similar mix of audiences, it built a theatre-in-the-round structure in Ife town far away from the campus. Under the direction of its original preceptor Ola Rotimi, the group of performers from indigenous traditions was called "Ori-Olokun." The center was similarly named "Ori-Olokun Centre." By 1975, the University dissolved the Institute of African Studies and the members of the center were relocated to the Department of Dramatic Arts in a new outfit called "UNIFE Theatre." Wole Soyinka wrote and directed his plays *Death and the King's Horseman*, *Opera Wonyosi*, *Requiem for a Futurologist*, and various political skits for this company. He also directed them in such plays as *Biko's Inquest*.
6 See Adedeji, J. *The Alarinjo Theatre: A Study of Yoruba Theatrical Art From its Earliest Beginnings to the Present Times*, unpublished Ph.D. thesis, University of Ibadan, 1969.
7 Adedeji, J. "Alarinjo: The Traditional Yoruba Theatre" in Ogunba, O. and Irele, A. (eds) *Theatre in Africa*, Ibadan: Ibadan University Press, 1978.
8 Adelugba, D. *Nationalism and the Awakening of the National Theatre of Nigeria*, unpublished MA thesis, University of North Carolina, 1968.
9 See Adedeji, J. "Alarinjo: The Traditional Yoruba Theatre."
10 Clark, E. *Hubert Ogunde: The Making of the Nigerian Theatre*, Lagos: Oxford University Press, 1979; Owomoyela, O. "Folklore and Yoruba Theatre" *Research in African Literature*, 2 (2), Ibadan: University of Ibadan, 1977.
11 See Adeyemi, M. *Iwe Itan Oyo-Ile ati Oyo Isisiyi abi Ago-d'Oyo*, Ibadan: Colonial Office, 1914; Johnson, S. in Johnson, O. *The History of the Yorubas*, London: Routledge and Sons Ltd., 1921 and 1966; Law, R. *The Oyo Empire (c.1600–c.1836): A West African Imperialism in the Era of the Atlantic Slave Trade*, Oxford: Oxford University Press, 1977.
12 See Adedeji, J. "Alarinjo: The Traditional Yoruba Theatre."
13 See Adedeji, J. "A Yoruba Theatrical Performance" *Research in African Literatures*, 2, Ibadan, 1971.
14 Freed slaves from North America founded Liberia in 1821 and began settling in large numbers from 1822 through a repatriation scheme by the American

Colonization Society. Through trade and other movements they began to settle in other West African cities including Lagos. Other freed slaves from Brazil settled in Lagos. These immigrant groups brought diverse cultural practices with them to the coastal cities.

15 By 1884 the German chancellor Bismarck, at the behest of Portugal, called a meeting among 14 European nations to make decisions on how to map out zones of resources in Africa. The meeting took place through December 1884 to January 1885. Austria-Hungary, Belgium, Denmark, Holland, Portugal, Russia, Spain, Sweden-Norway, Turkey, and the United States were represented at the conference. Britain's ambition was to own an area spanning Cairo in Egypt to the Cape of Good Hope in South Africa. It had Ghana, Nigeria, Gambia, and Sierra Leone in West Africa. France had the largest part of West Africa while Portugal took Angola and Mozambique, Italy decided on Somalia and parts of Ethiopia, Germany had Cameroon, Namibia, and Tangayika, and Spain the Equatorial Guinea.

16 See Soyinka, W. *Myth, Literature and the African World.*

17 See Echeruo, M. "Concert and Theatre in Late Nineteenth Century Lagos" in Ogunbiyi, Y. *Drama and Theatre in Nigeria: A Critical Sourcebook*, Lagos: Nigerian Magazine, 1981, pp. 357–369; Olusanya, G. *The Second World War and Politics in Nigeria (1939–53)*, Lagos: University of Lagos/Evans Brothers Publishers, 1973; and Coleman, J. *Nigeria: Background to Nationalism*, Berkeley: University of California Press, 1958.

18 Nkemdirim, B.A. *Social Change and Political Violence in Colonial Nigeria*, London: Arthur Stockwell Ltd., 1975.

19 Barber, K., Collins, J., and Ricard, A. *West African Popular Theatre*, Bloomington: Indiana University Press, 1997, p. 4.

20 Jeyifo, B. *The Yoruba Popular Traveling Theatre of Nigeria*, p. 121.

21 Barber, K., Collins, J., and Ricard, A. *West African Popular Theatre*, p. 4.

22 Ogunde, Hubert *The Daily Comet*, March 12, 1947.

23 Clark, E. *Hubert Ogunde: The Making of Nigerian Theatre.*

24 *Daily Service*, April 25, 1947.

25 Ibid.

26 See Clark, E. *Hubert Ogunde: The Making of Nigerian Theatre.*

27 Ibid., p. 31.

28 Excerpts from the play are taken from Clark, E. "The Hubert Ogunde Theatre Company", MA thesis, Department of English, Leeds University, Leeds, 1974, pp. 257–259.

29 Ibid., p. 262.

30 Ibid., p. 257.

31 Clark, E. *Hubert Ogunde: The Making of Nigerian Theatre*, p. 83.

32 Fanon, F. *The Wretched of the Earth*, p. 33.

33 Coleman, J. *Nigeria: Background to Nationalism*, pp. 258–259.

34 House of Representatives Debates: Official Report, Federation of Nigeria, Volume II, Session 1957–58: pp. 728–739.

35 See Barber, K., Collins, J., and Ricard, A. *West African Popular Theatre*, and Kerr, D. *African Popular Theatre: From Pre-colonial Times to the Present Day*, Portsmouth: Heinemann/James Curry, 1995.

36 Nkemdirim, B.A. *Social Change and Political Violence in Colonial Nigeria*, p. 50.

37 Ibid., p. 42.

38 See Ajayi, J.A. and Crowder, M. *The History of West Africa*; Adeyemi, M. *Iwe Itan Oyo-Ile ati Oyo Isisiyi abi Ago-d'Oyo*; Johnson, S. in Johnson, O. *The History of the Yorubas*; Law, R. *The Oyo Empire (c.1600–c.1836): A West African Imperialism in the Era of the Atlantic Slave Trade.*

39 Jeyifo, B. *The Yoruba Traveling Theatre*, p. 123.
40 Bhabha, H. *The Location of Culture*, p. 241.

5 Theatre, democracy, and community development: Ahmadu Bello University and the Nigerian Popular Theatre Alliance

1 Etherton, M. "Popular Theatre for Change: From Literacy to Oracy" *Media Development*, journal of WACC, XXXV (3), 1988, London: World Association for Christian Communication publications, p. 2.

2 Kidd, R. *The Popular Performing Arts, Non-formal Education and Social Change in the Third World: A Bibliography and Review Essay*, The Hague: Centre for the Study of Education in Developing Countries, 1982, p. 2.

3 As in other African countries, Nigerian universities in the 1970s became hotbeds for radical political activism and advocacy against neo-colonial governments, particularly military dictatorships. Left-wing politics permeated scholarship, particularly the humanities' questioning of a social reality that was spectacularly inequitable. Ahmadu Bello University was at the center of such radicalism in Nigeria. Its academic staff and student unions were constantly at the forefront of regional and national protests. Despite the oil boom of the period, workers in urban centers and peasants in rural communities experienced the most oppressive social reality. The drama work was based at the Faculty of Arts and Social Sciences, which developed a reputation for its diverse socialist approaches to education, civility, and democratic rights. Scholars such as Bala Usman, Abubakar Sokoto, Mahmud Tukur, S. Kwungwai, and international left-wing intellectuals like Bjorn Beckman, Okello Oculi, Yusuf Bangura, and Patrick Wilmot had developed vibrant theories and practices articulating colonial and postcolonial reality in Africa and the Third World. Despite intense socialist activities in the faculty, it will be too simplistic to assume the kinds of theatre produced are socialist. Rather, it provided a forum for various political attitudes among staff, students, and community members with a common focus on engendering democracy and subjectivity.

4 Abah, O.S. *Performing Life: Case Studies in the Practice of Theatre for Development*, Zaria: Klobal Communication Systems, 1997.

5 Freire, P. *Education: The Practice of Freedom, Writers and Readers Co-operative*, London, 1976 and Maguerez, C. *La Promotion Technique du Travailleur Analphabete*, Paris: Editions Eyrolles, 1966.

6 Etherton, M. "Popular Theatre for Change: From Literacy to Oracy," p. 3.

7 See Boal, A. *Theatre of the Oppressed*, Theatre Communication Group, New York, 1979; Freire, P. *Education: The Practice of Freedom, Writers and Readers Co-operative*; Constantino, R. *Neo-colonial Identity and Counter-consciousness: Essays on Cultural Decolonization*, London: Merlin Press, 1978.

8 A typical project involves first-year students spending an initial three to four weeks in a "participatory observation" exercise, during which they study the community in relation to their newly adopted one in the university. Data derived from the research is used in an open-ended performance involving and inviting audience participation. The performance text is itself an index of the students' own development. In taking theatre to the community, they expose their own fears, conceptions, and misconceptions of the community. Long hours of dialogue follow up such presentations.

In the second year, students go beyond taking theatre to the people by creating theatre with such people. Spending weeks with a base group and non-government development agencies, they research social issues affecting structural underdevelopment and use performances to entertain while communicating such issues. Successes at this level of the course have laid the foundation for the networks referred to earlier as ZAPTA and NPTA. This course is pursued simultaneously with studies in literary drama and, in most cases, students subject the plays developed to literary interpretation. By the third year, students create projects for specific communities and most of these emphasize the students' skill in literary and non-literary theatrical traditions. At this stage, they have a choice of specializing in children's theatre, directing, or acting with a community focus.

9 A record of this project is derived from video recordings of the rehearsals and performance. My class journal provides additional information on the process.

10 Jenkeri Okwori played Sauna, I played Dauda, and Jummai Ewu helped develop improvised scenarios. Jenkeri Okwori still teaches Community Drama at Ahmadu Bello University in Zaria, Jummai Ewu teaches Drama at Nene University College in Northampton, England.

11 A record of this project is derived from journals my students and I kept.

12 A title bestowed on Muslims who have fulfilled the obligation of pilgrimage to Mecca in Saudi Arabia. The feminine version is "Alhaja" or "Hajia."

13 Nigerian Popular Theatre Alliance Mission Document, Zaria, 1989, p. 1.

14 Etherton, M. "Popular Theatre for Change: From Literacy to Oracy," p. 3.

15 Abah, O. and Mike, C. *Theatre for Development Reports: Whispering Springs, Badagary,* 1995, p. 12.

16 Ibid., p. 11.

17 *Theatre Outreach Reports: April–December 1991/January–June 1992,* Lagos, p. 27.

18 *A Report on the Use of Drama for EPI: The Ojo Local Government Experience 18th–27th January 1993,* Performance Studio Workshop and Collective Artistes for the Performing Arts, p. 1.

19 Ibid., p. 10.

20 Project SISTER HELP brochure, Performance Studio Workshop, Lagos, 1997, p. 1.

21 Desai, G. "Research Resources on Popular Theatre and Development in Africa" in Eyoh, H.N. *Beyond The Theatre,* Bonn: German Foundation for International Development Education, Science and Documentation, 1991, p. 179.

6 John Arden: dramatizing the colonial nation

1 See dedication to Arden, J. and D'Arcy, M. *The Island of the Mighty,* London: Eyre Methuen, 1973, p. 1.

2 Arden, J. *Encore,* 20, May/June, 1959, pp. 41–43.

3 Some of their co-authored plays are *The Happy Haven, Ars Longa, Vita Brevis, Friday's Hiding, Soldier, Soldier, The Royal Pardon, Harold Muggins is a Martyr, The Hero Rises Up, The Ballygombeen Bequest, The Island of the Mighty, The Non-Stop Connolly Show, The Little Gray Home in the West, Vandaleur's Folly, The Manchester Enthusiasts,* and *Whose Is the Kingdom?*

4 Arden, J. "Telling a True Tale" in Marowitz, C. (ed.) *The Encore Reader,* London: Methuen, 1965, p. 128.

5 Lugard, F. *The Dual Mandate in British Tropical Africa,* Edinburgh: Blackwood Press, 1922, pp. 618–619.

6 Arden cited in Page, M. *Arden on File,* London: Methuen, 1985, p. 22.

7 Guha, R. "On Some Aspects of the Historiography of Colonial India" in Guha, R. (ed.) *Subaltern Studies,* Volume 1, New Delhi: Oxford University Press, 1982, pp. 1–8.

8 Arden, J. *Plays One,* New York: Grove Press, 1978, p. 43 (my emphasis in italics).

9 Ibid., p. 39.

10 Ibid., p. 36.

11 Ibid., p. 42.
12 Ibid., p. 108.
13 Ibid., p. 108.
14 *Sunday Times*, October 25, 1959.
15 Bryden, R. *The Unfinished Hero*, London: Faber, 1969, pp. 98–99.
16 Eric Keown, "At the Play", *Punch*, October 28, 1959.
17 Hall, S. in Hall, S. and Jefferson, T. (eds) *Resistance Through Rituals*, London: Routledge, 1991, p. 44.
18 Hall, S. "On Postmodernism and Articulation: an Interview with Stuart Hall" in Grossberg, L. (ed.) *Journal of Communication Inquiry*, 10 (2), 1986, p. 53 (emphasis mine).
19 See Chapters 1 and 2 on Wole Soyinka's *Death and the King's Horseman* and Femi Osofisan's *Once Upon Four Robbers* respectively.
20 Arden, J. *Plays One*, p. 20.
21 Ibid., p. 21.

7   David Edgar: the nation's theatre and its anticolonial scribe

1 David Edgar cited in Swain, E. *David Edgar: Playwright and Politician*, New York: Peter Lang Publishers, 1986, p. 335.
2 Edgar, D. *Destiny*, London: Methuen, 1988, p. 317.
3 Spivak, G. "Three Women's Text and a Critique of Imperialism" *Critical Inquiry*, 12 (1), 1985, p. 243.
4 Edgar in Itzin, C. *Stages in the Revolution*, London: Methuen, 1980, p. 139.
5 Cited in Peacock, D.K. *Thatcher's Theatre*, Westport: Greenwood Press, 1999, p. 2.
6 Edgar in Itzin, C. *Stages in the Revolution*, p. 146.
7 Edgar, D. "Ten Years of Political Theatre" *Theatre Quarterly*, 32, Winter 1979, p. 27.
8 Edgar in Itzin, C. *Stages in the Revolution*, p. 140.
9 Ibid., pp. 140–141.
10 Ibid., p. 143.
11 Ibid., p. 143.
12 Bull, J. *New British Political Dramatists*, London and Basingstoke: Macmillan, 1984, pp. 151–194.
13 Margaret Thatcher cited in Kavanagh, D. *Thatcherism and British Politics: The End of Consensus?* Oxford: Oxford University Press, 1987, p. 247.
14 Cited in Itzin, C. *Stages in the Revolution*, p. 146.
15 Ibid., pp. 144–145.
16 Dirks, N. (ed.) *Colonialism and Culture*, p. 3.
17 Edgar, D. *Destiny*, p. 327.
18 In Derrida, J. *Writing and Difference* (trans. Bass, A.) London: Routledge and Kegan Paul, 1978.
19 See Bhabha, H. *The Location of Culture*.
20 See Hazewell, C.C. "The Indian Revolt" *The Atlantic Monthly*, December 1857. Also online at http://www.theatlantic.com/issues/1857dec.revolt.htm
21 Edgar, D. *Destiny* p. 324.
22 Ibid., p. 330.
23 Ibid., p. 331.
24 Ibid., p. 345.
25 Ibid., p. 333.
26 Ibid., p. 336.

27 Ibid., p. 344.
28 Renan, E. "What is a Nation?" (trans. Thom, M.) in Bhabha, H. (ed.) *Nation and Narration*, London: Routledge, 1990, p. 19.
29 Anderson, B. *Imagined Communities: Reflections on the Origin and Spread of Nationalism*, New York: Verso Press, 1991, pp. 6–7.
30 Edgar, D. *Destiny*, p. 346.
31 Ibid., p. 354.
32 Ibid., p. 355.
33 Ibid., p. 356.
34 Ibid., p. 391.
35 Ibid., pp. 366–367.
36 Ibid., p. 378.
37 Ibid., p. 404.
38 Edgar, D. "Towards a Theatre of Dynamic Ambiguities" *Theatre Quarterly*, 9 (33), Spring 1979, p. 15.

8 Caryl Churchill: decolonizing the nation through gender and class

1 Churchill, C. *Cloud 9*, London: Pluto Press, 1979, p. 3.
2 Caryl Churchill interview with John Simon in "Sex, Politics, and Other Play Things," *Vogue*, August 1983, p. 126.
3 Bull, J. *New British Political Dramatists*, New York: Grove Press, 1983, p. 1.
4 Case, Sue-Ellen and Forte, Jeanie K. "From Formalism to Feminism" *Theatre*, 16, 1985, p. 65.
5 Michelene Wandor in "Free Collective Bargaining" *Time Out*, March 30–April 4, 1979, p. 14.
6 Caryl Churchill interview with Geraldine Cousin in "The Common Imagination and the Individual Voice" *New Theatre Quarterly*, IV (13), February 1988, p. 4.
7 Hanna, G. *Monstrous Regiment: A Collective Celebration*, London: Nick Hern Publishers, 1991, pp. xxvi–xxix.
8 Ibid.
9 Caryl Churchill interview with Lynne Truss in *Plays and Players*, January 1984, p. 8.
10 Churchill cited in Aston, E. *Caryl Churchill*, Plymouth: Northcote House Publishers, 1997, p. 37.
11 Churchill interview with Jackie Kay in *New Statesman and Society*, April 21, 1989, p. 41.
12 Churchill, C. *Cloud 9*, p. 3.
13 Ibid., p. 4.
14 Ibid.
15 Aston, E. *Caryl Churchill*, p. 80.
16 Churchill, C. *Cloud 9*, p. 4.
17 Aston, E. *Caryl Churchill*, p. 32.
18 Churchill, C. *Cloud 9*, p. 44.
19 Ibid., p. 23.
20 Ibid., p. 51.
21 Ibid., p. 52.
22 Ibid., p. 38.
23 See my Introduction to this book.
24 Tiffin, C. and Lawson, A. (eds) *De-scribing Empire: Post-colonialism and Textuality*, London: Routledge, 1994, p. 6.

25 Cited in "Narratives of Nationalism: Being British" in Carter, E., Donald, J., and Squires, J. (eds) *Space and Place: Theories of Identity and Location*, London: Lawrence and Wishart, 1993, p. 145.
26 Churchill, C. *Cloud 9*, p. 17.
27 Ibid., p. 91.
28 Ibid., p. 81.
29 Ibid., pp. 81–82.
30 Ibid., p. 83.
31 Ibid., p. 92.
32 Ibid., p. 99.
33 Ibid., p. 105.
34 Ibid., p. 111.
35 Said, E. *The World, the Text, and the Critic*, London: Faber, 1984, p. 169.

9 Monstrosities, deviants, and darkies: Monstrous Regiment, Gay Sweatshop, and black theatre

1 Bhabha, H. *The Location of Culture*, p. 172.
2 Said, E. *Culture and Imperialism*, New York: Vintage Books, 1993, p. 333.
3 Ibid.
4 Ibid.
5 Kershaw, B. "Performance, Community, Culture" in Goodman, L. and de Gay, J. *The Routledge Reader in Politics and Performance*, London: Routledge, 2000, p. 136.
6 Hall, S. "New Ethnicities" in Baker, H., Diawara, M., and Lindeborg, R. (eds) *Black British Cultural Studies*, Chicago: University of Chicago Press, 1996, p. 168.
7 Ibid.
8 Kershaw, B. "Performance, Community, Culture," p. 136.
9 Said, E. *Culture and Imperialism*, p. 406.
10 Barker, C. "Alternative Theatre/Political Theatre" in Holderness, G. (ed.) *The Politics of Theatre and Drama*, Macmillan, London, 1992, p. 32.
11 Hanna, G. *Monstrous Regiment: A Collective Celebration*, London: Nick Hern Books, 1991, pp. xxiv–xxviii.
12 Ibid., p. xxvii.
13 Churchill, C. *Vinegar Tom*, New York: Samuel French, 1978, p. 38.
14 Ibid., p. 24.
15 Ibid., p. 52.
16 Ibid.
17 Hanna, G. *Monstrous Regiment: A Collective Celebration*, p. lxxi.
18 Ibid., p. lxxv.
19 Greig, N. *The Dear Love of Comrades* in Osmet, P. (ed.) *Gay Sweatshop: Four Plays and a Company*, London: Methuen, 1989, p. 3.
20 Ibid., p. 31.
21 Ibid., p. 24.
22 Ibid., p. 41.
23 Osmet, P. *Gay Sweatshop: Four Plays and A Company*, p. ix.
24 Interview with Itzin, C. in *Stages in the Revolution*, p. 234.
25 Mercer, K. "'1968': Periodizing Politics and Identity" in Grossberg, L., Nelson, C., and Treichler, P. (eds) *Cultural Studies*, New York: Routledge, 1992, p. 429.
26 Ibid.
27 Bhabha, H. *The Location of Culture*, London: Routledge, 1994, p. 172.

Conclusion

1 Said, E. *Culture and Imperialism*, p. 380.
2 Jeyifo, B. "The Nature of Things: 'Arrested Development' and Critical Theory" in Mongia, P. (ed.) *Contemporary Postcolonial Theory*, New York: Arnold, 1996.
3 Alibhai-Brown, Yasmin "In the English Arts, a Merry Racial Blend" *New York Times*, July 21, 2002.
4 Ibid.
5 Said, E. *Culture and Imperialism*, p. 72.
6 Freire, P. *Pedagogy of Hope*, New York: Continuum, 1998, p. 8.

Index